AMERICAN HERETICS

REBEL VOICES IN MUSIC

BEN MYERS

CODEX

American Heretics: Rebel Voices in Music
by Ben Myers

Published in 2002 by
Codex Books
PO Box 148, Hove, BN3 3DQ, UK
www.codexbooks.com

ISBN 1 899598 23 5

Designed and typeset by
Surface Impression Ltd

Printed in the UK by Biddles Ltd

Contents

About the author

Ben Myers was born in the north-east of England in 1976, and has worked as a music journalist since he was a teenager. His reviews and interviews have appeared in *Kerrang!*, *Melody Maker*, *Bizarre*, *Uncut* and *Careless Talk Costs Lives*, and have inspired death threats on more than one occasion. He has appeared on numerous TV and radio shows as a 'cultural commentator'. His short stories and poems have appeared in a number of small press publications.

Ben Myers lives in Peckham, London, where he is writing his first novel and planning a band which will destroy all music. Forever.

Contact: bigbenmyers@btopenworld.com
www.benmyers.com

Acknowledgements

Special thanks and eternal gratitude to: my parents Geoff and Dorothy, my siblings Kathryn and Richard, and Kara Leith Cooper.

For many different reasons, I would also like to thank: Davey James Atkinson, James Batty, Anton Brookes and all at Bad Moon, all at Catshit Mansions, Shawn Crahan, Nancy Cutmore and Bob Charlton, Helen Dobson, Dulcie and Pinky, all at Ethic Internet, Dan Fante, Fat Mike, Martyn Goodacre, Steve Gullick, Gerald Halligan, Jeremy Hammett, Hayley and Peter (here's to your latest addition...), the K! freelance crew, Lisa Johnson, Allen Jones, Kelly Jones, Simon Keeler at Cargo, Michelle Kerr at Roadrunner, Hanif Kureishi, Anthony Luke, Ian MacKaye, Anna Maslowicz (for September 11th assistance), Chris McCormack, Manson and Ms Von Teese, Kerry May, Kas Mercer at Mercenary, Lee Milmore, Bob Mitchell, Mörat, Ronald Myers, Jeff Noon, Marc Ollington, Scarlet Page, Cosi Pole and Nick Stevens, Shane Rhodes at Wrecking Ball Press, Nadia Shami, Stewart Smith, the Smiths (the family, not the band), John Robb, Chris Thompson, Everett True, Cathi Unsworth, Chrissie Yiannou.

An extended devil's horn hand manoeuvre to Phil Alexander, Paul Rees, Jason Arnopp, Scarlet Borg and all at *Kerrang!* and *Planet Rock* weekly.

Introduction
birth of the heretic

"American adj. *belonging to or characteristic of America*
Heretic n. *a dissenter from an established belief or doctrine"*

From the *Oxford English Dictionary*

"I think if you know what you believe, it makes it a lot easier to answer questions. I can't answer your question."

President George W. Bush[1]

I DON'T KNOW what it all means.

I don't know the technicalities.

I still can't tune a guitar.

When I sing, small children weep. But still there's something about music that pulls me in time and time again. Wherever I have been, whatever has happened, there has always been a song or a sound to remember it by. Music has always been there for me.

As I sit here, blindly fumbling for words to describe the indescribable, my ears are ringing. Transcribing these hissing tapes with the blinds down and the windows open, thousands and thousands of words day after day, I've missed all the good bands who've passed through town recently. Yet, each and every show of the past ten years – in darkened rooms across the world – resonate in my ears. It's times like now, late at night when even the endless South London symphony of sirens and passing trains seems muted, that the cold echo of feedback buzzes somewhere inside. Images flash through my mind of young men and women hell-bent on celebration, destruction. So many bands plugging and rocking out beneath the flickering strobe-lights, legions of wide-eyed converts drawn to their glow like moths. If I even attempted to describe all the bands, I'd be typing until my fingers became ragged stumps.

Because it's more than just the music. It's about everything that goes with it. Everything. The style, the attitude, the politics, the hunger to howl above the squall of the mundane crowd with their chill-out albums and production line pop. It's no coincidence that I hate pop music because it stands for what's popular. The popular people are boring and never have the guts to stay the distance.

So here's where the unpopular people get heard.

The people who are walking gods in a god-less age.

Only these gods walk the earth. They shit, they piss, they play guitars. Some of them are ugly, some of them stupid, and all are flawed. But our gods speak the truth. You wouldn't trust them to water your plants, but their intentions are pure. The more erudite of them inform and educate the listener whatever consequences they might bring upon themselves. Our gods play heavy and loud, just like gods should. They are worshipped by millions who pay money to be healed by them. These converts queue for hours just to touch their gods, to hear a word uttered from their lips. And when the gods plug in and rock out, the people lose their minds, shake loose their troubles and inhibitions to unleash the demon inside, until finally, sated and satisfied, they tumble out of their badly-lit churches and into the streets where their epiphanic talk is filled with big ideas and plans, a new found camaraderie just when they thought they were alone.

The rest of them – the people still stuck on the rules and regulations of the more recognised religions – go to their church. We go to ours. If everyone accepted this, perhaps there would be no problems in the world. The crackpot dictators of the East and West would feel no desire to greed, persecution or conflict, and the gods of music would be left alone to do their beautiful electric thing.

That's why I wrote this.

Actually, I just listened to a few records, saw some bands, consumed some drugs and did a bit of typing.

But if we want to blame something for this addiction to the evil powers of hardcore, punk rock, heavy metal, rhythm and blues, then blame America.

"We ought to make the pie higher."

President George W. Bush[2]

BLAME AMERICA. That was the original title for this book – for this series of conversations with a bunch of disparate Americans who have made their names screaming until their eyeball veins pop, night after night, year after year; for those who suck the very marrow out of life and use the empty bones to bash out a beat, sending messages to their people, controversy and heresy be damned – Blame America seemed the perfect title.

"Blame America," these boss-eyed, gap-toothed, guitar-toting freaks shout to anyone who will listen. "Blame America, not us. America made us. You made us."

But then some crazy stuff happened. Terrorists. Planes. Visions of Allah in dollars. Dust clouds swelling into the sky. Screams. Tears. Tributes. Flags flapping in the wind. And knees jerking all over the place.

Suddenly 'Blame America' was no longer plausible as a title for a book.

In the wake of September 11 2001, when rational debate was substituted for blood lust, it seems like art is needed more than ever. And as the most accessible of art-forms, music might provide a few answers. Rock stars mean more to the younger generation than any politician ever will. Trust me.

And it's there in America – land of the free, perpetuator of a dream long since passed its sell-by date – that all the most kick-ass music is being made.

Never before in recorded history, has a society enjoyed such a boom-time period as America in the late twentieth and early twenty-first centuries. Never before has a nation offered its people such a vast expanse of material goods to consume alongside the widespread credit with which they shackle themselves to faceless corporate loan sharks.

One glance at the statistics informing us of the ever-increasing levels of obesity in America, suggests that the goose is getting fat. The people are housed, clothed and due to chow down on a plate of fried chicken after a hard day's work of being American. Just as decreasing unemployment figures often reflect a decrease in state pay-outs to those in need of assistance, the figures telling us of a thriving society are also in need of interpretation. They act as a smokescreen for the current universal truths of increased homelessness, drug dependency, and illiteracy, for failing healthcare systems, greater individual debt, a world run on high interest credit, an insulting minimum wage and continually treating minority groups as inferior. As writer/film-maker Michael Moore poignantly pointed out in his recent book of the same name, the world is still run by Stupid White Men.

Yes, the goose is getting fatter by the second – but how long can its heart hold out?

Right now, America seems like a country living on borrowed time – and by extension, perhaps the same is true of Britain and Europe. Freedom of speech, the exchange of vital basic ideas, and the encouragement of new forms of expression, seem more necessary than ever. I can smell change in the air. Slipknot may be a group of theatrically masked, heavy metal merchants, but they genuinely want to lay the taste-making, major label music business to waste and begin again. That they will fail gloriously and acrimoniously is highly likely, but it's the thought that counts. Henry Rollins may be a bull-necked gym freak, but at least he has formed his own bullshit-free alternative mini-empire; at least he's not a gung-ho redneck with an itchy trigger finger. Put it this way: if a hammy sub-John Wayne or an ex-alcoholic illiterate can make it to the White House, then there's hope for any fucker.

"I think we agree, the past is over."

President George W. Bush[3]

Down in the underground, vast networks are forming. Around the world, punk rock is still unsurpassed as a genre within pop's vast culture of radical dissidence. It's over 25 years since the Sex Pistols released 'God Save the Queen' and changed everything; now, punk rock is whatever you want it to be. As *American Heretics* shows, it's an attitude to be adopted and manipulated. It's that spirit that is the one link between the American artists in a collection that draws together a mix of voices who go against the grain, and at the very least, are living proof that you don't have to fit into someone else's social structure.

These are the musicians whose work has permeated the mainstream and held an influence over that all-important demographic: youth. It's the young who will always inherit the earth, so it stands to reason that we should listen to the rule-breakers who they hold in such high regard. This is not an overview of a specific genre, neither is it a biography, and yes, there is a regrettable lack of female voices.

Instead this is a document of the times, of a bunch of disparate people whose lives I've been fortunate enough to dip into from time to time as they holler their way into the new millennium. It is a collection of conversations, warts and all. Snap-shots to be laughed at in later years. It is a series of moments in time laid down on paper – the closet to truth you can get without freeze-framing the moment, without being there.

But let's not get precious here. After all, everything is disposable, nothing is sacred and rock stars are full of shit too. Things move on. In five years time new things will have happened. New bands will be turning heads, new voices emerging. New people gaining power. This is just as it should be.

And after it has all gone, the music will ring on in our ears, only this time we will get to decide the outcome. Nothing is predetermined; the power is ours.

So go write your own book. Go form your own band. Call in sick and listen to *Appetite for Destruction* all day, if that's what reminds you you're alive.

Here are the opinions of a cross-section of the most inspiring musicians who have done just that.

Those we call the American Heretics.

Ben Myers
September 2002

Notes
1 Reynoldsburg, Ohio, 4 October, 2000, from Dubya Says: Home of the George W. Bush quote library, www.columbiacentral.com/dubya.
2 South Carolina Republican Debate, 15 February 2000, source as before.
3 On meeting with John McCain, *Dallas Morning News,* 10 May 2000, source as before.

Ian MacKaye (Fugazi)
steady diet of nothing

*"If I am a fundamentalist then I'm
only fundamental about tolerance,
openness and joy."*

*"These are our demands:
we want control of our bodies,
Decisions will now be ours.
You can carry out your noble actions,
we will carry our noble scars."*

'Reclamation', 1991

IN THE LATE SEVENTIES, 15 year old Ian MacKaye's Team Sahara, a teen collective of skaters from Georgetown, Washington DC, who sported a uniform of black and gold T-shirts, were offered sponsorship and places on the in-store team of The F & R Sunshine House, a skate shop in the affluent Virginian suburb of Bethesda. Ultimately, it meant that the confident teenager and his gang of lower middle-class road rats – who also included the slightly older and physically stronger Henry Garfield (later Rollins) – could get a tonne of cool free shit for continuing to pursue the endless possibilities that the asphalt terrain of the capital offered to those unafraid of cuts, bruises and the occasional baton-wielding cop.

Anyone who has ever skated knows that it means more than just a frivolous way to pass the time. Skating is about seeing your urban surroundings through new eyes and reinventing it as your own playground; it's about subverting

Photograph: Martyn Goodacre

architects' blueprints and making them your own. Where others use handrails to steady themselves, you use them to launch yourself. Where others sit, you slide. Where others walk, you fly with the wind in your hair. Skating is an expression of pure, untempered energy that requires nothing but the get-up-and-go to do it. And in the seventies when skating was still a goofy attempt at surfing inland and not yet a bona fide sub-culture, it was still very much an unquantifiable pursuit – sport, hobby, toy, menace to society, or what the hell?

In a move that would set the tone for the rest of his life, MacKaye put his size seven foot down and affirmed Team Sahara's non-aligned, independent stance. No company, however small, would commodify *their* fun.

This interview took place on the phone, March 2002.

Was there a point where you realised what you wanted to do with your life?
"No, because I don't think about things like that. Never. I'm not a futurist. I don't think anybody has any fucking clue what's going to happen in the future, so I never wondered about what I was going to do. All I have ever really wanted to do is live in the present moment. This doesn't mean that I live entirely for the moment, but rather just make sure that I'm doing the right thing for the time. My theory is that the future is a point just around the corner, yet you never quite get to see it and therefore you can never bank on it or against it. But what you do have control over is the vehicle which you are riding in, and you should take care of that vehicle so that maybe one day you can get around that corner and meet that future. Obviously, I'm a fairly responsible guy anyway. I don't burn my bridges."

Plus that live-for-the-moment, carpe diem attitude that is such a big part of rock 'n' roll is often interpreted as some sort of hedonistic, fatalistic approach to life, which of course you have proved doesn't have to be the case at all.
"Yeah and because of that I'm quite confident about the future – I just can't pretend to know what it will hold. So all along I have never had a plan. I didn't go to college because I wanted to continue what I was doing in the Teen Idles or Minor Threat and live in the moment completely. Actually, the real reason I never went to university was because at the age of 16 or 17 – probably when I was in 12th Grade – I realised that if I was to be hit by a car I would have spent the majority of my cognizant hours in school, so it seemed kinda crazy to go back to school again after leaving. I wanted to wake up in the morning and really live, yet I was finding the educational structure that I was in a little crippling. Plus, at that time I also felt that American universities were indoctrination camps

– that you basically went there to learn how to fit in. I didn't fucking want to fit in."

So do you feel this way about the current US college system?

"I don't know because I have never been, but since you're asking me I would have to say that higher learning in America is probably even more institutional now than back when it was more of a concern for me. The same could definitely be said for college radio, which is something I know a little bit more about. Certainly 20 years ago college radio stations were places where kids could engage in a creative approach to something useful and entertaining, whereas now it's really just a training ground for people who will go straight into commercial radio. In college radio now they have to follow all sorts of rules and everything seems so scripted – including which songs are going to be played. And when something is so uniformly scripted one has to wonder who is writing the script in the first place? That's when you realise that the people writing the script are writing it for every fucking thing. And it's creepy."

What can you tell me about your background and the influence that your parents have had on you and your work? Didn't they write a book together at one point?

"Yeah, basically all of my family are writers. My father's father was a magazine writer who was based in London during World War II and was involved with the propaganda and information people. He also wrote a few books about generals, plus some true crime books and some mystery books. My grandmother was a mystery writer, a front-line correspondent during the war and she also wrote a column called 'Can This Marriage Be Saved?' here in DC for a magazine called *Ladies Home Journal,* which was really considered to be the first of the advice columns. My mother's father was a sports writer for a newspaper here in Washington and his wife was an English teacher and magazine writer. Then there's my mother who wrote for magazines and is a historian/journalist who conducts immense amounts of unpublished research that is stored away for future use, and my father who has been a newspaperman for 25 years. He's now an editor who continues to run a Seminarian journal. My parents actually met at a school in DC called Sidwell Friends, which is a Quaker school, and they wrote a book[1] about the place together in the 1970s. My older sister, another word champion, is a poet, my other sister is a linguist, my brother studies English and my youngest sister is a writer too. The written word has a lot of weight around the house. So, yeah, I guess it's safe to say that this background had a profound effect on me."

> *"How many times have you felt like*
> *a bookcase*
> *sitting in a living room gathering dust*
> *full of thought already written?"*

'Furniture', 2001

INSPIRED BY the near-religious live shows and 'positive mental attitude' philosophy of local Rasta-punks Bad Brains who were fronted by the iconic HR (a band who did more for race-relations and the breaking down of boundaries within music than a million Bonos, Paul Simons or Stings could ever dream of) whilst in high school, MacKaye formed The Slinkees, who in turn quickly morphed into the Teen Idles. With MacKaye on bass, Rollins was offered the position of singer, but declined because his girlfriend didn't approve. Some tough guy.

Too young to play proper venues, and with the threat of harassment always nearby thanks to the anti-social nature of their finger-pointing speeded-up punk, the Teen Idles formed the core of the G-Town punk scene, an instinctive close-knit self-protecting youth movement which sneered at the dope-addled, long-haired seventies burnout contemporaries. This was a time when the wrong haircut or a ripped T-shirt was enough to warrant an ass-whoopin' from less progressive people. MacKaye found the band shows in DC – usually in community halls or basements in order to circumnavigate the stringent licensing laws and hard-line ID approval – before taking a Greyhound bus cross country in order to play shows in San Francisco and Los Angeles where the likes of The Germs, Black Flag, Flipper, Circle Jerks and Dead Kennedys were reclaiming punk rock back from the British and turning it into something faster, uglier and hungrier. Energised by the trip and the new-found realisation that there were teenagers and early twenty-something's just like him and his Georgetown friends 3,000 miles away, MacKaye embarked upon a mission to record everything that was happening around him with the release of Teen Idles' *Minor Disturbance* EP. The cover depicted a pair of crossed fists with big black 'X's penned on them – a satire of the DC bar policy of ear-marking all underage gig-goers so that alcohol is prohibited to them.

Needing a name for their own one-off label, MacKaye chose Dischord.

You've been running Dischord records as an independent label for 22 years now – how have you survived in a time when the major labels seem to be increasingly gaining control over things and therefore forcing smaller labels into liquidation?

"We put our first record out in December 1980. The most obvious reason is the fact that we have some bands that have proven to be relatively popular, in particular Minor Threat and Fugazi. Minor Threat still out-sells every band on the label and that's pretty crazy when you think about it."

Minor Threat still sell more records than Fugazi?

"It's hard to compare because Minor Threat only had one CD whereas Fugazi has eight or nine. Put it this way, in the last six months the Minor Threat *Discography* has sold 20,000 copies. We also still sell tonnes of cassettes and some vinyl, so in total it's probably topped half a million copies, whereas Fugazi's *13 Songs* sold less but still sold more than our newer records. It's weird."

But there's a lot more to Dischord than just being an outlet for the bands you play in?

"Well, I just wanted to be straight-up about that from the get-go. To some degree the timing of the label was pretty good, which obviously helped us define who we are and what we did pretty early on. We happened to stumble into punk rock or it stumbled into us at a time when it was definitely of the moment. It was happening there and then. A lot of those early bands became defining bands and Minor Threat is definitely one of them. We never had a mission or board meetings because we weren't interested in running a label, we just wanted to document our friends here in Washington. In the very beginning the initial concept was to put out the Teen Idles single and that would be it, but then people started saying, 'Well, what are you going to do with the money?' because there was a lot of sensitivity about selling out – early on punk rockers weren't even interested in putting out records, that's how hardcore some of them were. To some people, merely releasing a record was selling out. So we decided that any money would be spent communally in releasing our friends' records. This music was fucking important to us and it remains fucking important to us and fortunately we had the good sense to document it. We could not have known that this would be something I'd be discussing 20 years later. But we were interested in what was going on in LA, or maybe someone there might be interested in DC, so things grew naturally through word of mouth and mutual interests. Of course, Washington DC has no rock 'n' roll business and never has had, so we weren't effected in the same way that people in, say, London, Chicago, LA or San Francisco were and still are today. We had no bad influence because the industry machinery wasn't in place. For instance, in London bands get involved in the whole promotional aspect of rock 'n' roll and the way the machine works is really established. In this city we had to do everything ourselves because basically it's a city saturated with the federal government. The fact of the matter is, though, there are a lot of people in Washington DC who don't give a damn about the government. It just happens to be the factory in town and when the wind changes we have to deal with their smoke, but for the most part we go about business ourselves. We don't ask for their permission or guidance because they don't have a clue.

"Having no real idea or plan we approached things organically. We'd make a record, figure out the costs and sell it for a reasonable price so that we didn't lose money. We didn't bother with lawyers or contracts – that was the rock 'n' roll business and we were punk rockers. We didn't need their blueprint or their schematic to figure out how to run a business because it really is very simple. In fact, it was so simple that it surprises me when people struggle with running a record label. I actually think about this a lot because when I very first started playing music in high school there were other kids who would be considered to be in the more successful bands, though they never did anything but play cover songs at parties. And they used to ridicule us because they said that we couldn't play our instruments – that may have been true but we were fucking playing shows and they were not. We were touring and putting out records and they were not, so who the fuck were the real musicians?

"The same thing applies to running the record label as some people tend to see Dischord as like a boutique operation or some weird cult, but the fact of the matter is while they're sitting around talking about things or trying to figure out how much to pay their lawyers, we're releasing records. We never sat around waiting for things to happen, we just put out records, because that's what labels are meant to do, right? This kind of fragmentism or straight-forwardness enabled us to focus on what we really wanted to do, rather than focusing on some lame business agenda."

I remember reading interviews with you around the time of the great grunge gold-rush of 1991 where, as some sort of warning to new, young so-called 'alternative' bands, you named bands who had sold millions in the eighties yet were practically unheard of and historically irrelevant only a few years later. Do you feel vindicated now?

"Yeah, I think I referred to awful bands like Ugly Kid Joe or Loverboy[2] – long-forgotten bands who are meaningless today. For instance in the early nineties a lot of people in so-called alternative bands thought 'Oh, we're all going to be rich!' and they loosened their belts a little because they thought they were going to get fat, when really they got so skinny their pants fell off and that was the end of many of those bands. The early nineties was like a big period of bloodletting in music because there was a sudden surge of cash largely inspired by Nirvana. All of a sudden we saw all these major labels come storming into the valley with bags full of cash, but by the time they left it was almost as if most people had forgotten to grow their own food.

" 'Vindicated' is not necessarily the word I would use because I don't wish ill on these bands. What I was talking about was just trying to get people to think about what really has value and what doesn't. Obviously, if someone wants to be in an extremely popular band that no one will remember in years to come, that's fine because someone has got to do it. But I also think that many bands were missing the mark in terms of making something of any real substance."

Whereas you have eschewed financial success for critical and, more importantly, lasting success?

"I'd say so. I think that in American culture – and British culture, for that matter – there is such an emphasis to define all success in terms of finance and cash, but really that way of thought just plays right into the entire corporate, market-place structure. If making money is the ultimate form of success, what do people do with all their cash? They spend it in a market place which thrives on money and consumerism and which perpetuates this notion. That's why success will never be defined by, for example, volunteerism, because they can't sell you anything as a result. Volunteerism is not reliant on a marketable product."

Plus, of course, musical success is rarely judged by the influence that a band can have or the fact that it is has provided a good career to people who might otherwise have done nothing with their lives.

"Right. And if you look at all the Top 10 lists of records, movies, books or whatever, it's always going to be the biggest selling ones and that just doesn't equate goodness to me. Frankly, if something sells right across the board I mostly likely think one of two things. Firstly: if it's homogenous enough to appeal to people across the board with all their varied tastes, then the chances are it's going to be bland. Secondly: once again it's just proof that advertising works. That's no great surprise, is it? Certain types of music are really no different to, say, Twinkie's or certain brands of soda pop – they only sell well because they have a very cohesive type of advertising. So, in other words, there are occasionally records or bands that sell well and may even fall into the genius category, but largely… it's just a bunch of bullshit."

IN 1980, MacKaye and fellow Teen Idle/Dischord co-conspirator Jeff Nelson formed Minor Threat. Physically and musically lean, angular and stripped down (the rigours of skating and an alcohol-free diet, coupled with raging teenage hormones makes for an endless energy supply) Minor Threat quickly became the leading light in the nascent hardcore movement. Through songs like 'In My Eyes' and 'Straight Edge', MacKaye laid down a loose manifesto for a new generation of pro-active punks bored with pretty much everything that had gone before. The straight edge scene had a uniform (shaved heads, cheap T-shirts, Vans trainers), a naïve ethos (those who aren't fucked up on drugs get more things done), a diet (endless cans of corrosive soda and, later, vegetarianism) and a clear goal: to exist as a unified musical entity completely independent of the established music industry. Minor Threat's *Discography*[3] compilation on Dischord is one of the most pure, perfect and positive-minded examples of rock 'n' roll ever released.

Knowing what you know now, if you were given the chance are there any things that you would do differently with Minor Threat?

"No, I don't have any regrets about anything in my life. I actually feel in some way that that band was as perfectly executed as it possibly could have been. I was actually just talking to Bob [Weston] from Shellac about it this morning. I was telling him that during the band's demise there was a point where the aspirations of the four individuals parted ways. It wasn't that these aspirations weren't always present, there just was no possibility of executing them, so they weren't a pressing concern. Look at it this way: let's say you and I go on a trip in the desert and you love swimming but I hate it. If we're in the desert, it's not an issue. But as soon as we get to a place with a pool problems will arise. In the beginning of Minor Threat we were just a punk band that no one gave a damn about so the issue of signing to a major label was non-existent. Later, towards the end of the band, some of these aspirations became problematic because we finally got to that place with the pool and some people wanted to swim, but some of us did not. This then brought about a stylistic shift in the band because once some members had decided to take a swim they then had to figure out what would be the most attractive suit they could wear, you know? And it was a bathing suit that I objected to whole-heartedly! Basically, we just disagreed as a band about where we wanted to go and the decision to knock it on the head when we did was great. I know that Minor Threat split at the right time."

Part of the attraction of Minor Threat is that you left behind a pretty flawless legacy – a collection of short, sharp original-sounding songs for a new generation to pick up on.

"I can actually think of a number of bands who didn't make the decision to split and either went on to soften the intense impact of their work by putting out a series of confusing messages or muted weirdness, or conversely, continued being a band that no one really cared about."

Whereas Minor Threat have steadily got bigger since you split up without having to endure all the bullshit that goes with it.

"Definitely, we're way more legendry now than we ever were when we existed, which is weird, but cool too. All bands have a beginning, a middle and an end and you can't fuck with that. Obviously, though, the members of bands can then conceivably do something to sully a band's reputation, as is often the case.

"This is interesting and I was talking about it only yesterday. Here's a funny story. When I first got into punk rock in 1979 we would go to the record store and pick up any import singles that we thought looked even vaguely cool. One time we picked up a couple of singles by the band Skrewdriver[4] – the original line-up. At that time, politically they certainly didn't appear to be a Nazi band, like they became later. They were just this punk band singing songs like 'You're So Dumb'. Tough guys, yeah, but not really that hardcore. And I loved Skrewdriver. They put out this EP, broke up and I just thought 'Wow, what a cool band!' so in interviews that I did in 1981 I'd tell people that I really liked this band Skrewdriver. But in 1984 they reformed and suddenly they were these serious National Front, Nazi guys! It wasn't even the same guys – just the singer Ian Stewart – but none the less it made everything that they had previously done stink. They immediately tainted their early work and it was just incredible because there I was going round telling people how great this Nazi band were. See, that's the thing – when a band breaks up it's hard to screw with what you had, but on occasion the behaviour of the members of that band can really, really have dire effects on the band's work, their legacy. Conversely, if people go on to do really interesting things it can work the other way. I think Fugazi's work has a lot to do with the continued interest in Minor Threat."

Like it or not you're seen as something of an iconic and influential figurehead in underground music and still regarded as the man who founded straight edge. What is the biggest misconception people have about you?

"I think people think that I'm a hardcore fundamentalist, when I'm not at all. Or if I am a fundamentalist then I'm only fundamental about tolerance, openness and joy. That's where I'm coming from. A long time ago, it became clear to me that the point of all the yelling and screaming in punk rock was that we were dissatisfied and not at peace with life and that things might change if we yelled at them enough and kicked up a stink. If that was my belief, it seemed that it would be absurd to not actually be happy because you have to practice what you preach. You can't say that you want change and then not even attempt to have it in your own life, so I think essentially people would be startled by just how much more approachable I am than they probably think. I'm a pretty easy-going person."

Another misnomer about you – and indeed much of the first wave of US hardcore – is that you lack humour. To me, many of Minor Threat songs were satirical, cheeky and full of teenage humour, as were Black Flag's 'TV Party' and 'Six Pack' or Dead Kennedys' prankster songs like 'Too Drunk To Fuck'. To me, it's subversion through easily digestible humour.

"You're absolutely right. I'm extremely dry. I'm a prankster and I'm a dry motherfucker, yet people tend to take so much of what I do so seriously that they don't always get the joke. That's a big misconception that people have."

But then at the same time, straight edge had a pretty blunt aesthetic: shaved heads, the rejection of the trappings of all that was good about previous youth cultures – alcohol, cigarettes, drugs, casual sex – and an over-riding sense of male-dominated physicality and confrontation. Maybe that's where your image stems from?

"Yes, and it's also because anybody who shares an opinion is suddenly seen as if they're giving orders, which is something which I never really did. I was always just saying what I felt, whereas lots of artists in music over the years have run from opinions, particularly nowadays. Look at how things are now lyrically in rock music – it's incredible to me how far musicians will veer to get away from committing to any kind of point of view in their lyrics. At the moment things are really oblique and pretty shocking, frankly. I want my lyrics to speak, to sing. I want them to make sense to people so that I can engage them. I think since the early nineties there has been a steady desire amongst a lot of punk bands, so-called punk bands or whatever-the-fuck bands to not take risks or go out on a limb. I mean, just look at the lyrics that punk bands were singing in the early eighties compared to the bands of today."

"Lights out for the cynical sharps for their wide-eyed foils and all attendant props supporters of flash and pan-fried fucks who grease like cops throwing round their weight and I feel dangerous and vexed swinging two ton second guess and every motion just cuts too cruel… too cruel."

'Caustic Acrostic', 1998

Minor Threat split in 1983. During their three year existence they released two albums, toured the States and inspired a new breed of bands. They got out just as hardcore – somewhat predictably, given it's subterranean, elitist existence – began attracting jocks more interested in the physicality of the mosh-pit and the potential for violence rather than bringing about any real change. Worse still, rules were being applied left, right and centre.

Like British punk before it, hardcore quickly became predictable and, for the most part, boring. Once something becomes public knowledge it becomes misinterpreted. Straight edge spawned endless arguments over who was 'straighter' and soon prompted tales of beatings over wayward cigarette smoke. Plenty of good bands still exist to follow the design for life as laid down by MacKaye in 1981, but even more still go through the motions in an often stagnant, fashion-led scene. That said, the straight edge hardcore of today is still a genre that has largely thrived without interference from the major labels who generally swarm down on any new movement – be it grunge, gangsta rap or pointless latter-day punk bands like Sum 41 and Blink 182 – like a swarm of locusts, sucking it dry and stripping it of all energy and magic and selling back the bare bones and empty husks to a wider, more impressionable audience already headfucked from relentless corporate advertising campaigns and the constant flicker of MTV, an outlet whose projected lifestyle contributes to the kind of increased peer pressure that leads to high school massacres. Perhaps hardcore's limited commercial value and relatively ugly, brand-free aesthetic is one of its main strengths.

Unlike the keeping-it-real gangsta kids or fans of modern 'grunge' abortions like Creed and Staind however, the hardcore kids of today don't have to buy their music and their culture back from the few unseen fat cats who make the decisions at the 'Big Five' record companies, MTV, Nike, or Pepsi-fucking-Cola. Sometime it's hard to listen to music or eat a burger without wondering which company your money is being filtered back to and who had to sweat blood for chump change and your privilege. Sometimes it's hard not to get conspiratorial when all you want to do is rock.

Hardcore though, for the most part, is still a self-sufficient genre that operates efficiently through it's own network of labels, bands, fanzines, distributors and promoters. It is free enterprise at it's best. America should be proud.

By 1984, those who got into the scene right at ground level in DC decided to leave the many new bands to bash out their simplistic machismo anthems. As with any true innovators, the desire to progress and reinvent was a strong one for MacKaye and friends, so rather than making themselves comfy in the rut in which them found themselves stuck, they decided something needed to be done. Something new for themselves.

Anyone reading an interview of this nature probably knows that Minor Threat were the definitive hardcore band and Fugazi are one of the most influential bands in alternative music in the nineties and beyond, but they may not know so much about Revolution Summer, a scene that you were involved in whose influence has perhaps only recently come to fruition in the hardcore bands of today.

"Revolution Summer seems to have taken on a mythical quality. In the mid-eighties there was a breakdown of a bunch of the original DC bands, like Faith[5], Minor Threat and Insurrection[6], and there was a bunch of boys and girls kind of at a loss and without any focus. The Washington punk rockers were like a tribe and we were all thick with each other; we were a cell within a much larger punk scene. But we weren't that happy with what was going on in the DC punk scene – it just seemed like it had turned really macho and dumb. Violent too. At the same time, though none of us wanted to straighten out and have to go get a job because we were punk rockers, we just didn't relate to what was being called punk rock by a lot of kids here in Washington. So we decided we wanted to do something we felt good about. We wanted to be creative and re-energised. We weren't interested in trying to take back the punk scene – they could have it – when we could just start another one. Something new.

"I was just one of a few dozen people in a crew of friends. There was actually a couple of meetings/get togethers/parties where we talked about what we could do. At one point, we decided everybody should start a band or a fanzine or just get something new going by October of 1984, something we referred to as 'Good Food October' – the idea being that we would all get active by that time. But it didn't happen and everyone was bummed, so someone said, 'OK, by the next summer we'll have a musical revolution. Get your shit together and get active.' Hence the Revolution Summer of 1985. We put up flyers in the places that we hung out basically saying, 'come on, get it together!' And it worked. There was a definite swell of energy."

What about the fact that all these bands were promptly tagged 'emo', thereby handily pigeonholing what you were doing? I mean, even within music as extreme and non-commercial as punk and hardcore, there's a tendency to categorise and attempt to package something whose essence is its spontaneity and unwillingness to replicate anything that has gone before.

"Well, the emo thing is a different matter. The term 'emo-core' was a disparaging one that stemmed from a comment someone made about us saying we didn't play hardcore punk, we played 'emotional hardcore', so we immediately rejected it because we were aware that it wasn't complimentary. It was like the term 'punk rock'[7] – it was originally meant as an insult but then kids adopted it and turned it into their own thing. But I never referred to Embrace[8] or Rites of Spring[9] as 'emo-core'. Ever. That's just insane. I mean, Rites of Spring are one of the greatest fucking bands of all time, yet a lot of people ridiculed and maligned them. They thought Rites of Spring were a bunch of cry babies or something when in fact they were bold, seriously bad-ass and their shows were just... epiphanal. Beyond any other bands in DC at that time, they were the ones who people were really psyched about and when they played everybody immediately wanted to go out and form their own band. Rites of Spring's music kicked people's asses and they wanted to return the favour. They were an incredible band but unfortunately because of this jokey tag of 'emotional hardcore' people still didn't get it. I don't think people realise how intense these shows were and how hard these guys rocked, which is a drag, but that's the way it goes."

And now emo has been established as yet another punk rock sub-genre. Not so long back, the *NME* did an emo special where they had cut-out-and-keep emo kids with their own accessories. I mean, talk about missing the point!

"Yeah, I heard about that. That's the British music press for you. I'm really not at all surprised by that."

*"This is three minute access, so pop
   the question:
Will we leave the last place burning?
Or do we just get leaving?
Red-light, red-light my mind moves
to refuse that filter.
Are you still surprised?*

'Exit Only', 1991

DECEMBER 1998. I've just arrived in Fairfax, Virginia, 40 minutes drive outside of Washington DC, to interview a fat white rapper with a Sinn Fein tattoo and a pacemaker, when I get wind that Fugazi are playing. Tonight. In DC. A home-town show. Fu-fucking-gazi. Book the cab, I'm just going to change into my dancing shoes...

Leaving a dozen junket-drunk so-called journalists, taste-makers and photographers to their ever-increasing bar tab, me and the only other fan/writer present who appreciates a good band over a dull night in a dull hotel with dull people namedropping dull bands, navigate our way to Georgetown University. The cab costs us $60 – a bargain price to see Fugazi anywhere. We hit the campus and spend too long trying to locate the right building. Down winding tarmac driveways. Along the halls of academia. Time is ticking. The capital's hot-bed of learning. Across well-trimmed lawns. Breaking into a trot when we hear the faint doof-doof of a bass drum. Silent planes above cutting through the clear Virginia night. Beyond them, just stars and satellites plotting our destiny and tracking our movements. Sweat on my back. Lungs raw (shit, I've gotta get fit, discipline, less-weed-more-speed). The music getting louder. Through a doorway now. Stuffing dollar bills in the hands of the bored girl with the little red cash-box. Charging into a too-bright hall.

No fancy lights, no theatrics, no dumb gutter punks at the punk rock show. Fugazi are onstage, hunched over their instruments. No one is speaking, smoking, drinking or interacting. They're just staring at the sparse spectacle of four non-descript men hardly making a sound, yet are still emitting hypnotic electro waves out over our heads. Singer Guy Picciotto spread like spilled spaghetti across the stage. Ian MacKaye plucking baby-notes from his guitar, dripping down onto the front line. Bassist Joe Lally feet apart and poised. The inactivity and silence lasts forever and I look around at the misfits in knitwear and horn-rimmed specs, tall skinny boys with fringes and short dumpy girls with paperbacks stuffed in their back pockets and clips in their hair, heads nodding, poetry in their eyes – true punk rockers. None of this spit and sawdust macho shit. *Bong!* drummer Brendan Canty taps his big bell and the song bursts into life, a maelstrom of sounds, a symphony of electricity like snapped cables writhing in the wet dead dirt of America, dark funk rumbling beneath it like a layline coming to life. They reach a cymbal-crashing crescendo and cut the song dead. Kill it without prejudice. The band exit and the crowd drift away.

Fugazi meant "fucked up situation" in Vietnam.

Now it means quality control. "No bullshit."

MacKaye formed the band with Rites of Spring's Picciotto and Canty and bassist Joe Lally in 1987. In the subsequent 15-plus years Fugazi have been responsible for some perfectly-packaged and vital underground releases, albums and shows that have influenced everyone from big leaguers like Nirvana, Rage Against the Machine and At the Drive In to hundreds of lesser known bands currently criss-crossing the globe in their own little post-punk pods.

Entirely self-managed, Fugazi have a policy of only playing for affordable ticket prices and often opt to play benefit shows rather than the usual circuit of venues run by profiteering promoters. They have played in 50 US states and every continent in the world, selling somewhere in the vicinity of half a million records on the way. And that's without TV or radio airplay and very few mainstream interviews.

Fugazi continue to divide opinion within punk rock – which, for better or worse, is often an elitist and highly critical scene – even though you're one of the few quality assured bands. I know that when I buy a Fugazi album that a) it will be different to the last one and b) it'll be great. Fifteen years on from the band's formation, how does criticism effect you?

"How do I deal with criticism? [Laughing] I don't give a fuck! Honestly, if you like the record that's great and it makes me happy to hear you say that, but if someone doesn't like it, that's alright too. I don't give a damn. I don't care. If some kid wants to slag us off in his punk rock fanzine then… whatever, it makes no difference to me. There are plenty of people out there who have had a problem with me or maybe even hated me right since the beginning, but I can't be bothered by them, I don't care…

"Look: I don't confuse myself, my work or my bands with anything that is necessary for life. Music is not oxygen, it's not water and it's not food, so on that level it doesn't matter. People aren't required to like me and that's fine. There are five billion people in the world and I know I won't come close to meeting a hundredth of them. Put it this way, four billion people could hate me but it wouldn't change my life at all because if I don't interact them, then what does it matter? Fugazi's best selling record has probably sold about half a million copies – it was probably the first album – and that's roughly… what? One-seventh the population of London or something? It's not that big of a deal, so if some kid says in a fanzine, 'Oh, Ian is a fundamentalist prick', of course on one level I'd like to meet this kid and straighten his ass out, but I'm not going to write him a letter and I'm not going to defend myself because it doesn't make any difference to me. If I was going to get hung up on bad reviews I wouldn't be doing this interview today. I would have been a basket case about 15 years ago. I just don't respond to it. My general reaction is 'So what?' and then I'll continue doing what I do."

I've recently spoken to people like Marilyn Manson and Slipknot to see what the bands who influence today's teens have to say – do you think these so-called cutting edge bands use their platforms wisely?

"I don't really know anything about those guys. I don't think I've heard either ones of those bands, in fact. Clearly kids are effected by them, but they're really not my cup of tea. I know all about the Columbine High School shooting and the tenuous link to Marilyn Manson, of course I do, but I also think that some people are perfectly happy to trade on chaos and profit from the proliferation of it. But the profiting is very well organised so they can't be that chaotic. Put it this way, Marilyn Manson is not a crusty. The crusties… now, they were chaotic and insane. Not that I think that's any better because it isn't, it's just that there's something particularly insidious about people who preach total anarchy and chaos. Anyone who is involved in music and touring, or especially if they're playing in arenas to ten or twenty thousand people who have each paid $25, then it's all highly orchestrated. It's not like Manson is kept in a cage until show time, you know? It's a business that trades on chaos. But do I think someone like Marilyn Manson is responsible? [Laughing] Oh, I don't fucking know! I guess I don't really spend much time thinking about it. It's, like, do you want me to talk about wrestling or something because to me it's part of the same thing? If I asked myself whether wrestling is responsible, I'd probably say no, but it really doesn't have a place in this interview, does it? And does Marilyn Manson? No, not in my opinion because to me he's just another aspect of that same form of entertainment."

Given that you're from such a large family of writers and your punk rock childhood buddy Henry Rollins is having a fair stab at literary immortality, have you ever considered writing yourself?

"I've thought about it a lot and I think that some day I'd like to do some writing if I can get past this question: who gives a fuck what I have to say? That's something I have to answer for myself. In terms of music and lyric-writing things are clearer and I know who I'm singing to – just as right now we're doing an interview where I'm speaking with you directly and I understand who I'm talking to and what I'm talking about. I recently did a public speaking thing where I took questions from a group of a couple of hundred people and I found myself in a bit of a quandary because it really wasn't clear who I was speaking to in the room. There were some 15-year-old kids but also 50-year-old men, so it was difficult. Some of the people there were acutely aware of the minutiae of my work whereas others had never heard of me, so I didn't know whether to get up there and say, 'So, I used to play in this band called Minor Threat…' or whatever. I feel the same about writing. I like the idea of it but I'm not sure that I'm armed to do it yet."

A lot of Fugazi's lyrics lend themselves to poetry anyway. Regardless of the music, they look good on the page.

"Well, thanks. Ever since I was a kid I've written poetry and treated it as a craft. But also I'm loaded with fucking opinions or impressions or feelings. I think about stuff so much that it eventually comes out, which is what poetry is, I guess."

I gather that Dischord is planning to release a box-set to commemorate two decades of punk rock business – how's it coming along?

"I'm still working on it. It's a massive project to undertake, but one that is very cathartic. I'm having to go back through all the old releases and I'm finding it pretty interesting purely because I never think about Dischord in terms of longevity and because I just concentrate on work on a day-to-day basis. Like right now today I'm doing exactly what I have always done, which is basically sitting in my office returning calls and taking care of what needs to be done. That's what I was doing in 1981, 1985, 1990, 1995… and now. It's what I do. Every once in a while I do have an opportunity to stop, look around, and think 'Wow, I got a lot of stuff done!'"

Finally then, here's a question I've never heard you been asked before. What do you do for fun?

"Well, you know I'm really not a hobbies type of guy and I'm not frivolous in any way. I do love to play music and I play outside of the band for enjoyment. Basically though, I spend a lot of time with my family, who are very close. Aside from one of my sisters who lives on the West Coast, we all live in DC and meet up to have dinner every Sunday night. It usually turns into a big discussion of some sort and it's great. Obviously, I'm also part of a big, old, deep community of friends so there's always something going on. Never a dull moment…"

Notes

1 According to Director of Publications and Sidwell Friends Quaker School alumni magazine editor Matt Jennings, William R. MacKaye and Mary Ann 'Ginger' MacKaye published *Mr Sidwell's School* (1983) and were both members of the class of 1951. Both are still involved in the school, with Ginger MacKaye sitting on the schools' alumni magazine editorial board. "I had no idea their son was in Fugazi!" says an excited Jennings.

2 As their name suggests, Loverboy were a lame Canadian hard rock band who had three multi-platinum albums in the 1980s, a perfect example of a massive selling, yet ultimately worthless corporate band. Their definition of 'hard rock' is my definition of 'soft rock'.

3 *Discography* is a compilation of Minor Threat's career spanning a 26 song/50 minute output – their first two seven inch singles, three EPs: *Minor Threat* (1981) *Out of Step* (1981), *In My Eyes* (1983) and their parting *Salad Days* EP. Collectively, it is a brutal burst of songs, stripped down and fuzzed-up like The Ramones, but with pop culture references replaced with personal politics, and where violence and goofy teenage boy humour jostle for space. By lacking the standard formulaic rock 'n' roll clichés – guitar solo's, over-slick production, unnecessary extra instrumentation, a willingness to soften the edges for easier consumption – *Discography* is very rock 'n' roll indeed. Jeff Nelson's guitars may recall a passing nod of kinship to the anti-Clapton/guitar hero, cheap-and-cheerful buzz-saw thrashing of Johnny Ramone or The Buzzcocks' Pete Shelley, but they're angrier and altogether more biting, while drummer Lyle Preslar keeps the whiplash beat at a constant throughout and MacKaye unleashes a series of diatribes that suckerpunch topics such as senseless violence, toxins, inverse racism, betrayal, regret and apathy into submission. In all these respects, *Discography* is a triumph.

4 Formed by Ian Stuart Donaldson (1958-1993) in the north-west of England in 1977 from the ashes of Tumbling Dice, Skrewdriver became the archetypal working class skinhead figureheads for the burgeoning rise of the National Front-led racist far right. Skrewdriver's first single 'You're So Dumb/Better Off Crazy' was released in 1977 by prominent punk label Chiswick and one early roadie included future Madness singer Suggs. Their career as a cult band for that minority of ugly British bulldogs who weren't aware that rock 'n' roll has always essentially been a more Marxist inspired left-wing movement is perhaps best represented by this, a mere footnote in history. Nothing more.

5 Faith (1981-1983) featured Alec MacKaye on vocals. Their debut album was a split release with Void and their self-titled album (Dischord, 1982) features all their recorded works. Worth checking out.

6 Pre-Rites of Spring DC band featuring Guy Picciotto and Brendan Canty. An early MacKaye-produced demo was, according to Picciotto in Michael Azerrad's *Our Band Could Be Your Life: Scenes from the American Indie Underground 1981-1991,* "lamentably terrible, one of the worst bands in town" and so bad that only keen archivist MacKaye held onto a copy. Incidentally, unbeknown to them at the time, MacKaye and Picciotto were at the same 1979 Cramps show that they both claim changed their entire outlook on life.

7 The general consensus is that the term 'punk' is derived from prison slang for a forced, submissive homosexual or 'bitch' and was clearly originally a derogatory term. The epithet appeared a number of times before the musical genre crystallised, most notably in the work of writer William Burroughs, himself an influence on numerous early punk performers like Patti Smith and Richard Hell. The term 'punk' was then believed to be first appropriated alongside this new form of music by writers Legs McNeil and John Holstrom for their milestone comic/fanzine of the same name. Says McNeil in *Please Kill Me: The Uncensored Oral History of Punk* by McNeil and Gillian McCain (editors): "The word 'punk' seemed to sum up the thread that connected everything we liked – drunk, obnoxious, smart but not pretentious, absurd, funny, ironic, and all things that appealed to the darker side." The zine's first cover feature was an interview with Lou Reed conducted at a show by The Ramones at CBGB's. Very punk indeed. A year later the term crossed the Atlantic and the rest is history.

8 Vastly under-rated post-Minor Threat/pre-Fugazi band (1985-1986) featuring MacKaye on vocals. Their self-titled 1986 release on Dischord is another important post-hardcore record, not to be confused with the Leeds, UK-based, floppy-haired no-marks of the same name.

9 Rites of Spring (1984-1986) featured future Fugazi members Guy Picciotto and Brendan Canty. As with Embrace, their self-titled debut (Dischord, 1985) and subsequent four-song single are seminal releases of the generally musically arid mid-eighties and still a strong influence upon today's underground post-hardcore scene.

Rage Against the Machine
guerrillas in the midst

*"We're dealing with this huge,
monstrous pop culture that has a
tendency to suck everything that is
culturally resistant into it in order to
commodify it, pacify it and make it
non-threatening…"*

"Ya Basta!"
("Enough is enough!")

Battle cry of the Zapatista Army of
National Liberation, 1994

RAGE AGAINST THE MACHINE formed at the start of the 1990s and swiftly provided a much-needed antidote to all those second-generation (post-Nirvana) grunge bands who advocated apathy and premature smack-induced death as viable lifestyle options. The impact of their self-titled debut album in 1993 was immediate. Their combination of differing ethnic backgrounds with socialist politics, immediately gave them a distinct advantage over their blank-eyed, slack-jawed contemporaries. Frontman Zack de la Rocha's mother was an anthropology graduate and his father, Beto de la Rocha, an artist and member of the political group the 'Los Four' who depicted Chicano history through their

art. Guitarist and Harvard Political Science honours graduate Tom Morello's father was a member of the Mau Mau guerrilla army which freed Kenya from British colonial rule and his mother is a founder member of anti-censorship organisation Parents for Rock and Rap. In it for the powder and the pussy, Rage Against the Machine were not.

Living in an LA rife with racial unrest circa the Rodney King incident, where the service industries and sweatshops are still reliant on cheap immigrant labour – and where a mere few miles divides the millionaires of the Hollywood hills and the down-trodden minority neighbourhoods of Compton, Inglewood and so forth – certainly provided Rage with all the lyrical ammunition that they needed. This new musical fusion that brought their city to life was a sound that was to change the shape of rock music in the nineties and beyond, and take live performance to a whole new level. With raised fists and a defiant stance, Rage Against the Machine took their brand of protest music to the world. In years to come songs such as 'Bullet In the Head' and 'Killing In the Name' will remain two of the defining musical moments of the 1990s, as timelessly potent as *Kick Out the Jams* or *Anarchy in the UK*.

Such protest music has been at the heart of rock 'n' roll since its inception, and anyone who says politics and music don't mix is clearly tripping. Of course, music is political. Everything is political. Farting on an overcrowded rush hour tube train is political if it's done in protest at the over-priced bovine-like conditions within which you find yourself and over which you have no real control. And the punch in the mouth that you receive from your less understanding citizens for your little anti-social act will be political too. That's what politics and protest is about – getting involved. Vocalising your discontent. Changing things for the better.

Given that rock 'n' roll was primarily born out of a form of black American blues music which sang of slavery, hardship and oppression, it stands to reason that modern hard rock's roots are entangled with those of the protest song. Naturally, if we can pin-point the birth of rock 'n' roll as some time in the early 1950s (when a good looking white fella drew together blues and gospel, stole the spirit, packaged the idea and sold it so brilliantly to a generation of listless post-war kids) then the protest song clearly dates further back in time to when man made his grievances heard by randomly hitting inanimate objects together.

And given that there are only really two forms of music – that which celebrates and that which protests – 'the politics and music don't mix' argument which so many critics seem fond of is a redundant one, a short-cut to thinking which also determines that, for example, sport and politics don't mix, to which you only need reply with two words: Mohammed Ali. (Those who put forward such an argument are generally the people who are more interested in what

Madonna's kids and oafish husband are wearing as opposed to all the admirable work she has done in knocking down gender, religious and sexual boundaries; they are those who consistently miss the point.)

Hip-swaying, quiffed-up rock 'n' roll gave birth to the political protest song via folk music and Bob Dylan, whose song 'Maggie's Farm' Rage Against the Machine later covered on their *Renegades* (2000) album. Dylan turned things on their heads and invested meaning into music that was previously all about 'Blue Suede Shoes' and 'She loves you, yeah, yeah, yeah...' At a time when the nation was changing, Dylan effectively mixed up beat poetry and images of old Americana in a classic troubadour style. He not only captured the feeling of the moment but also vitally suggested alternative solutions too.

Post-Dylan, the sixties were littered with protest singers and floppy-hatted doppelgängers. It was only when the relative innocence of the early sixties gave way to the inevitable red-eyed come-down that the Fab Four were superseded by the equally influential MC5 and the Stooges, the hippies turned into the more militant yippies, and the peace, love and brown acid of Woodstock gave way to the hate and war undertones of Altamont and the imminent influx of heroin into rock 'n' roll. For the first time, politics in American rock music began to pose a real threat to the establishment – most likely because it was now white, middle class kids who were spouting the radical rhetoric.

Cold war paranoia, materialism, disparity in wealth, American apartheid, the growth of the Women's Movement and the Vietnam conflict all provided an identifiable cause for many a troubled youth. At the end of the decade, insurrection on the streets of LA, Paris, Washington and London showed how much the times had already a-changed, with rock music, as ever, reporting back from the front lines and into bedrooms across the world. Even the pearly-teethed Beach Boys had links with Charles Manson. Rock 'n' roll became nastier and the protests became louder and more focused. The seeds for a generation of politicised, literate bands were being planted. The term radical was applied to anyone who stopped to question the status quo – including various parents of Rage Against the Machine members.

In the seventies everything was amplified. The music became louder, dissenting voices became angrier. The most important protest music of the decade can be divided into three sections: Bob Marley and conscious reggae, the Sex Pistols and nihilistic punk and Sly and the Family Stone-inspired (possibly the first ever inter-racial, male-female band) colourful, sloganeering funkateers, who managed to bring fun, wigs and leather to the proceedings. A special mention should also go to the dino-journalist's favourite, 'What's Going On'[1], the most soothing depiction of social upheaval ever recorded.

*

1980s America is generally credited with spawning the 'Me, me, me!' generation. Money and personal gain, AIDS, nuclear bombs, Reagan and Bush Sr and widening race/class divisions were all on the agenda. The growth of hip-hop at the start of the decade was about taking the power back, only for MTV to pop up and take the power back again by slowly co-opting a wholly black genre to line the pockets of the white-run industry. It was the decade in which the future members of Rage Against the Machine came of age. Surprisingly, in such sickeningly selfish economic, political and musical climates, mainstream protest songs (I refer to 'mainstream' protest songs because those which are restricted to their own underground genres rarely make a lasting difference) were less memorable. There were worthy exceptions: N.W.A.'s 'Fuck Tha Police', Public Enemy's entire eighties output, Madonna's 'Papa Don't Preach', U2's 'Sunday Bloody Sunday', Bruce Springsteen's anti-Vietnam effort 'Born In the USA' (albeit a decade and a half too late) and Twisted Sister's 'We're Not Going To Take It', plus punk bands like the Dead Kennedys and Black Flag, discussed elsewhere in this book. The 'Do They Know It's Christmas?'/'We Are the World' releases showed that the protest record could now be manipulated into the Career-Saving Charity Record[2]; that way it's not just the starving, fly-tormented African kids that gain something out of it… but Sting does too!

It is in the canon of the angry young man that Rage Against the Machine belong – that group of people for whom music, rather than party politics, is the chosen medium through which to inform and change. Drawing together punk rock and hip-hop, two ideologically similar genres, their recorded output represents many dissenting voices of the populace, the band admirably utilising their air-time/column inches as a mouthpiece for those who feel that a vote once every four years is just not enough involvement. The fact that we've recently seen 'rock 'n' roll' presidents and prime ministers means very little – they're merely further examples of 'the power of good PR' – indicating that protest in rock 'n' roll and its many offshoots is more necessary than ever. Anyone who read of the blanket banning of hundreds of songs on US play-lists post September 11 ('Ob-La-De, Ob-La-Da'? for fuck's sake!) would surely agree that the possibility of musicians cutting through the futility of conflict to unearth greater truths about the world around us, is still very much a threat to those in power.

In late 1999 I got a chance to interview Rage Against the Machine. Rumours abounded that they were about to split. An entourage of management and record company representatives clucked around and created just enough chaos and confusion to justify their existence. The interview was off. The interview was on. Anyone who has been in the court of the chart-topping, major label rock star will know that this is standard tactics… but Rage Against the Machine?

Finally, after much needless to and fro-ing from the many lackeys in attendance, I was given the green light. Consummate gentlemen and engaging subjects, they didn't disappoint. Ladies and gentleman, the most subversive band to permeate the mainstream. The greatest musicians. The best of their time. Rage Against the Machine.

This interview took place September 1999 in a London hotel.

What did you do before the band took off?

Timmy C (bass): "I'd known Zack for a while and we've always jammed together, although for the most part I've always been a kind of social hermit. A lot of my adolescence was spent in my bedroom just playing along to records in order to learn how to play bass. I played in a few bands jamming with people, but none of it was too serious. Then one time I played with a drummer who happened to be the last drummer in Tom's old band, Lock Up[3]. I played with him for years in Irvine where me and Zack are both from, before he hooked me up with Tom. Then, later, Zack hooked up with Tom and Brad. I wasn't there at the time because I got to the stage in my life where I didn't think that I was cut out for music, I was floundering. I think in order to have success everyone has to go through a period like that that – one where you have to question whether music is or you. At that point I really thought that it really wasn't for me as a profession, but then of course the phone rang asking me to jam with this new band… and that was it."

Zack, I remember owning the one single, 'No Spiritual Surrender', that you did with your old hardcore band, Inside Out.

Zack de la Rocha (vocals): "Really? Right on!"

How do you look back on that time now?

Zack: "There was really not that much of a difference in what we did with Inside Out to what we're doing now in Rage. Both were political acts, just on a different scale. If anything, it's just an aesthetic difference."

Is it true that you had a song called 'Rage Against the Machine'

Zack: "Yeah, we did, but it never got recorded. We performed it at the last Inside Out concert that we ever gave. At the time it was certainly a different scenario because we were playing to 100 people as opposed to 100,000. I think within that scene there was a certain set of ethics that I carried over into Rage Against the Machine. I mean, at that time we were putting the music out ourselves, so that was obviously another distinct difference. What was important to us in Inside Out, and the thing that we carried on into Rage, was that music should not be a medium in which kids are super-exploited. If a kid wanted to identify with a band, they didn't have to go out and spend a month's worth of pay on a T-shirt or a concert ticket. Things have to be affordable."

So was it like a Fugazi thing, where prices must be kept to a minimum?
Zack: "Absolutely. I'm pretty removed from that time now so it's hard to elaborate on what it was like, other than remembering that I was playing with some of my best friends in the world and things like playing up and down the West Coast, the little hardcore tours. Playing places like [legendary Berkeley, California punk dive] Gilman Street. It was an exciting time for me."

Are you still in touch with old friends from the hardcore scene?
Zack: "Oh yeah, definitely. For the most part they're into what we do in Rage. I think the members of Inside Out have all gone on to contribute in our different ways and all stuck to our original ethics. A friend of mine, one of the first guitar players in Inside Out, is now running a free interactive website in which he broadcasts demonstrations, protests and dialogues from around the world. He's trying to create an alternative source of media for people to engage in. We've all moved forward in different ways."

How much has living in LA defined the band's approach?
Brad Wilk (drums): "I was actually born in Portland, Oregon, then moved to Washington, then LA for about nine years, then Chicago, then back to LA. Personally, I have a love-hate relationship with LA, and I have definitely been there long enough to let the things that would normally bother other people just wash over me. In the middle of all the phoney, back-stabbing entertainment music industry bullshit, there are actually lots of little pods of greatness to experience. Plus, it's such a cultural melting point... all that LA scenesters shit is in your face if you want it to be, but that city has definitely had a large effect on every one of us in the band, both musically and politically."

What are your memories of Rage Against the Machine's first ever show?
Brad: "It was a pretty amazing LA club show in a place called Jabberjaw and it's still one of the highlights of our career. This was 1991. What we did was rehearse for about three months, consciously said 'fuck the record companies' and instead put a tape together to sell at shows, although to

be honest we really had no idea that any record company would even be interested in a band like us. But at that first show, the reaction from the crowd was so intense and so right on with what we were portraying that it was one big communal celebration of frustration and anger. It was a remarkable feeling for a debut show. It was afterwards that I realised that we had something special, whereas beforehand I hadn't been completely sure. I guess I realised the effect that we could have on an audience. That feeling never goes. I love it."

Timmy: "I agree. I still get psyched every time I listen to Rage Against the Machine. I think the lyrics are sick, the guitar playing is sick, the bass and drums are sick. We've definitely got a more of a groove element happening these days. Personally, I listen to a lot of hip-hop and over time that's gradually become the type of music that I want to play. I don't even listen to heavy music these days and instead have been listening to Snoop, Ja Rule, Westside Connection, TLC, Foxy Brown… I love all that hip-hop radio stuff and I hear it within our band. It's my dream to turn on an LA hip-hop station and hear Rage."

Have each of you established your own roles within the band?

Zack: "I think all of us do things individually which, when we come together, contribute to the band as a whole. For some of us, it's strictly to make great hip-hop/punk records and to some of us it's a form of activism that we feel is necessary given the turbulent nature of our times. I think that everyone does what they have to do in order to make sure that we can continue a dialogue with young people about the things that aren't normally addressed – particularly right now in America where you have a very narrow control over the information that reaches young people about the things that are drastically affecting their lives."

Timmy: "The life-blood of Rage Against the Machine is progression; to constantly get better and never take any steps backwards. We record albums, but I think we play the music better live and that, ultimately, is what we've always been about. We're currently self-managed, which would be really intimidating to a lot of musicians. It's nice though, it's exciting and it's empowering because we can do whatever the hell we want. I'm liking that. Even people giving me their opinion of our songs and entering into a discussion about who we are and what we do excites me. The prospect of what we can achieve is exciting and when that goes away we'll be over."

Zack, you deliberately chose not to do interviews during the early part of the band's career – why was that?

Zack: "One of the things that I wanted to ensure was the protection of this band's integrity; that we were actually walking what we were talking… before we were talking. Our words had to be backed up by our actions because we're dealing with this huge, monstrous pop culture that has a tendency to suck everything that is culturally resistant into it in order to commodify it, pacify it and make it non-threatening. It's happened to so many bands in the past. I think that what's important about my decision not to engage in interviews is based on that very idea: whenever I was involved with the media it revolved around my actions, whether discussing the conditions and the situation of the Zapatistas[4] or going to Geneva earlier this year to present the case of Mumia Abu-Jamal[5] to the Human Rights court. Those were the things that I chose to discuss because I think that it's important that artists in my position should set an example through their actions because there is a such a fine line between the promotion of a product and the promotion of an idea. So, in order to protect that integrity I decided to refrain from interviews, although there was a little misunderstanding as to why I made that decision. But also, I think there's a time when the music and the lyrics have to speak for themselves."

That's true. When I saw you on your first UK tour, your lack of interviews only made me pay extra attention to the lyrics. You were something of an enigma.

Zack: "And that was definitely my approach. It felt like we needed to raise the volume for those whose voices aren't heard. There was a time when we became popular that I think we probably could have sold two or three times as many records that we did, but I think it would have been very destructive for the band, I really do. Our first tour was on the West Coast opening up for Public Enemy, then we opened for Pearl Jam and were subsequently given the opening slot on the Lollapalooza tour. It was at that point that we got into a discussion as to whether we were going to makes videos as a way to assimilate information, as opposed to promote the music as a product. At first I was very opposed to the idea but ultimately choosing to do them was, I feel, the right decision to make – but then again, what would have happened if we had sold seven million copies of the first record? Would the actions of the band be taken with the same emphasis? I don't think so. It all comes down to a difference of opinion and that's where me and Tom don't necessarily agree. We have different approaches as to how the politics of the band are addressed."

Is that conflict a healthy thing?

Zack: "Absolutely. We agree on 99% of the things that we address and the ideology behind the band, anyway. Tom and I just have different approaches and ultimately that contention has served us well."

Now that you do interviews, why do you tend to do them individually – does that come from the band or from the label? Or do you all just have too much to say?

Zack: "Yeah, it's primarily the latter! I just tend to feel more comfortable doing interviews on my own. I think from Tim or Brad's perspective it's purely a musical situation – not that they aren't political people with a desire to express things in their own right – I just think the emphasis for them is on good music and they're more engaged in our efforts and experiments in documenting this fusion of hip-hop and punk that we create. Because of that it's usually easier for us to bring in our own relevant discussions and what-not. It's kinda weird I know, but that's how we tend to do things."

It took four years to write and record your third album – what was the reason for it taking so long?

Tom Morello (guitar): "Well, we toured for all of 1996 and then deferred making any decisions about our future by touring again in 1997. We did some shows with U2, a tour with the Wu-Tang Clan and a lot of US festivals, so we were always busy."

What was it like touring with the mighty Wu-Tang?

Tom: "It was… dramatic. They only actually made it through about half the tour – it was a great half, but they had never really toured properly before. They had nine members, plus satellite members and I think they ended up having some internal difficulties that made it a problem for them to stay out for a full two months. It was a pretty forward-thinking, challenging tour. It was the first time anywhere that we've encountered resistance from local authorities over Rage Against the Machine shows. I think it was a combination of our politics and it being a rap group that terrified middle America."

What type of resistance were you met with?

Tom: "What happened was that a local sheriff's department in Colorado was faxing the local promoters about the anti-police sentiments of one band and [laughing] the dangerous blackness of another band! Whatever. We managed to intercept one of the faxes so we knew exactly what they said about us and what their intentions were. They tried to shut down several shows in the North-West and certain local officials filed injunctions because they thought we were going to incite riots or something, none of which were successful, I should add, thanks to the First Amendment[6]. It was really the first time that we encountered that type of hatred and opposition – normally it's reserved for devil worshippers."

Is being in the studio an enjoyable experience for Rage Against the Machine?

Zack: "With us? Never. It's never enjoyable. Actually, I take that back. Because we take so long between records we usually develop our own conceptions of what a great record will sound like, without actually writing continuously together during that time for number of reasons, the first of which are our political engagements outside of the band. For me, it got to a point before the last record that I didn't feel recognised to a certain extent, amongst the four of us, as to what my contribution was. Up to that point, I had written about half of Rage's music as well as all of the lyrics and as a songwriter I suppose I wanted some respect, I wanted my props. It's not about self-aggrandisement or money, I just wanted that recognition. So for our third album we took a different approach. The band spent three months writing and recording the music, then I came in with the lyrics. In times past, things got a little trying but ultimately that tension has become a fundamental part of our chemistry and I wouldn't change it for a thing."

To me, the importance of Rage only continues to grow. Along with Nirvana, you were probably one of very few bands responsible for creating your own genre in the nineties. Do you agree?

Tom: "Well, that's great, but I'll let you writer guys sort that out. Obviously, the genre of music that we began in 1991 has now come to commercial fruition, but I still like to think that it's obvious that we stand apart from other groups in the rap-rock genre, as much as I like a lot of them. Zack's lyrics have nothing in common with the other bands and while other bands incorporate DJs I think we still sound like a pretty unique group. I mean, it's very kind of you to lump us in with Nirvana. Over the course of our time as a band we've only made three albums and a live record, and I think that now due to a greater level of solidarity in the band we've made our best record yet. Timmy and Brad play the deepest funk together and there's a musical cohesion there. It's got some of the angriest anger and some of the raw punk rock and hip-hop sounds on there. It feels great. We were rocking the songs last night at a secret gig and the place just exploded."

Brad: "There's a part of me that wants to agree with you here and say, yes, we're highly influential, but I just don't feel it. I appreciate it when people say that though. It feels nice just to be even asked a question like that. I suppose we have influenced a lot of bands who are only starting to surface now – which I guess makes our music all the more viable – but our music definitely sets us apart from everyone else."

Are there any bands who you wish hadn't heard Rage?

Brad: "That's a question! To be honest with you, I haven't bought records by Limp Bizkit or Korn or any of those bands who've taken on our sound because I myself didn't want to be influenced by those bands when we're recording. It's only now that I realise that in a way those bands are our rivals – it's healthy competition for us."

Zack, how do you approach writing lyrics?

Zack: "I try to place myself in settings in which the environment around me is conducive to trying to create a more realistic picture of what it is like to live in America, what the American experience really is. Also, I try to write about some of the experiences outside of America. On the last album I tried to raise the volume of voices of people who are trying to fight for their own liberation, which to me is the essence of what I do as a poet; I try to take my own experiences as well as other people's and make them tangible through song. Over the course of the last two or three years, I have travelled to Mexico where the people are now engaged in their second revolution of the century. I think there's a distinct difference between artists that talk about politics and artists who directly experience something and allow it to filter into the poetry of whatever it is they are writing about.

"So in Mexico at the beginning of 1994, the Zapatista Army of National Liberation announced its presence to the world by seizing eight principalities within the southern state of Chiapas, with the hope of raising attention about the domination of the peoples by the 70 year ruling party of dictatorship, which of course is supported by the United States. It was also to shed light upon the very inhumane conditions that the people are living in down there. For example, over the last ten years 150,000 people have died from curable diseases. There's one teacher for every 1,000 people. There are more veterinaries for the pets of rich landowners than there are doctors to aid the people, the majority of which are my indigenous people. Also, the Zapatistas were responding to the globalisation of the capitalist economy because these are people who, in the eyes of the World Bank, the IMF (International Monetary Fund)[7] and Wall Street, are completely disposable in the world economy purely because they don't have the economic base within their communities to buy the products that are being shipped into Mexico en masse as a result of the passage of the North American Free Trade Agreement. Also, these people are not seen as a viable source of labour from the various corporations that are buying up the land that they have owned and fought over for over five centuries, so they're in a very precarious position – right on the edge of a cliff so to speak. They are being shoved out by the global economy and their response is to seize new territory and announce their presence to the world because in this particular historical period they have been a relatively faceless and nameless group of people. Now though, they're the major protagonists of giving birth to democracy – real democracy – in Mexico. Of course, their struggle has been an inspiration to me, not only as an artist but as a Mexicano. Their voices have definitely filtered into our latest record, *The Battle of Los Angeles.*"

Rage have always informed their fans about such issues that most would previously be unaware of. Do your political concerns share an equal billing with your musical concerns?

Zack: "There are so many voices and so many who are doing exactly what we're doing, but because we're at an intersection where art and commerce collide the massive mergers that have gone on between the major record companies have developed into a new format, a vacuum in which to sell this very poppy, very commercially-orientated music – all these one hit wonder bands. Because of that the five major record labels have predominantly ignored a number of great bands, whether that be a Brazilian activist band or Asian Dub Foundation – people who, like us, also see music as a viable weapon in terms of politicising young people who may not have yet responded to the times and conditions in which they live. It's very important that music occupies that space. I can't say that Rage is the most important band in opening people's eyes to global concerns, we just happen to be the band who have been able to create this open space within pop music and try to set in motion a new era where more dissident voices within commercial music can come and be a part of the dialogue."

You must be proud of the position that you have achieved then?

Zack: "Yes, but it comes with great responsibility too. Nirvana were an interesting band because for every one of them, there was ten or fifteen Bush's following in their wake! And you can kind of see that thing with Rage – where there's many not-so-great bands trying to emulate the sound and aesthetic."

Do you see a big difference between current American society and other English speaking countries, such as the UK?

Zack: "To a certain extent it's true, there are certain fundamental differences, although realistically Tony Blair isn't much of a departure from Clinton or Bush or any of those people."

Tom, your guitar playing is very distinct and you've openly advertised the fact that the band do not revert to using samples or synthetic sounds – you play it all. How do you feel when you consider the influence that you've had on a generation of players?

Tom: "I think that it's natural. I am neither particularly proud of myself nor do I disparage anyone who is influenced by my sound. If you listen to a band that you like on a fairly regular basis then their influence is inevitably going to seep into your playing. It's very strange to hear it in other bands though. For example on this new record there are times when I'd be doing a guitar break and I'd look into the control booth and everyone would be laughing at me because my style is a little… unorthodox. My thinking about the instrument has moved so far away from the traditional rock solo approach that that type of playing makes perfect sense to me, but maybe they were expecting something else."

What is the most dangerous situation you've found yourselves in as a band?

Brad: "I can easily tell you which moment was the most intense and that was when we were tear-gassed on our bus right before we played at Christiana[8] in 1996. I remember the cops coming in and trying to incite a riot by shooting off this gas at kids who weren't even doing anything. It was purely because they don't like the idea of Christiana because of the liberal nature of its society. I'd never felt tear gas before yet despite the police's best efforts the show went ahead. It was probably the most intense show I've ever played and I've never felt so alive in my life after being threatened like that. It was a very emotional experience. We certainly weren't expecting that."

Tom, what can you tell me about the time you were jailed for your involvement in the Guess jeans demonstration?

Tom: "It was Christmas 1997 and we'd been working with Unite, the garment workers union, who were battling sweatshops and particularly the company Guess who make jeans and have sweatshops in Los Angeles and all over the country. So what we did was, through Unite we purchased the billboards that Guess normally use outside of shopping malls. The day they went up, the Guess attorneys managed to intimidate the company who actually erects billboards into taking them down, and we were amazed that they had the power to do that. So then we bought radio spots on all the alternative radio stations, and encouraged people not to buy Guess jeans that Christmas because of their collusion with the sweat-shop lords. Again, bar a couple of exceptions, the Guess attorneys were able to prevent the radio stations playing our adverts. We knew we had to do something else, so there was a demonstration at Santa Monica where we broke past security at this mall to demonstrate against those shops selling Guess products and were carted off to jail. It was for civil disobedience. It was pretty successful in the aftermath – I mean the people at Unite are the people who do it and we just gave them a bit of publicity. But, as a result, some workers who had been wrongly fired and others who had been jerked off by the company were given back-pay, basically because the boycott did effect the company's bottom line. It was a case of simple organising, one on one. We're still involved."

How did the infamous naked PMRC[9] protest (in which all four band members appeared gagged and naked onstage) come about?

Tom: "That was a moment, man. We had thought about doing it a few days before, but we decided to wait in order to pick the right city in which to stage our protest – in this case Philadelphia, home of the Liberty Bell and all of that. It seemed appropriate. As there is now in the wake of the Columbine shooting, back then there was a high level of censorship in the arts and entertainment in the US. At that time the 2 Live Crew were being censored and we decided we should do something as high level as Lollapalooza '93 to… well, basically it was Situationist shit-stirring to cause a bit of buzz. We stood on stage for 15 minutes and let me tell you, 15 minutes is an eternity when you're standing butt-naked in front of 30,000 people. That is a long-ass time! Because we were opening the whole show, for the first five minutes people were going crazy. Then, five minutes in people were, like, 'OK, where's "Bullet In the Head" then?'

"We're looking at them, they're looking at us… for another five minutes. Then they start getting pissed and the booing begins, the middle fingers are raised and they start throwing coins, which was terrifying. The majority of the crowd were really angry, pissed off and upset, but that was our exact point: you may not be able to hear controversial music on mainstream radio or TV, but you don't just sit there waiting for it. You have to act if you want to hear it, which is what we prompted them to do. We walked offstage and, of course, the police came to arrest us and put it this way, Rage Against the Machine's biggest fans are not members of the Philadelphia Police Department. Luckily I got out because I was able to hide out on Fishbone's tour bus where naked black men are a regular occurrence. There you go."

You were involved in party politics before the band – is it something that you would return to in the future?

Tom: "Well, it was really just a day gig, something that my degree could get me because I was woefully unemployable at the time. That was really the last gasp of thinking that that kind of parliamentary set-up was worth being involved in on my part. I got to see first-hand how it works in the belly of the beast. Even though the senator I worked for was a particularly progressive one, the degree to which America is a cheque-book democracy was painfully obvious, but there was also a great deal of hypocrisy at play. I'll give you an example: we had this one idiotic woman call up because she was incensed that Mexicans were living in her neighbourhood and all of a sudden she wanted to do something about it. At the time I was living in a Latino neighbourhood and I gave her a piece of my mind. I told her that it was far better to have a neighbourhood full of Mexicans than loud-mouth racists like herself. I thought I was doing good work for the senator but I got chewed-out all the way up and down the party line. They were pissed, you know? I thought that that was why I got into politics – to do the right thing – but it was painfully obvious that it just doesn't work that way. Any real substance of change – whether it's in workers rights, civil rights or women's rights – will not come about from having rulers who sit around benevolently doling out gifts. It's their force to organise people at a grass roots level."

So will your pursue things as an activist after the band?

Tom: "You know what? I can see Rage playing at the White House sometime. I think we'd have to have a major overhaul to do that, but it'd certainly be a nice place to have a record release party though – the Oval Office."

As a guitarist you've collaborated with a lot of people. Which has been the best?

Tom: "That's easy. The best was with The Prodigy when we did a song called 'One Man Army' for the *Spawn* movie soundtrack. It was awesome. That's the non-Rage song I'm probably most proud of because basically what Liam [Howlett, The Prodigy] did as the person who assembled it was put together a Prodigy-esque song entirely from my guitar playing, as opposed to going down the normal sampling route."

You played with Jimmy Page on Puff Daddy's version of 'Kashmir' too...

Tom: "Between you and me – actually it doesn't have to be between you and me at all – Jimmy Page doesn't even appear on that track. He played on it, but they didn't exactly use his part."

That's sacrilege. What was Puff Daddy like to work with?

Tom: "We were in Los Angeles and Jimmy Page was here in London, so it was meant to be done via satellite or something because I don't think either of those guys gets on a plane for anybody! That is a crazy world that Puffy lives in. But yeah, I spent a couple of days with him and he was great. He was very musical, he had a lot of ideas about the production... but it's a very different world to the one in which I'm used to operating. I just went in and set up some mics and started rocking, which is something Puffy may and his people may not be used to. But The Prodigy project was definitely fun."

Rage Against the Machine also collaborated with Snoop Dogg too.

Timmy: "Yeah, Tom, Brad and I worked on a song for a benefit record. Fuck man, I've forgotten what the benefit was for... anyway, it was a cool-ass song called 'Snoop Bounce', that had Charlie Wilson from The Gap Band singing some of the vocals. We spent a couple of days writing the song, recorded it, then called up Snoop to come on down. Charlie Wilson did his weird shit then Snoop Dogg came in and fucking went off, laid it down, one take. He smoked a lot of dope, brought a lot of people, turned off all the lights then... boom! He went off. Snoop Dogg's got skills, definitely. He's got style."

Tom, what's your preferred reading material?

Tom: "As far as reading a serious tome, I'd choose a Noam Chomsky reader. As for lighter fare, I'd have to admit to a guilty pleasure in liking the distinctly non-Rage Against the Machine book, *Watership Down* by Richard Adams. I read it as a kid and I reread it from time to time when I'm feeling down because it's a book with a great spirit. Actually, when I was a little kid, about 13 or so, my Mom brought me to Europe and I made a checklist of all the things that I wanted to do. These things included visiting The Matterhorn, Loch Ness, the Black Forest and Watership Down because there's an actual map in the book. We found the place, but sadly there were no rabbits."

What do you get up to outside of music?

Tom: "Lately there hasn't been anything outside of music. I enjoy the occasional game of American touch football. I hang out with friends, family and have some completely unmanageable dogs who control a great quadrant of my life. I enjoy Muscle Cars, which are late sixties/early seventies big-engined American cars that go ridiculously fast. Growing up I was never the least bit interested in mechanics – I liked the colour of something but that was it – but now I find myself strangely interested."

Timmy: "I have tonnes of spare time, hell yeah. I race mountain bikes, I'm on a football team. During our last hiatus I spent a lot of my time on my pull-up bar everyday doing what I call my jail-house work-out. I work out religiously. You know, I meet a lot of people who hear Rage and say, 'Fuck man, I love to work out to your music!' I'm the guy in the band who hears that and goes, 'Yes! That's dope. That is killer'. I'm not afraid to say that is basically it for me. I work out, I'm in better shape than I've been in my entire life and I think it's going to lead me some place positive."

So which bands did you turn to as a teenager?

Timmy: "For me, there was just The Clash who were politically happening and I also liked the Sex Pistols because my politics have always basically been: 'fuck you'. I was like the living embodiment of that song 'Bodies' by the Pistols. When me and Zack were kids we listened to that over and over and it's crazy because we now have a song as powerful and influential as that ourselves. That's fucking dope. I feel empowered when we're on a big stage saying 'Fuck you, I won't do what you tell me!' I mean, what a simple, powerful gesture. There's something extremely powerful about looking out into the audience and everybody is giving you the finger. If they're jumping in unison it's even better…"

Away from the music, do you socialise with one another?

Brad: "You know, because we spend so much time together as a band when a tour ends we tend to go our separate ways just to preserve our sanity, so that we all want to come back to it again further down the line. Having to deal with the non-music aspects of the band can begin to interfere with friendships, so any time away from one another is pretty important. When I'm not playing I try and do sports… OK, maybe it's not so cool but I'll admit it, I play tennis once in a while. I really enjoy hiking, reading and I've got a small space in my house where I do other types of recordings. Even when I'm not touring, 75% of my time is spent working on music. I've been working with groove samplers with my girlfriend who used to sing in the band Seven Year Bitch and I also have a couple of friends who I get together with to jam on a telepathic level

– no discussion goes into it. We just play and connect and see what happens. That to me is a pretty amazing thing to do. It's so different to writing traditional songs with a band and it provides a nice contrast."

You have a reputation for being very intense freedom fighters – po-faced, some would say. How true is this perception?

Tom: "This is a question we're asked a lot. While the work that we do is deadly serious, on a day-to-day basis there's some funny motherfuckers in this band. When we're playing a show we're deadly serious. I guess that's the side of us that the public sees."

Brad: "We all have our intense moments, but there is somewhat of a balance. It's not like we get up in the morning and rage against the milk carton because we can't get it open! The fact that we don't put our lives out there completely in the open I suppose means there is an element of mystique to us. It's easier to open up when you're talking about politics or organizations than actually talk openly about yourself."

Timmy: "To Rage Against the Machine everything is a sporting event and we're on the same team. All other bands and anyone who we are playing with is the competition, it's as simple as that. Friend or foe, they're all the competition. Whether it's onstage rocking or in the back of the bus playing Sony Playstation, it's on! Hey, I'll screw anyone on Tekken, man."

How do you handle the day-to-day rigour of your heavy touring schedule?

Brad: "It gets pretty heavy but, you know, I could also be sitting in a sweat-shop sewing sleeves onto a shirt, so I can't help feeling that I'd be whinging about a dream come true if I were to complain. Touring can get real tedious but I wouldn't trade that hour and a half on stage for anything."

Rage are probably the most exciting, explosive and subversive band I've ever seen. Do you still get off on the pure thrill of playing live?

Tom: "We've woefully underplayed the UK in last few years and the British fans were really our first when 'Killing In the Name' took off. We always love playing and it's great to be back here again. There were crazy scenes when we first came here, so there's a definite affection. The Reading Festival, Brixton Academy… those have beem some of our best ever shows. We're psyched. Playing the small club last night was a real reminder as to what it's all about. I don't mind playing big shows – I'm not one of those purists who insists on an 'intimate' environment, even though I think we managed to create an intimate environment at Glastonbury – but it is different when the front row is closer than you are from me now. We always try and do those kind of shows as a warm-up."

Have you ever thought about leaving the band when things have got particularly hard-going?

Timmy: "No, but I think about what it will be like once all this is over. My job has been to deal with the relationship between four people whilst going onstage and dealing with my own personal insecurities. That's it. That's my role. Hopefully there'll be something out there for me to do after the band, because I do worry about it. I don't worry about the money, but rather feeling good about myself and doing something I want to do. It's going to be hard after this to match everything we've achieved in Rage. I mean, playing in Rage is a skill and a craft. It's no different to making a cabinet."

Excuse me?

Timmy: "Well, at the end of the day I get the same satisfaction at looking at something that I've made as I do from the music. I just love anything that's artistically inclined. I wasn't really bummed about never making it as a cabinet maker, which was my original intention. As I become more of a veteran on the scene I still ultimately have to deal with the level of insecurity which has always been higher than the excitement level. I guess it's just human nature. I guess it's just the way that I am. If anyone tells you that they're secure with being on such a large stage in front of such a large audience, I say that they're talking bullshit."

What about you, Zack?

Zack: "I don't think that in our heart of hearts we were ever ready to destroy this gift, you know? Right now we're taking this day by day but I don't see any reason why we can't continue to do this, primarily because we've really overcome a lot of the tensions that existed within the band around the mid-nineties. There were definitely some very serious tensions back then, but now we're talking much more, discussing things and acting more as a collective than we ever have. Because of that, I see no reason not to continue into the future."

Postscript: Less than a year later after typically incendiary performances at the likes of the Reading Festival and LA's Grand Olympic Auditorium (captured on the succinctly-titled *Live* album), in October 2000, Zack leaves the band and issues a statement claiming that, "our decision-making has completely failed. It is no longer meeting the aspirations of all four of us collectively as a band." Tom, Tim and Brad succinctly vow to continue: "We'll keep it loud, keep it funky, and most definitely rock on..." Whatever the future movements of these four men (and I suspect we haven't heard the last of them) their mark on modern rock music and the power of the protest song is unarguable.

Notes

1 See note 2 below.

2 The most recent high-profile example of which is undoubtedly Paul McCartney's post-September 11th effort, 'Freedom' (thanks Paul, but don't al-Qaeda also say you have to fight for freedom?)... and you still tell me he's one of the greatest songwriters of all time? That said, hearing Fred Durst's 'rock mix' of Marvin Gaye's 'What's Going On' surely brought tears to the eyes of even the most hardened anti-Western extremist. Tears of pain.

3 LA-based punk/funk band who released one far from impressive album for Geffen, the amusingly-titled *Something Bitchin' This Way Comes* (1990).

4 On New Year's Day 1994, the day the North American Free Trade Agreement (NAFTA) came into effect, 2,000 indigenous people from several groups came out from the mountains and forests of Chiapas, the most Southern state of Mexico. Masked, armed and calling themselves Zapatistas (after the legendary people's revolutionary Emiliano Zapata) they carried out a daring revolt, protesting the heavy-handed treatment by the government and its patrons. The spokesmen for the indigenous Indians was the mysterious and articulate figurehead 'Marcos'. Through their resourceful use of the internet, which could not be censored by the Mexican state, the Zapatista people all over the world soon heard of the uprising. These masked rebels from poverty stricken communities not only demanded that their own land and lives be given back, but were also intent on highlighting neo-liberalism and the "death sentence" that NAFTA and other Free Trade agreements would impose on indigenous people. They demanded the dissolution of power, the development of 'civil society', and encouraged others the world over to take on the fight against the enclosure of people's lives by capital. Public sympathy in Mexico and abroad was overwhelming, and the protest in Chiapas proved to be an extraordinary popular uprising which was to change the landscape of global resistance today.

5 Former award-winning radio journalist sentenced to death for the alleged murder of Philadelphia policeman Daniel Faulkner in 1981, who was believed to have been beating up Abu-Jamal's brother at the time. A follower of the Black Panthers and vocal opponent to Philadelphia's mayor Frank Rizzo, Abu-Jamal's case has prompted protest and support from many quarters, largely due to him receiving an inadequate trial and four eye witnesses identifying a third party perpetrator. The facts of the case remain unclear, yet following a stay of execution in 1999, Abu-Jamal arguably remains America's most known death row political prisoner, where he remains to this day protesting his innocence and continuing his writing career. See www.freemumia.org for full details of the case.

6 "That Congress shall make no law abridging the freedom of speech, or of the press, or the right of the people peaceably to assemble and consult for their common good, and to petition the government for a redress of grievances."

7 Aim of the IMF: "To promote stability and orderly arrangements among member countries."

8 Copenhagen's Christiana/Kristiana (spelling varies) is an old army barracks zone now operating as a well-organised independent republic/squat community – imagine a hybrid of Camden market, Glastonbury, San Francisco's Haight-Ashbury and Amsterdam's coffee shop culture. A mere 20 blocks by three blocks in size, it has its own rubbish collection and recycling system. And lots of drugs on sale too. In a commendable/cunning show of goodwill and trust the local authorities realised that they had no control over the drug use in the area, so decided to make it no longer a part of Denmark, therefore freeing it of certain Danish laws with the consequence that soft drugs can now be smoked freely, but hard drugs are outlawed. Police and cameras are also allegedly banned from the area, although clearly this is open to abuse. Certain travel guides recommend that tourists do not visit Christiana at night, but aside from the stereotypical bongo-playing hippies and their malnourished dogs lolling around, this visitor had a whale of a time. Or so he's been told.

9 Following a meeting at St Columbia's Church in Washington DC in early May 1985, Tipper Gore, Susan Baker and 20 wives of influential Washington politicians and businessmen formed the Parents' Music Resource Center. The PMRC's goals were to lobby the music industry for: lyrics printed on album covers; explicit album covers kept under the counter; a record rating system similar to that used for films; a rating system for live concerts; reassessment of contracts for performers who engage in "violent and explicit sexual behaviour on stage"; and the formation of a media watch by citizens and record companies in order to pressurise broadcasters to not air "questionable talent." The PMRC's persistent lobbying and persecution of numerous musicians led to the introduction of the ubiquitous PARENTAL ADVISORY EXPLICIT LYRICS stickers.

Casey Chaos (Amen)
bleed American

*"My body is a temple and I'll
destroy it if I want to…"*

ONE OF ROCK MUSIC'S GREATEST ATTRACTIONS is its level of physicality. Performed live by individuals, many of whom would be incarcerated, institutionalised or running the country were it not for the saving grace of the deadly rhythm; extreme, loud and aggressive rock music in its multifarious forms can't help but take over its players and is capable of inducing reactions in its audience usually only ever achieved by costly narcotics.

Extreme music and its delivery, is all about the movement, the explosion of muscle, the violence in the air, the endless possibilities in defining a moment. It can't be staged. Yes, Wagner or Mahler might rock too but, dude, they weren't much to watch[1]. It's about the interaction between band and crowd, the spontaneity of the movement, the shortened distance and common bond linking everyone in the room.

Casey Chaos, singer with LA-based band Amen, understands this. Amen aren't the greatest band on the planet and they aren't the most original, but in Chaos they do have a frontman with a complete conviction to derangement and mayhem, a whirling dervish of a focal point. It's to a wailing wall of raucous metal and punk riffs that Chaos worships nightly on stages across the world, each Amen show an anything-goes stint in the nowhere zone. It's as much about the ugly presence of five men finding their personal space and letting go as it is about everyone getting together and having a jolly good old time.

Whether it's metal, hardcore punk, experimental post-rock, fucked up industrial noise, post-lobotomy gabba techno, whether it's The Clash or Mogwai, Napalm Death or Guns N' Roses (only circa *Appetite for Destruction,* mind you), by their very definition these forms of aural chaos and blunt polemic poetry rely

on two vital components: a gratuitous – nay, vulgar – amount of volume and a delivery so powerful that it borders on the potentially fatal. The hairs on your neck prickling. Heart attack music. A case in point – which is better: Axl Rose, speed skinny in 1987, dripping from his microphone like treacle, howling blue murder through narrow, venomous eyes; or some rich dufus riding his Harley onstage to his grand piano for a 12 minute jam of some questionable Wings number, only to miscalculate his timing and tragically crush his knackers between the ivories and his roaring engine, with only a pair of skimpy cycling shorts for protection?

Exactly.

This actually happened.

See what people do when they get 'successful'? A simple slap upside petulant Mr Rose's head early on in his career and all this could have been avoided.

Chaos – by his own admission a troubled teen – was raised by his stripper mother in Florida. His absent father had been in Auschwitz during WWII. From the age of ten he recalls being constantly surrounded "by people fucking and doing drugs." In his early teens, he took refuge in skateboarding, quickly earning a fierce reputation and a new name. He also developed a coke habit before quickly graduating to heroin. At 15 he cleaned himself up but was soon diagnosed with a lung disorder that still hampers his performance today.

Cutting his teeth with numerous hardcore and punk bands, Chaos formed the LA-based Amen with a bunch of seasoned scenester miscreants. Erroneously lumped in with the burgeoning nu metal movement, they have been signed and consequently dropped by numerous labels – all biographical detail that is relatively inconsequential here. They've released a couple of strong albums that have found success, particularly in Europe, and prompted former Sex Pistol Steve Jones to confess, "Amen are more pissed off than we ever were."[2]

The key to Amen is not the sales figures, but the event and the quasi-religious fervour upon which it is based. Chaos writes blunt polemics about the ugliness within modern American life and the unwanted by-products of The Dream, lights them up and lobs them into the squall at his feet. Live shows are cacophonous dins of middle-finger sloganeering and dumb riffs, Chaos; a death-bent skater without a board, an intelligent guy twisted out of shape by liberty, freedom and the pursuit of happiness.

They're the latest band to look around and wonder what the hell is going on, with Chaos biting the very hand that tries to contain him.

These interviews took place November 2000 by phone and December 2000 at The Mean Fiddler, London.

How have things been going?

"Things have been great over the past year – we got to come over to the UK and play the Reading and Leeds Festivals and all sorts of other shit. We did that *Kerrang!* sponsored show in the Virgin Megastore, which was like a cool, intimate gathering, but I don't think I could get over the fact that just a few metres away people were buying their DVDs or whatever. I guess it's now an ideal place to play. The Reading Festival was our first proper gig in the UK and it was just the sickest vibe ever. All those free-thinking individuals coming together to form a sense of unity in one single place is fucking brilliant."

Has constant touring sharpened the band?

"I've noticed the change in my body from all the damage I'm incurring, that's for sure. People ask me what they can expect from an Amen show and I just say stuff, 'Come see the one-eyed freak show,' because that's what it feels like to me and I don't know how long it's going to be around for. I don't know how long I can do this for at this level. And to be brutally honest with you, the minute it becomes likes a routine or a job or an act I'll just stop. I don't give a fuck. I don't care about the money because there is none and I definitely don't care about the fame. Being in this band is a mode of expression, and the minute it stops being an expression and becomes a job is when it will be over."

You sound pretty jaded right now – is this down to the demands that you put on yourself?

"It just gets tedious sometimes, you know? I get up in the morning and I can't walk because I've fucked up my leg doing some stupid shit. When you're damaging yourself on tour you're not giving yourself proper time to heel. I mean, my ankle's still fucked up from [Belgian festival] Pukkelpop. I went to see a doctor and he told me I had to stay off my leg, but there's no way that I can because we've got all these dates lined up. Also, I've got all this fibrotic tissue that's formed a giant lump in my leg and shows no signs of going away… whatever. Poor, poor fucking me. Ha, ha, ha!"

Being on a tour bus for months at a time must have its strains. All that testosterone in a tin can on wheels.

"Yeah, but we try not to masturbate on the day of a show. Hey, you've got to keep your chi! I'll tell you something that is totally true. I find the male body so disgusting that I couldn't turn myself on if I tried – and I have tried plenty of times, believe me. It just doesn't seem to work. I've got to have that interaction with a female because when I look at myself it's like 'Ugh, God! Why?' If I was a woman, I probably wouldn't leave the bedroom but being a man, masturbation is difficult for me. I rarely do it. Women though are perfection for me – they're the true walking gods. I love the way females interact, the way they talk. Everything."

Do you think the heightened physical sense of your performance relates back to your days as a professional skater?

"Oh yeah, without a doubt. I think anybody who does something like a physically extreme activity, which is what skateboarding is, with a certain degree of passion and conviction, they're always going to push yourself that little bit further. Maybe you can do an eight foot air out the top of a ramp and want to go to ten feet, but to do that you have to push yourself and max-out as much as possible. And obviously, when you're testing your own limits and capabilities you're going to eat shit and damage yourself in your attempts. That's basically the circumstances that I was brought up in. Probably my happiest memory from that time was quitting drugs at 15 and knowing that I could do it and move on. Everything was about pushing myself as far as humanly – and inhumanly – possible in order to express myself. I just wasn't sure how to do it. That led to me screaming in hardcore punk bands, but now as a I get older I find I'm able to focus and direct that energy and that anger a bit better."

So you're saying that the Casey Chaos of today is a mellower version of the mohawked leader of many a ropey punk band?

"Yeah, absolutely! I was way more violent when I was playing in hardcore bands. I used to punch our guitar player whenever he made a mistake onstage. Back then, I had a lot of misguided energy controlling my actions, whereas now I try and package things so that I can go through my day and not really feel any hostility towards anyone."

How long have you had your assumed name?

"Since I was ten, when I started skateboarding. Everyone was much older than me but when I look back at old videos or posters I now realise I was doing lunatic shit back then. Everyone used to go, 'Aw, man, that was chaotic!' when I did something cool so 'Chaos' quickly stuck."

Do you think you live up to it?

"I don't know. I'm not out of my mind or crazy but my life is definitely chaotic in the sense that crazy shit just seems to happen to me. Like I've got a black eye right now from falling into a guitar. That wasn't planned."

What's your real name?

"Chmielinski. A good Polish name."

Was religion a part of your life, growing up?

"When my mother moved us to Florida she made some new friends and whatever denomination they were, we'd go to their church. Baptist, Catholic, whatever. We went to them all. And they all had the same book, but their own interpretation. It was confusing for me because you'd hear one thing at one church and something contradictory at another and whenever you asked questions they wouldn't be able to answer them. I'd ask 'Why?' and they'd say 'That's just the way it is'. I guess the *Bible* is a an interesting book, although events have been so distorted and chapters have been lost over the years, so that it's hard to swallow it. There's a book out there called *The Lost Books of Eden* which claims to be the sections that were omitted from the *Bible* for not being Christian enough, so basically we get the edited version. The boring stuff."

What music were you listening to back then?

"Well, I wanted nothing to do with the tobacco-chewing, flannel-wearing rednecks who listened to bad rock 'n' roll, so I came to it all pretty late. Then one day a skater played me some Black Flag and I thought I'd discovered God. It was music with meaning. Punk rock led to metal, black metal, goth… but now I listen to anything that is pure or real."

I'm currently writing a piece about the act of self-mutilation within the context of rock 'n' roll performances, and have recently read a lot of letters from kids who wrote in after your show at Reading saying that, yeah, they do it too. What reaction do you get from fans when you push yourself so hard that the performance turns into out-and-out self-destruction?

"It depends. A lot of nights kids come up to me afterwards and say 'What happened? There was no blood tonight!' It's not something that's planned and I don't do that type of thing for anyone other than myself. Sometimes it happens because I can't breath properly or I feel that I'm not giving as much that I can and my mind starts wandering, so in a weird way doing those things keeps me in my place. As far as the reaction I get from people, well… if everyone did things just because someone else did then we'd be in trouble. For example, we'd have to ban pets in America because it was dogs that told the serial killer Son of Sam to go out and kill people. What I mean is, everyone is going to find excuses for their own actions when really it all comes down to being a good human. That's the test, really. You've got to ask yourself: are you a person or a human being?"

When it's all going off and you start slashing yourself with glass or leaping off lighting rigs do you feel the pain or is it – like Iggy Pop once said – pure adrenalin taking over?

"I never feel anything on stage. When we played London recently I was on crutches, but as soon as that fucking music kicked in I just smashed the crutch, threw it into the crowd and it was on. I was really limping a lot that day. I went to some place… Camden Market, is it? Well, I was trying to see the sights of London but I was limping and getting so pissed off because I could barely walk and the crutch was hurting my arm and I was ill that it finally came to a head that night and I smashed the crutch and went for it anyway. I really don't think when I play and that's the very reason that so many stupid things happen to me."

As it's generally something that people do in private and don't like to advertise, is the self-mutilation something that you've always done off stage too, or is it all purely because of the music?

"To be honest, I did it a lot as a kid. It predominantly came from the time when I broke both my arms skateboarding and I was pretty much housebound and couldn't do anything. Through music I'd finally found the right outlet to unleash my anger, but because I was incapacitated I'd get so pissed off, and hate everyone around me, that nothing felt real. In cutting myself though there was a real release – of both frustration and endorphins, which have been proven to be released on such occasions. It's a rush. You're high. You can trace it right back through history to ancient scarification rites, and even now with the various modern primitives – the people who bring the idea of mutilation to whole new levels."

At what age did you start cutting yourself?

"I began doing it as a child. There were times that I'd be so pissed off that I'd punch walls and still not get the release that I required so I'd take a fucking bottle and smash it or take a fucking knife from the kitchen and cut myself up without any thought to it. It's almost like jacking off or something, you know?"

It's like a great unspoken secret that goes on way more than people

suspect at all levels of society – from bedroom dwellers to princesses. And, aside from suicide, it's the ultimate expression of self-loathing and call for attention.

"And it's one of the truths of our society that when you do self-mutilation as an adult there's almost an art to it, but when you're a misguided youth who's pissed off and probably doesn't have good parenting it becomes a problem, and one which we as a society – particularly American society – don't always wish to address. The fact that we don't always recognise or acknowledge that people are doing these things to themselves is just as much a problem in modern American society as what it is they are actually doing. Society currently has a habit of avoiding addressing such problems, as we don't like to admit to what's going on. I suppose at least in seeing me doing this stuff people aren't alone in their feelings. Personally, I have no tattoos or anything like that – just a belief structure. What I do is purely self-mutilation. My body is a temple and I'll destroy it if I want to."

Because a lot of Amen's work plays heavily on childhood imagery – or images of children – are you worried about getting associated with the hordes of angsty nu metal bands whose sole lyrical message is moaning about how hard it was growing up in nice suburban Californian towns?

"Musically and lyrically we're different from those bands, but a lot of people do have this whole 'loss of innocence' thing going on. Children are probably the purest form on the planet so a lot of people have picked up on that imagery and either make it a bit more intricate or bastardise it. The image of children that we used on the first album cover [*Amen*, Roadrunner 1999] came to me in a dream, so I can't really explain why we use the imagery that we do. I like the cover of a record to compliment the subjects we're covering within the music, so the songs and the art go hand in hand for us."

But even though you're more of a punk band in intention and delivery you're still associated with lots of nu metal bands and all the directionless fake-angst imagery that goes with them.

"I don't have an image, do I? Hopefully the music is what people connect to, because every time we play it's like it's the last show that we'll ever do. Hopefully what we do comes across as honest, and hopefully our integrity has contributed to whatever it is that we have achieved. I honestly think music is the most powerful medium out there, period. It's a worldwide thing, and although I'm not sure whether it can change the political world, it can change humanity on a piecemeal, individual basis.

A lot of American music right now is very materialistic and formulated towards fame, and lot of bands form to get rich and famous – live the American Dream. But if we can bring music back to what life is really about and we show a bit of integrity in what we do, it can definitely change people for the better. If you can change the way someone thinks on a personal level, they will then, hopefully, convey that feeling to their friends and so on. It's a level of simple communication. Then if we all convey a message to our children, the whole world changes. Music changed my life when I heard it. When I was growing up I thought the whole world consisted of Bon Jovi until I heard Black Flag and thought 'What the fuck is this?' "

You tend to write all of Amen's songs even though you don't play an instrument onstage.

"Right. From when I stopped skateboarding, I've been picking up instruments that were lying around the house. I got myself a four-track studio and wrote and wrote constantly – it became the new outlet for my aggression. I've got so many songs written. At least 500. When Amen first formed we used to get together in the garage and I'd pick up instruments that I can't even play, press record on the machine and try and create something. We have a song called 'Here's the Poison' that was completely written and recorded on the spot, it came together through the eye contact between us. When I gave the band the finger, they stopped. That's how it works sometimes. I'm not a musician though. I just make noise. One thing you can be certain of is that this band will never be money-motivated, will never be commercially viable and won't be heard on TV advertisements. That's not the type of music we're interested in making."

Outside of music what else are you in to? Beyond the obvious who else inspires you?

"A lot of movie directors. Harmony Korine[3] is the greatest film-maker alive right now. Stanley Kubrick. Alejandro Jodorowsky, who isn't making movies right now, but is definitely a huge inspiration. David Lynch. Oliver Stone makes great blockbusters. I thought *Natural Born Killers* was great. There was nothing controversial about it whatsoever, it was just an entertaining film. I thought *Titanic* was more controversial because it was so insulting."

People like Harmony Korine – who I agree is one of the best film-makers out there – thrive in the underground. If they worked for a major studio they'd be sucked into making sub-standard films. A film like *Julien Donkey-*

Boy would not get backing from your big companies, would it?

"Oh totally. Have you seen his film *Gummo*? *Gummo* is America. But, yeah, he's an independent film-maker whereas all the Hollywood studios care about now is these awful, themed blockbuster movies, regardless of the content. All that matters is what stars they can get, what movies they can remake and what thoughtless stories they can come up with. One of my best friends works at 20th Century Fox and he invites me to all these big red carpet premier things. One time he invited me to see *Independence Day,* where everyone was all dressed up and all the stars were out in force, but the type of place where you're not even supposed to leave the seat if you want to got to the bathroom. You've got to sit and endure it like it's some sort of interrogation. And I'm sitting there looking at the screen thinking, 'What is going on here?' so I just got up and walked out and when my friend caught up with me and said, 'What? You're leaving?' I said, 'Yeah, I'm getting the fuck out of here! This movie is one of the worst things I've ever seen! I can't be bombarded with this... this, barrage of shit. I have better things to do with my time.' Hollywood consistently just wants to cash in on some lame idea, it doesn't care about quality."

Amen have had lot of conflict with record labels. What advice would you offer to new bands – particularly one of an extreme nature?

"Don't listen to anyone. Listen to your heart and if anyone tells you to do anything, tell them to fuck off. If you're a female you're going to have a lot of people trying to manipulate, glamorise or commercialise you, whether you're doing country, trip-hop, heavy metal, whatever kind of style. Follow you heart. Who cares what's hip at the moment? Who cares if your songs don't sound like what's 'happening' right now? Follow your heart. In the long run nothing else matters."

I know that you're interested in art and work on your own images.

"Yeah, I create... things. When we were working on the first album I was doing some art stuff and Ross [Robinson, Amen producer] came in and started freaking out at what I was doing – 'Oh, man, this stuff is amazing!' I was basically living in a tiny pitch-black room that wasn't much bigger than a cupboard and I covered the walls with images and my own pictures. Then my friend who is a photographer suggested I exhibit my stuff and we found a gallery who wanted to do it, but I knew that we were going to be on tour the whole time, so it never came off. Maybe one day..."

As you're now signed to Virgin[4], how much input do you have in the overall packaging of Amen releases?

"After we finished the last album, the band had two weeks off, but I spent the time mastering the album, dealing with the label, doing the artwork, laying out the lyrics, making artwork for propaganda campaigns… It's a love/hate thing, but we just want to make sure that something which has Amen on it doesn't end up with, like, pictures of *NSYNC or Coca-Cola or something on it."

Which other bands or artists would you most like to play with?

"Oh, there's a lot. Emiliana Torrini, At the Drive-In, Queens of the Stone Age, Slipknot, Rollins Band. We'll play with anyone as long as they're not some fake band. We've become good friends with Slipknot actually – they're like a big, strange family who we've got close to. We like Raging Speedhorn, Mortiis, lots of black metal. All sorts of stuff really."

One ongoing issue within the world of rock music is age restriction at gigs, whereby kids' options are pretty much limited due to licensing laws, profitability and so forth. Basically, underage music fans aren't as commercially viable because they don't spend as much on alcohol in clubs even though they are rock music's life's blood. Is this something you encounter a lot?

"Oh yeah, it's totally ridiculous. Music should be open to everyone. Sometimes in America they let underage kids into clubs, but don't allow them to go anywhere near the stage, yet it's the older fans who are less likely to really get into it and let themselves go, so it's self-defeating. When I see that it isn't an underage show I don't really want to play. Music is music and it should be exposed to everybody, right? Age means nothing to me. A person is a person. When I was 15, I was older than any ancient, secret Chinese guy because I lived a ridiculously speeded-up life. I saw way more than, like, some guy sitting in his rickshaw who gains respect purely because he's old. I don't believe in age discrimination. I think that as long as parents are bringing their kids up right, it really doesn't matter what some band is singing about, whatever the age of the listener."

What was your take on the recent farcical Bush/Gore election?

"I thought it was embarrassing, a circus, a diversion plan and so typically American. It was perfect that we were in Europe to release an album [*We Have Come For Your Parents,* Virgin, 2000] whose general theme is the many examples of hypocrisy that we see in modern American life. It was a great advertisement for what we sing about. Personally, I would never vote for either George W. Bush or Al Gore because they're just professional liars. If anyone I would have voted for the Green Party's

Ralph Nader, purely through lack of choice. I'm not really interested in the grand scheme of party politics, I'm more interested in the personal politics of sex, religion, addiction. Getting in touch with people. I don't care who the president is, because, you know, maybe I'm going to have to pay more taxes but I'm still going to do my own thing regardless of who is in power. The President has almost become like the Queen, it's just a title and all the real power lies with the House of Representatives. The President is what Mickey Mouse was to Walt Disney – just a spokesperson, a figurehead. To me, [laughing] the president might as well be Ronald McDonald or the Hamburglar!"

Bill Clinton, who recently vacated his position as leader of America, was called the first rock 'n' roll president. Now that his term is over, how true was that description?

"Evidently the Clinton administration improved the economy, but like everyone else all I really know about is the Monica Lewinsky thing. He should have just come out and been honest about it all instead of saying that a blow job isn't sex. I don't know, I just try and stay alive on my own two feet and not worry about the sex life of powerful men in their fancy mansions."

What are the major differences between American and British society?

"In America we live in a violent society. It's the most violent country in the world because people cannot get along with others who are different. If you're young and you're different then you're the freaks in the trench-coats at Columbine, the outcasts who everyone makes fun of. In Britain it seems like it doesn't matter so much how you look. People seem to accept individualism more easily. We've played with all sorts of different bands in the UK – acoustic bands and trip-hop bands – but in America that would never happen. It's like the Reading Festival – you got Stereophonics and Oasis playing with the Foo Fighters, Limp Bizkit and Ween. In America, things are way more packaged because the people are sheep. Like at the Ozzfest or the Warped tours, it's all music of a certain type, whereas in Europe it's all thrown in together."

Describe Amen in three words.

"Unpredictable. Dangerous. Nice. No, wait, nice sucks. Human is better."

Notes

1 In my mind, the greatest rock 'n' roll performers in the world are not necessarily the greatest singers. So long as they've got the moves and strike deadly like a cobra, who cares if they can't hit the high notes? Who cares if they fluff their lines? What matters is he's wearing see-through PVC pants and a horse's tail and... he's coming this way! I am, of course, referring here to Iggy Pop, a man as culturally and musically influential as Elvis Presley and arguably more successful, considering he is not only alive, but still skinny too.

2 This quote was used on Amen's then official record company biography, Virgin Records, 2000.

3 As a teenage skateboarder in Manhattan, Harmony Korine (born Bolinas, California, 1976) was introduced to film-maker Larry Clark, who commissioned him to write the screenplay for his movie *Kids* (1995). An impartial fictionalised study of how quickly city children turn into corruptible adults, the film proved to be too real for many who baulked at the underage sex and violence. Korine, an eccentric young visionary, then went on to make the twisted white trash montage *Gummo* (1997) and the dark depiction of incest and collapse of the American family in *Julien Donkey-Boy* (1999) for the US wing of the Danish Dogma film-makers. Amongst many other projects he has also written a 'novel', *A Crack Up at the Race Riots,* which is full of Korine's fragmented black humour and trademark subversion of American everyday life. "My parents are Trotskyites," says Korine of his background. "They used to firebomb empty houses. They have kind of disowned me, my father more than my mother, because I refuse to make Marxist propaganda. But they're nice people." From an interview at www.angelfire.com/ab/harmonykorine/biography.html.

4 Amen parted company with Virgin in 2002.

Marilyn Manson
the god of fuck v the world

"I had to decide whether I was going to lie back and get fucked in the ass or if I was going to kick someone's teeth in. This record kicks people's teeth in..."

"The Machiavelli of the 20th century will be an advertising man, his 'Prince', a textbook of the art and science of fooling all the people all the time."

Aldous Huxley on his initial impressions of American society[1]

BORN BRIAN HUGH WARNER in Canton, Ohio in 1969, the ironic, iconic pigeon-chested stick insect who has been dividing opinion since the mid-nineties, is a clear product of America, only this time the Dream has been turned on its head.

Raised a regular – fucked-up, alienated, disenfranchised, confused – adolescent with a healthy fascination in the dark side (as opposed to a regular, fucked-up sports-obsessed jock with a fascination for sweaty all-male activities that involve wearing shorts) Warner's pre-Manson years were spent questioning the hypocrisies presented to him on a daily basis at Ohio's Christian Heritage School and developing a fascination with the apocalypse that, he was assured

by teachers, was about to hit any day.

The music of Black Sabbath, Dio, Alice Cooper and Judas Priest provided a suitable soundtrack and a smokescreen for a world that suggested perhaps mankind didn't necessarily have to live by the *Bible's* rules. Damned by his school teachers as Satan's music, Manson naturally investigated further, discovering David Bowie, Iron Maiden, Kiss, horror films, comics and, most disturbingly, the inane fantasy world of Dungeons & Dragons. "If every cigarette you smoke takes seven minutes off your life," he later wrote, "every game of Dungeons & Dragons you play delays the loss of your virginity by seven hours."

If Marilyn Manson is a product of pop culture's flirtation with the dark side, then it's because society made him that way. To understand his importance, you have to understand where he came from and what he had to fight against. In the UK no one gives a shit if you're a Satanist. I have personally had afternoon tea with a group of Satanists on a quiet Saturday afternoon in a perfectly middle class suburban housing estate where the car-washing neighbours would clearly prefer bone china to ancient pewter challises. No bother. They didn't seem to bat an eyelid to the comings and goings of the black-clad figures who play in one of Europe's biggest black metal bands (and, no, it wasn't Cradle of Filth). Transfer this scenario to, say, Alabama or Kentucky or West Memphis and it's a different scenario.

Here in the UK, where our philosophical and theological development extends a little further back than a paltry few centuries, and where we have, this far, managed to evade the persistent hard-sell of TV evangelists who sport shit-eating smiles and Klan robes under their pin-stripes, most would put it down to the usual English eccentricities. 'Oh, my! Doesn't he look dapper in all that black! Satanism you say? Good work, old boy. Best of luck to you.' In the States though, where the comedic social control system known as all of Organised Religion is as important as food and guns, anyone who directly challenges the status quo by laying down with Lucifer is practically begging for an ass-whoppin'... shee-ut.

America in the 1980s, when the young Manson hit his turbulent, squeaky, sweaty-palmed teen years, saw not only the rise and fall of politicised and marginalised hardcore punk rock, the birth of MTV in 1981 and an economic boom that saw a reappraisal of the American Dream but also the return to a society of wholesome family values, the like of which had not been since the 1950s when the McCarthy witch trials set out to quash individualism, free speech and those goddamn Commies. Unless you were a new wave nancy boy, a yuppie white soul singer or a ridiculous, preening glam rock peacock, it was not a great time to be a rock star with a solid agenda.

The Cold War, and the questions thrown up by the Vietnam conflict, had developed into a paranoid nuclear age as terms like 'meltdown' and 'fall-out' and the stunning facts of The Bomb entering the national vocabulary. It was new territory. And at the helm of this new good ship Conservative was one Captain Ronald Wilson Reagan, out to make his mark on a country corrupted by the loose morals and indulgences of the boho sixties and the hedonistic seventies. Along with clueless Ron, came the inevitable high-powered sycophants and financial supports – the anonymous CEOs, the benefactors with business agendas, the post Billy Graham TV evangelists, the low-ladder senators and congressmen fuelled by greed and fame, the church-going citizens chasing a long lost Suburban/Utopian dream, the bigots, racists and the burgeoning cut-throat capitalists – all drunk on their own dreams of a whitewashed world of conformity and regularity and guaranteed good seats in heaven come judgement day. Life to them was a Norman Rockwell painting made real. Russia was an unknown entity. Hell, to most Americans (only 5% of whom own a passport) the rest of their country – never mind the world – was an unknown entity.

But as with any great shift in moral standards where the artist is inevitably first in the firing line, the underground – the true lifeblood of America – fought back. The seeds of artistic and political rebellion had been planted as far back as the jazz era and had moved through the Beat Generation, the hippies, Vietnam, feminism, the Black Panthers, Jimi Hendrix, Watergate, punk rock; an army of activists, entertainers, writers, dope-heads, artists, sexual freedom fighters and all-round freaks providing a voice for all those existing on the margins, away from the mainstream.

For the artists, the 1980s was the biggest challenge yet. Tipper Gore, wife of future failed presidential candidate Albert Gore, rose to prominence with the Parents' Music Resource Center (PMRC), a watchdog organization which, along with Jesse Helms, introduced an amendment to tighten up obscenity laws. They were swiftly granted the power to label albums with their immortal 'Parental Advisory: Explicit Lyrics' stickers, thereby tapping into Middle America's fears that their culture was being swamped with the advocation of drugs, sex and violence. In reality, the stickers merely served as a handy signifier to kids that, the chances were, they were purchasing a rather cool release.

Perhaps unsurprisingly, the decade saw the emergence of two very different, yet equally effective, forms of music. Heavy metal had diversified from the big, bludgeoning riffs of Zeppelin, Sabbath etc into thrash, speed, black, death and industrial metal, while the hedonism of the spandex-sporting, hairspray-toting LA-centric glam rockers proved that, for many, the thrill was in the sheer hedonistic abandonment of it all. Deep in decaying New York, rap music had taken breakdancing and graffiti – two of the simplest, free-est expressions of the individual – to the world, before hardening into gangsta rap and the defiantly territorial East and West Coast cliques. Somewhere in the middle, skateboard culture vaguely linked these two new strands of youth culture. Metallica, Black Flag, N.W.A., Slayer, 2 Live Crew and Public Enemy were the true enemies of the state and heroes to those in the know.

Out of all this came Marilyn Manson & The Spooky Kids, the concept unleashed by Brian Warner in 1990, then a recovering journalist and struggling writer of horror stories. Public interest in American bogeyman Charles Manson, since his involvement in the high-profile slayings of 1969, had seen something of a resurgence with Manson Sr becoming a leering, sinewy icon for everyone from the nihilistic post-punks to the rich eighties wastoids normally found lounging round pools in a Bret Easton Ellis novel. To this day, Charles Manson still represents a totem of anti-establishmentarianism at its bluntest.

Marilyn Manson became the chosen name to reflect the bipolar aspect of human nature – the perfectly doomed all-American glamour and rapid downfall of Hollywood's most resonant daughter as equally a potent image as the shadowy, swastika-eyed Manson now festering in his cell somewhere. And just as the all-white starlet Monroe had a dark side, so too Charlie had an intelligent, creative and articulate side. Strange then than most critics have only ever picked up on the more corrupted side of Warner's creation. Perhaps this tells us something about the public's natural propensity to gravitate to that which they know will ultimately repel them. People want to be shocked by their fellow man's transgressions. After all, that's what religion was invented for. And rock 'n' roll.

After a number of years on Florida's underground goth-industrial-fetish-metal circuit, Marilyn Manson's band was signed to Nothing Records (a part of the vast Interscope empire) by Nine Inch Nails' visionary leader Trent Reznor, who the young Manson had interviewed in a journalistic capacity. They released *Portrait of an American Family* (1994) and *Smells Like Children* (1995) to moderate interest, but it was 1996's *Antichrist Superstar* record and attendant single 'The Beautiful People' that provided the band's international breakthrough. An autobiography, *The Long Hard Road Out of Hell* (1999) further fuelled the Manson myth and solidified his position as more than just a caricature frontman – he clearly had a lot to say about American life.

After an attempt at a Bowie-esque reinvention on *Mechanical Animals* (1998), Manson found himself as public enemy number one following the Columbine High School massacre in Denver the following year, despite the killers actively disliking Manson's work. After a self-imposed year of solitude, man and band returned with *Holy Wood (In the Shadow of the Valley of Death)* (2000), the third and final album in a cycle which saw the self-styled 'God of Fuck' (a phrase taken form a Charles Manson lyric) rise from shock-rock contender to an often-quoted and reliably erudite representative for America's disenfranchised. Which bring us to an all-white ultra chic Sunset Boulevard hotel room where the air-conditioning is on maximum and I'm waiting for the phone to ring.

I'd spoken to Manson once before over a bad mobile phone line as he proceeded to share with me the bare details of the new album he was writing, the tentatively-titled *Holy Wood (In the Shadow of the Valley of Death)*. And now I had been invited to do a proper face-to-face interview at his house in LA. It was the beginning of a return to action for Manson after the post-Columbine backlash, Clinton was on the way out and vacuous, over-marketed metal was almost as popular as vacuous over-marketed pop. Strange times. I packed my bags and flew to LA.

Seven hours after our scheduled interview time, I'm finally driven into the Hollywood hills, rattling with caffeine. Along a winding, dark road on warm Californian night, I'm dropped off at an anonymous looking back garden gate. Manson's publicist leads me past a long narrow pool, the mosaic pattern shimmering from the bottom of the dark water, and along a path into the shadow of a large and impressive hillside house. The back door of a quaint pool house building, recently converted into a studio, opens and Manson steps out, white claw extended. We shake hands.

"Look out for racoons," he says, nervously. "They keep raiding my trash."

The first part of this interview took place in August 2000 in Los Angeles.

This is the first proper interview you've done in close to a year. Why choose to talk now?

"When I began working on my new album, I made a statement on my website saying that my only contact with the outside world would be through that medium. Some people took that to mean that Marilyn Manson would never talk to the press again, but that's not the case. I have however made my website the place where people can find the truth that isn't filtered by the media – who tend to pick out just the parts that they want – and a place where they can get information first. I actually enjoy doing interviews because I used to do them myself when I worked as a journalist, but I do remember and always will remember those people who turned their back on me during the whole period of 1999. There was a lot of negative press against me and, like Santa Claus, I made my list. I also remember the people that have stood behind me."

Does the Internet appeal to your Renaissance man sensibilities? Is it another tool to assist you in spreading the word about who Marilyn Manson is and what he does?

"What I like most about the Internet is also what I like least about it – it's chaotic and you can't have any control over it. There's always a great fear that your record is going to leak out there, but I've taken a different attitude about things now, you know? I mean, only today I put a brand new song on my site. We're in the Information Age now. If it was the Ice Age you would want to give your child a warm coat and now because it's the Information Age you want to give information. Don't hide it from people – you need to explain things to them. I think the biggest fear about the internet, pornography, video games or violence in entertainment is that parents are no longer smarter than their children. That's where the fear lies and I think it's great because it has been a long time coming.

"One of my favourite films is *Wild in the Streets,* a very American film. It's about a rock star who runs for president and takes everyone who is over 30 and puts them in concentration camp with a load of LSD. Then, of course, he himself turns 30, so it's all very ironic. But in a way, that was kind of metaphorically what I wanted to do with my career."

So do you ever go into Marilyn Manson chat rooms? I bet it's tough trying to convince them that you actually are Marilyn Manson?

"Yeah, it is. Now I can communicate with my fans on a regular basis. Initially there's a danger that if you take all the adulation seriously – or take the negative comments to heart – you begin to think that you're something that you're not, or you end up with your feelings hurt. It's kind of like Andy Warhol's prediction that everyone will have their 15 minutes of fame – only now everybody thinks they have an opinion to express, so a website is an obvious outlet. Surfing the Internet is like hearing everyone's thoughts at once and it'll be interesting to see where things go in the future. I think we'll see a situation where the strong and truly creative survive because when you put the power of entertainment in the hands of everyone and not just the artists, eventually you'll have to weed it down. I don't like the idea of giving people the ability to remix your songs or whatever. If I put a song out there it's because I want people to hear it, whereas some bands put a song on their website and say, 'Hey, what do you think of this?' then they get feedback and change it. I think that's the death of art. That's when you lose your creativity. It's great to gauge people's opinions but you've really got to stick by what you want to do."

Judging from the demos you've played me of your new album, *Holy Wood* sounds like you taken the best bits from previous works and played on your strengths.

"That's a good compliment. That's what I set out to achieve. It's a record that is meant to conclude a trilogy of albums, a record that ties together my career to date. I see it as our *White Album* in so much as it's experimental, although it turned out a lot heavier than anyone probably expected. The *White Album* was a significant album for various reasons. It was one of the most important records of the late sixties and, to my knowledge, it's the first record that has ever been blamed for or associated with violence. And that, of course, is an attraction for me, what with me getting blamed for things all the time. I'm not necessarily sure that it's my favourite Beatles record, but there's a lot of it in spirit on my new record.

"A lot of the album was recorded here at home and some of it was done at a house that used to belong to Harry Houdini, which lent some extra magic to the situation I guess. We also did some more experimental recordings out in the desert. Acoustic songs, that type of thing."

Acoustic songs in the desert? It sounds like you're turning into Jim Morrison.

"No, that's more through a lack of electricity and a lot of absinthe."

If *Holy Wood* is part of a larger concept – the final chapter to a bigger story if you like – and something of an allegory, what subjects do the songs cover?

"Well, as an example, the first song 'God Eat God' strikes me as the beginning of the story where I imagine the character of Adam to be lost and contemplating things in Death Valley. Here, Death Valley isn't geographical, its more of a metaphor for the outcast – the imperfect of the world. Then the second song 'Love Song' is, strangely, a religious anthem of the religion that rules in this imagined world, although it's not that dissimilar to the reality of Christianity. It's a very fascist, commanding and demanding religion, which is reflected in the lyrics: 'Do you love your God? (Yes!)/Guns? (Yes!)/Government? (Yes!)'. These are rhetorical questions – you don't have a choice to say 'No'. Then the third song, 'Fight Song' is more related to the revolutionary aspect of the album. You've got a person who has grown up all his life thinking that the grass is greener on the other side and then when he finally does everything to be a part of this world that he thinks is perfect, he realises that it is truly exploitative and even worse than where he came from, so he feels betrayed. Idealistically, he thinks that he can overthrow us by starting a revolution through music and making a better world..."

This all sounds very autobiographical: confused and ambitious young man strives by any means necessary to elevate himself into a perfect world –

that of the adored and unobtainable rock star – only to find it's a far sicker and more morally corrupt place than an everyday, normal, relatively insignificant existence. The media turns on him, he gets fucked over, he gets mad, he comes back fighting…

"Yeah. When I wrote *Antichrist Superstar* it was grandiose of me to predict what was going to happen to me in achieving fame, but now it's like the old 'art imitating life' argument. The story itself, in some ways was not about me, but in many ways was very much about me. As things went along, *Antichrist* began to write my life and I became what I had feared as a child. I guess *Holy Wood* is autobiographical in many ways but I don't know which came first: did the story write me or did I write the story?"

I think you've been writing the story with you in a starring role all along, only perhaps you underestimated the stupidity of the many detractors who enjoy cameo roles in the Marilyn Manson soap opera.

"The more distance I get from this, the more I realise there's a lot of me in there. I could have done songs like these ones back when I was writing *Mechanical Animals* but I don't think I had the musical wherewithal to accomplish it. I think the new album shows a real growth in the band and my songwriting. Every step that I've made has been one that I'm proud of. No regrets.

"The best way to look at *Holy Wood* as a concept is to see it as about someone who is an innocent in the world who gets given the forbidden fruit, much like the biblical story. And once they have that knowledge, this innocent tries to be idealistic and uses the knowledge to better his surroundings, to be a revolutionary. What happens is, the revolution itself ends up becoming another product of the things that he is fighting, so he realises that he is fighting himself. People will see the link to *Mechanical Animals* where the character of Omega was a satire of a rock star. They'll understand the delineation between the different characters on Marilyn Manson albums – and when I say characters, I mean the role that I play. And when I play a role it's something that I live. 'Characters' refers to it in layman's terms because I really don't ever feel like I'm living a role. Musically, my music at the moment is sheer muscle and bone. It sounds like it has skin. I wanted to make a really heavy, electronic album."

Is *Holy Wood* a record born out of the past year's events – specifically the fact that you were blamed for the Columbine High School massacre and the subject of an attendant witch hunt in certain quarters of the world's media?

"Absolutely. After Columbine and other random acts of nature that happened last year, that I got blamed for, I had to decide whether I was going to lie back and get fucked in the ass or if I was going to kick someone's teeth in. This record kicks people's teeth in.

"I don't know whether the sound or the story would have been any different without those events, but they gave me a real purpose, something to stand up for. It suddenly became necessary that the record had to be completed. You know, the album isn't necessarily about the high school shootings because some of it was already written, rather it's more about the reasons why things happen: the way America raises kids to felt like they're unwanted or dead already. It's also fuelled by the repercussions of what happened; the fact that music and entertainment have risen – or rather fallen – to an all-time low. Music has become very innocuous these days. Just to detract for a moment, one thing that I really loved about the film and the book of *American Psycho* is that the killer really finds all of his inspiration from innocuous pop music. That pleased me in so many ways."

When Bret Easton Ellis wrote *American Psycho* he was met with a lot of the same opposition that you have seen – perhaps because you both rip out of the heart of the American Dream and show the ugliness that lies beneath. That said, I thought the shock tactics of gratuitous violence were hilarious, much as I see humour in the work of Marilyn Manson.

"When I saw *American Psycho,* I laughed out loud in the cinema and people were looking at me like they were very upset! I think that's the worst part about the repercussions that I suffered after Columbine and that, although he has had a lot of positive and negative effects on America, also reflects the bad side to Bill Clinton's tenure as president – the fact that an overwhelming sense of political correctness now reigns and as a result people are really afraid to say anything. I think that anything you say is going to piss off a certain group of people, like with the way people reacted to Eminem. So, my way around that is to piss them all off. Basically, I don't want to discriminate, I want to hate every motherfucker that's in my way, if I may quote myself."

What do you think of Eminem?

"I got the record and I liked it. While I'm not generally a fan of rap music when I do listen to it I tend to go for the more extreme forms of it – stuff like N.W.A., Geto Boys or 2 Live Crew. The stuff that's very over the top. The King Diamond versions of rap. But not only am I entertained by Eminem, I am also thankful for him because no one can possibly complain about anything on my records ever again. I feel a camaraderie with him because he takes a lot of heat, plus in his song 'The Way I Am' he mentioned my name and managed to rhyme it with 'heroin' so, for no other reason than that, I was happy to oblige when he asked me to be in the video.

"This shouldn't be confused as any commentary on race division, but it seems that while heavy metal and rap music are blamed for lots of things in the black and white worlds, I'm often accused of being a terrible person, while you've got Puff Daddy arrested for guns and assault and being embraced as a hero or role model in the community. It's purely because I have opinions that people don't like to agree with. And sometimes I like to show my ass."

Presumably the artwork for your new album has a concept too?

"Yeah, a lot of is based on tarot and alchemy – things that I started studying ten years ago. A lot of people will put stuff on their album covers because they want something to simply look depressing or scary or whatever they're trying to achieve, but my artwork is always very significant and always goes hand in hand with the writing process of the album. The nature of this artwork is so intricate and in depth. For example, the title of the *Mechanical Animals* album was an anagram, almost in a *Rosemary's Baby* sort of way because when you mix up the letters it says 'Marilyn Manson is an alchemical man'. The imagery should be just as powerful and the music, which incidentally in this case has mainly been a collaboration between Twiggy [Ramirez, bassist] and John5 [guitarist] and I even played a little guitar and keyboards here and there. It's arrogant sounding in an art-rock sense, but it's not self-indulgent."

What brought about the end of your friendship with Trent Reznor, [Nine Inch Nails and Manson mentor].

"The termination of our friendship was down to equal ego conflicts in us both during awkward periods in our lives, both professionally and personally. I think we eventually resolved things, and although things probably aren't the same, I've always said that I don't have a problem with Trent."

Are you proud of the fact that you are considered such a challenge to the establishment – that many people see you as a serious threat to the well-being of a whole nation?

"On a smaller level, yeah, I think so. There are few people who have really gone out and there and challenged people through music. John Lennon did it and Elvis did it too, in a different sense. There's been the Sex Pistols, The Doors, The Stooges... people who have pushed that envelope, and not just in shock value but in true political sense."

Go on, admit it – you must get a hard-on thinking about the mayhem you've caused.

"What I mean is, when you create something like punk rock – or whatever type of rock it is – you can really reach out to people and change the way they think. I can't say that I've changed the way the world thinks but I have taken a stand when other people have been afraid to. I guess that's something to be proud of. I don't know... I just feel responsible, not necessarily because I care about the world because I'm not idealistic in that way, but I do care about people who remind me of myself and my fans remind me of how I was when I was growing up. There's no one there for them to say 'Hey, what about their rights? What about their feelings?' The normal white teenager does not have a support group other than Marilyn Manson."

If you're the Pied Piper leading kids today, who did you have growing up in the late seventies and eighties?

"Well, there was definitely escapism through music. Kiss were a band I could identify with, but only really in a cartoonish sense. Records like Pink Floyd's *The Wall* or Rush's *2112* provided an escape by taking me out of a world that I didn't really want to be a part of. Essentially, that's really what I set out to do with *Holy Wood.*"

Do you have any expectations as to how it will be received?

"When I started making it I actually had the attitude of 'I don't care if anyone buys this', purely because it's a very cathartic thing to do anyway. The early signs though are that it's a record that people need."

I'd say so. Since you emerged in the mid-nineties, metal has undergone a massive re-invention and resurgence thanks to bands like Korn and Limp Bizkit, who are considered, marketing-wise at least, your rivals and contemporaries. What do you think of these types of bands?

"I think it's all just a matter of waiting a few years and then looking back to see which music really mattered at the time. It's generally not usually the music that was really popular at that time that lasts. One thing we have seen is the rise in popularity of faux-angst music as a product in the record industry – all these people who are pretending to be mad about something, you know? You can definitely tell the difference between something that genuinely captures an emotion to something that only pretends to do that. I don't know, it's hard for me to have an opinion on these people."

*

The interview tape is paused for more absinthe and metal. Manson sits at the studio controls with a barely noticeable – yet proud – grin on his face, occasionally glancing over to gauge an opinion. Flickering candles cause shadows to dance across the wall. I flash the devil's horns sign back in approval. What is there to say in such circumstances, particularly when coherent speech is becoming increasingly difficult?

If this new album bombs and your sales figures were to drop drastically would you be content to exist as an underground, cultish figure like, say, Nick Cave or Henry Rollins?

"Hmmm. I think my only reason or desire to be part of the mainstream is that if you want to accomplish something truly subversive you need to do it in that forum, because otherwise you're just preaching to the converted. When my ideas start seeping into the minds of unsuspecting people within the mainstream it's very satisfying. It's equally as, if not more, important as getting a reaction from hardcore fans because it seems like there are very few forms of revolution left. It can be achieved through music, but not on a small scale. It stands to reason. I think the only band who have been overtly political and successful is Rage Against the Machine and they're far more political than I am. They really stuck to their guns and they have never diluted their message, so I've got to give them credit for that."

I wanted to ask you about your social life. Most of the pictures I've seen of you recently have been on red carpets at film premieres – is that the life you're leading now?

"It's strange because in the past year I've only been to, like, two parties. One was for my friend Johnny Depp's film *Sleepy Hollow,* which I went to because I wanted to offer some support to him and the other time was some other film party. But other than that I go through anti-social periods where I might not leave the house for three months, you know? It's amazing how a few photos around the world can misrepresent me in such a way."

So you're haven't turned into one of 'The Beautiful People' that you sing about — another Hollywood starfucker?

"Well, there was a definitely a bit of that within the Omega character that I created for *Mechanical Animals.* That was me being ironic and satirical and taking the piss out of Hollywood. I don't find it unreasonable to imagine why Charles Manson did some of the things that he did in this city. There's an overwhelming sense of aggravation from all directions in

Hollywood, but that's where I draw my inspiration from, whereas Charles Manson went off in a somewhat different direction."

Actually, I heard on the news today that one of the Manson family women was up for parole.

"Yeah, you know, it's something I got back into in the making of this album. That whole Death Valley area where the Manson family lived is very magical and the effect they had on this city was pretty powerful. It was like the day that John Kennedy died was the same day that Aldous Huxley[3] died and because they represented two extremely different things – polar opposites of the human condition – some believed their passing caused some sort of schism throughout the universe where everything suddenly goes a bit out there. That's kinda how I see the effect Manson had, because some people may argue that those murders killed Hollywood. That's what I think they set out to do. And some people, even my father who was in the army, would find more reason in what they did than what the US government did in, say, the Vietnam war. I mean, my father was sprayed with Agent Orange[4], which as a result not only gave him, but also myself all sorts of problems over the years. I was always a very sickly child because of the chemicals America used on millions in Vietnam. Were the Manson murders any worse than that? Probably not…

"Incidentally, there's an interesting tour spot on Hollywood Boulevard called The Museum of Death that people usually walk out of vomiting, it's pretty entertaining. They've got an interesting collection of stuff – things like Charles Manson's sweat-pants…

"I'll tell you about this new song, 'The Nobodies'. It's a very simple song but to me it really defines the way teenagers rightfully rebel these days: 'We are the Nobodies, we wanna be somebodies/When we're dead they'll know just who we are.' Its about the kid who lashes out, either hurting himself or hurting others. It's a song about how America has taught us that an obituary is just another headline and *Holy Wood* the album is not that great an exaggeration of what Hollywood the industry has become. What really bothers me the most – and this probably doesn't apply in Europe – is that if you're 16 you can get a job and pay taxes, yet you aren't allowed the right to decide what you can see. As far as censorship goes, kids are growing up faster. They're finding out what they like and don't like and it's good. Kids growing up in homes where they're made to feel like accidents or like they caused a break-up in the marriage are going to feel like they're dead already. People need proper love and respect when they're growing up."

Can I smoke in here?

"No."

Are you anticipating the usual madness and trouble that tend to follow you around on your forthcoming tour?

"Absolutely, because the time is right for it, particularly with a forthcoming presidential election."

How do you feel about the candidates George W. Bush and Al Gore?

"You know, I don't affiliate myself with any political party and I refuse to vote because I don't want to put my name on a list that puts you up for jury duty, but I find myself in favour of George Bush over Al Gore because he and his wife Tipper Gore have always been very destructive to the music industry with the PMRC. And now this week he announced Joseph Lieberman as his vice president – who, strangely enough, was quoted on the back of my book as saying Marilyn Manson's music was the sickest he had ever heard, and who has every intention of destroying my type of music. Because of that I would find myself leaning towards Bush. I don't know, I don't care – well, I do, but only about what's important to me and my right to live my life how I want. They're all so boring."

As a very visual artist do you have any particular plans as to what you're going to do live when you tour again?

"I want the stage set to be like Death Valley, again not in a geographical sense but somewhere abandoned where nothing lives, like how the album feels. We'll be playing our fair share of songs off all the albums. I don't want to be self-indulgent like so many bands recently who play really long boring shows. There's a fine line between being an artist and doing what you want – you still have to entertain people. You can't alienate them by jerking off for 20 minutes playing bullshit that people didn't even want to hear on the album, let alone live."

Surely a true artist can entertain or inspire people without compromising what they're doing and still maintain interest themselves?

"Yeah, that's what makes an artist. Because, you know, a lot people are just musicians. That's the real difference between someone like Billy Corgan from Smashing Pumpkins and I. While he's a brilliant musician, I don't think he's an artist, and while I know I'm not a brilliant musician, I think that I am an artist. An artist is able to create something… and sell it. But it's not about selling it to make money, it's about selling it to be heard. Let's listen to some more music. I'm pretty pleased with how it's all turned out. Funnily enough, you've caught me on the very day I've finished it. We've finished it just in time to release it on election day."

Which song that you have written are you most proud of?

"That's a difficult question to answer because it tends to change daily, particularly when you're writing new songs. I would probably say the song that means the most to me is 'My Monkey', off our first record[5] because it was the first song that I wrote. Some of the lyrics were derived from a Charles Manson song and I should give credit to 'My Monkey' because that's how all this started. Incidentally, while we're on the subject, let me get a Polaroid of you and my stuffed monkey."

Where did you get the monkey?

"There's a nice little shop called Necromance where I've bought a lot of interesting furnishings for my home: taxidermy items and many rare and bizarre medical collectibles. I actually bought the monkey from E-bay though."

So what would you never do for money or drugs?

"I can't really name a specific thing that I wouldn't do because I'm open-minded enough to listen to whatever you propose, but I would never do something that I didn't feel represented me or didn't feel comfortable with purely for the sake of money. In the end money doesn't equal the amount of hard work that you put in to establish a belief system that will always remain with you. There's been plenty of things that I've been offered that I haven't done, believe me."

What type of things?

"Commercials, advertising, playing shows with bands that I dislike, giving my songs to films that I don't like, appearances on television shows that I have no respect for. That type of thing."

Which Marilyn Manson band members have you engaged in sexual acts with?

"That's a good one. I have, on various occasions, witnessed John5 engaged in what I would refer to as 'inappropriate sexual acts'. I loitered for a moment to observe his style and technique, but sexual contact with my band members is something to be avoided. I mean, imagine having to wake up and actually cuddle one of them?"

What did you think of *Demystifying the Devil*, the unauthorised video of your life and the early years of the band?

"Hmmm, the *Demystifying the Devil* video. I think if I wasn't me I would have watched it. And I did watch it, but didn't find it particularly interesting or amusing. To interview a bunch of people who claimed to know me, or my ex-girlfriends, might provide a bit of insight, but you have to keep it in mind that those people interviewed probably have an agenda in order to achieve their 15 minutes of fame. And there's really not much to demystify. I'm not inhuman, I'm a person just like everyone else and a lot of the video footage that they had was quite old. I thought it was kinda boring. If I was someone who bought it I'd want a refund."

Do you think it's wise to tell your fans that drugs are cool?

"I don't think I've ever actually come out and said 'drugs are cool' it's just that a lot of people throughout history have considered legal drugs to be worse for people – cigarettes, caffeine and so forth. I mean, legal drugs kill far more than illegal drugs, right? So I can't say I've ever really promoted the use of drugs, but rather I've promoted the right to free choice."

How much do you weigh?

"I like to refer to myself as 'slanky' – that's slim and lanky. Right now I weight 138 pounds, the same weight I was in high school. I have weighed as much as 150 pounds, which is probably the proper weight for someone who is six foot one, but I have a very high metabolism. I manage to maintain my figure with a diet of apples and disco dancing."

Would you say that you are obsessed with death?

"I don't think of myself obsessed with death, although if I look at things subjectively I guess I do surround myself with a lot of death-like imagery, for example my taxidermy collection. I think in many ways everyone is obsessed with death or afraid of it. I think I've come to terms with death and my obsession is purely a desire to share my knowledge with others about my experiences in life… and that in life you're always facing death anyway."

When the time comes what will you choose – cremation or burial?

"Cremation because the band would like to snort me."

Why have you never had a female in the band?

"Because I'm sexist. No, I'm being sarcastic. There was one point where we almost hired a female drummer before Ginger [Fish, current drummer] but basically there have never really been any girls who have approached me about being in the band. I did have female back-up singers but I guess we've just never found a female to fit the role when there has been a vacancy going. It could probably get confusing."

Twiggy Ramirez, Madonna Wayne Gacy... do you have a stock supply of other starlet/serial killer names for future use?

"We did have a few after we made *Antichrist Superstar,* but I felt that it was something that was beginning to border on the expected or the predictable, which is always to be avoided."

What's your favourite food?

"I'd have to say steak."

I do remember reading an article by the French writer Roland Barthes devoted entirely to how the symbolic importance of steak is its rawness and that those who ate it were rewarded with a bull-like strength. That seems kind of fitting for you.

"I agree. I definitely think the appeal of eating steak is that it is something that once had hair on it, something that once lived. Drink-wise, I currently favour the absinthe, of course. You can't yet buy it in the States so I have to have people bring me a bottle or two whenever they're coming over from Europe. It's contributed to the album in a big way."

If you could spend an evening drinking this stuff with anyone who would it be?

"Jesus Christ. From what I understand he had a lot of interesting prostitutes for friends and the whole water-into-wine thing would be a real boon at any party. I believe Jesus would be the perfect host. Hey, you want to listen to some more of my new album?"

Interview terminated 2.19am.

Back in England in October 2000, I'm given a cell phone number and told to ring Manson in America where his God, Guns, Government tour is underway. Although the interview in LA was, I considered, something of a success, in my drunken state I'd conveniently forgotten to quiz him about a number of subjects which I had intended to broach. Also, I'd left my tape player recording the sounds of an empty room when Manson had kindly given me a full guided tour of his house, proudly showing me his collection of child-sized prosthetic limbs and a blackened, seven foot tall skeleton complete with an unnerving Goat of Mendes style head. His Doris Day memorabilia and teddy bear collection had evidently been secreted in a cupboard elsewhere. The result was one side of a tape full of conversation and the other full of cicada sounds, which are pleasantly hypnotic but don't make for a good rock 'n' roll music read.

After the usual false starts and Kafka-esque periods of waiting which seem to be inflicted on all who approach him, Manson was as cordial and mischievous as ever, despite a crackling phone line and the joint of strong skunk that I'd accidentally smoked minutes earlier.

Let's talk about other people who have inspired you. I mentioned this before, but in an attempt to understand where exactly you're coming from I was hoping you could elaborate on the list that you gave me of those people who you consider to be your heroes and villains.

"First, I'd go for the film-maker Alejandro Jodorowsky. After seeing films such as *Holy Mountain* and *El Topo* he gave me the encouragement to have a greater imagination when it came to making videos and to not be afraid to think of things that normally your consciousness would try and leave out. He, to me, is one of the greatest ever film-makers and his films and friendship have made the greatest impact on my art and my life.

"Aleister Crowley has been an obvious influence too. I think he represented everything that was great about being evil. He was a fellow beast that has inspired me to carry a torch that he lit a long time ago.

"Willy Wonka is a character who I've spoken about before, a character that I've always identified with and I paid tribute to him on *Portrait of an American Family* by recreating the boat-ride scene as an intro to the album. If I could be any one other character, I would love to be Willy Wonka, even if it was just so that I could just see up Veruca Salt's skirt... [dirty, lascivious chuckle] He's the most enigmatic character in a children's film. He was both Christ and Satan at once, a child trapped in a man's body."

Who else is there?

"Of everyone who I've ever read, I'd have to say that Oscar Wilde has got the sharpest, most bitter wit and I think I have a similarly dry sense of humour. He knew how to push the envelope and he was damn funny too. I've always been inspired by his writing and he was a particular inspiration in the making of *Holy Wood*. I don't have a particular favourite work, I just like his little aphorisms, his little one-liners.

"Despite the fact that we have a lot of dissimilarities, I find that I have a lot in common with John Lennon as far as some of the lyrical imagery that comes to mind and the reaction we have provoked from, for example, Christians. Plus, of course, a lot of his songs are what I grew up listening to. He was my favourite member of The Beatles and the significance that he had in music makes him a hero in my books. The most amazing songwriter, he blinked and earthquakes happened – that's almost a Lennon phrase in itself and is probably best left as an image. No further explanation needed.

"Anton LaVey, the founder of the Church of Satan, was a great friend who taught me a lot and who gave me courage to be what I am today. I suppose he was the changing of the guard – when Aleister Crowley left LaVey stepped in and now I hope to carry on that same tradition of challenging mainstream religions. Did he direct my career in any way? It's possible, but I can never try and guess what would have happened if I had picked a different path. Meeting him, though, and the encouragement he offered, definitely helped me to get where I am now.

"I'd also like to mention Egon Schiele, a painter who has most inspired my work, a mad artist that I draw inspiration from in my watercolours. I discovered his work in art class in high school and although he's not an artist that's particularly well known he really had a dark vision that has stuck with me."

You've got the film-maker Luis Buñuel down here too. Wasn't he associated with Salvador Dali?

"Yeah. Buñuel was sort of the director that came before Jodorowsky and he was from the same school of surrealist thought and film direction as Dali and his contemporaries. He was someone who filled his movies with subversive counter-culture ideas. If you watch his films they're not overtly shocking but they have some really powerful messages in them. There's one particular scene which I love that has a woman carrying a switchblade that is also a crucifix. His films caused religious riots and inspired a new approach to cinema."

The next one is a controversial choice – the scientist Jack Parsons, creator of the atom bomb. Why choose him?

"I've also chosen Jack Parsons because of his very significant influence on the world, and particularly America. Not only was he the man most responsible for the creation of the atom bomb… but he was a Satanist too, which people may not know. It's ironic that the person who created the power to destroy the world was doing it simply for that reason alone. He was a complex genius who used science to bring about the Apocalypse.

"For my final hero, I'd have to go for Friedrich Nietzsche – the one true voice of individuality. He's an obvious inspiration and *Antichrist Superstar* was definitely something of a musical tribute to his books, *Twilight of the Idols* and *The Anti-Christ*. I think he's somebody that many people have misinterpreted and whose simple philosophies were overlooked and I think there's still a lot to be learnt from his writing."

Do you think Nietzsche has been misinterpreted because of the way in which the Nazis appropriated some his 'only the strong survive' theories for their Aryan, uber-man vision?

"Yeah, to blame Nietzsche for what happened in World War II is like blaming the *Bible* for the many deaths that happened in the Crusades. Everyone is always going to have cause to explain why they act in terrible ways, even though everyone [laughing] knows it's really because of Marilyn Manson!"

That's because you're a very naughty boy. So that's the heroes taken of – who are the villains of Marilyn Manson's world?

"Like I've said before, Joe Lieberman. People like him are a danger to free speech. Then there's Rush Limbaugh on the other side, on the right wing with the Republicans. He's sort of a fat talk show host who just espouses his Christian morals onto everyone and he's equally as dangerous, but from another point of view.

"Likewise, Christian evangelist Pat Robertson is an evil man. I've heard he runs the 700 Club, which is a gay bar posing as a TV Christian ministry. I've been there and it's definitely a gay bar where they have bottom-less dancing, but Robertson is just afraid to admit it. I think it's a crime against God's nature what he does for a living."

Who else do you hate?

"Puff Daddy. He's responsible for the decline of music in the nineties. He's the true anti-Christ because he has destroyed everything that was good about the history of rock 'n' roll because when you sample other people's songs and try to make kids think that you wrote 'Kashmir' and not Jimmy Page, then you've upset the balance. By the same token I'd nominate Ed [Kowalczyk] from the band Live. He's a sub-celebrity that dared to challenge me and if he ever comes face to face with me again he will really hear 'The Dolphin's Cry'[6]. He was at a bar in Los Angeles and he told me that I was evil and that it was the house of love and I should leave. I don't really know what that means, I don't know how to spell his last name and he's so unfamous that it's worthless even to talk about him more. Let's move on."

There does seem to be a dearth of awful Christian hippy types doing the rounds at the moment. They're often described as grunge or post-grunge,

but to me they're a million miles away from bands like Nirvana or Mudhoney.

"Which brings me neatly to my next choice: the band Creed, because they are quite simply the Stryper of the new millennium. Only Stryper had better outfits. All that yellow and black! But yeah, I believe they're Christians and they promote goodness, which I think is a terrible thing to do for a living, particularly in rock 'n' roll. Also the singer's got an awful collection of chest hair. I also despise the actress Jennifer Love Hewitt, who has an awful collection of chest hair. No, once again she presents goodness, wholesomeness and she probably drinks milk. And even though it's not her fault, I still like to punch her in the tits. I should also mention Dolores C. Tucker[7], another person who is a dangerous threat to free speech."

I think I'm in agreement with your final choice from the list.

"Yes, finally I'd like to nominate Marilyn Manson because it's my job to be a villain. I make villains look good whereas all the other choices don't."

You've spoken out about your dislike of team sports a lot recently. Can you elaborate?

"When I was mixing one of the more violent tracks on the last album we were watching people rioting on TV in LA after the Lakers won the championship. They were setting fire to police cars and stuff. It was great. One of them had 666 on top of it and it was engulfed in flames as people savagely danced around it. Normally I would condone something if it wasn't some sort of act of revolution, but sometimes people just love to riot and loot for no apparent reason, particularly in LA. Then they'll try and blame it on poverty, yet everyone who I saw smashing the police cars were wearing expensive Lakers jersey's that cost at least 50 bucks. There's rarely a poverty issue. If it wasn't at a sporting event I would have condoned it more because I think people don't blame sports enough for violence in society even though that's where a lot of it comes from. When you train kids in school to be competitive, what do you expect? To me a rock 'n' roll concert has a soul to it, whereas sporting events are much more... base."

Yet sports in America embody the American Dream – that idea of striving hard and being the best team player, being a winner.

"Yeah. Sports, politics, religion and music are all the same in some ways. I find it strange when entertainment gets blamed for bad things that happen, whereas sport's heroes are highly respected and on the front of cereal boxes. What about all the people that are cheering 'Kill! Kill! Kill!' at football games as people bash the hell out of each other? It reminds me very much of *Gladiator* and the things we used to do when we weren't 'civilised'. To me sports are the opposite of heavy metal because metal has always been about thinking, whereas sport is all about physical prowess and the kids who excel at them are usually the ones who are less interested in learning. It's probably all stems back to when I was at school where I couldn't partake because I was too small. I would like to bring back feeding the Christians to the lions. One day, I think it would be a good sports reality TV show."

Do you have any more plans to do another book after the success of *The Long Hard Road Out of Hell?*

"Yeah, definitely, I'm working on something now, something fictional. The type of writers that I would model myself on are people like Burroughs, Kurt Vonnegut Jr, Philip K. Dick and Aldous Huxley. I've also been reading a lot of William Blake, things like that. I actually think you can understand more about someone though their fiction than through autobiography, which is why I think a novel will be particularly revealing. I think you can be at your most honest when you're lying."

And have you told any lies in this interview?

"Maybe, maybe…"

After a chaotic hometown show and a Christmas break at home in Holywood, Marilyn Manson's neverending world tour hit the UK in January 2001. Despite plenty of post-Columbine press coverage, the *Holy Wood (In the Shadow of the Valley of Death)* album seems to have stalled, but the tour sees some of the band's biggest shows across the States, Europe, the Far East and Russia.

At a UK show in Manchester, traditionally a city of pill-heads and mad men, I stand and watch a 50-strong choir clutching candles as they sing beatific songs of Christian protest, their angelic faces tilted to the typically unforgiving Manchester rain while 15,000 misfits of all shapes and sizes, from the north-west of England and beyond, trudge past them with barely a 'couldn't give a shit' second glance between them.

Boys dressed as nuns… girl-gimps on dog chains… stony-faced doppelgängers… hundreds of cheapo home-dyed hair kits running down young necks, speckling the sterile arena floor in Technicolor… the usual scenes.

In Birmingham, Manson performs while nearby a female friend sits out of sight beyond a speaker stack, her long pale legs opening and closing to flash her money-maker whenever he's back there taking a breather. At the Docklands

Arena in London, stoned and drunk on too much over-priced beer, I experience a strange moment where for a few seconds I have absolutely no idea who I am or what I am doing. Suddenly, it feels like my entire life has been spent standing in the middle of a crowd watching some band or other going through their rock 'n' roll exorcism and that everything else has just been time spent between the shows. This mini epiphany neither frightens or enlightens – it just feels like the crowd is quicksand and I'm sinking slowly, drowning in a whirlpool of hormonal goths. Ah, but at least I know I'm alive. Three days of hanging around waiting in vain for Marilyn Manson to show up and a mere three nights of pyrotechnics, stilts, chanting, costume changes, pointing, baiting, rebellion, middle fingers, groping, snogging, cigarettes, drugs and beer is more than enough.

The crowd swallows it all and goes nuts.

The day before the shows start, I meet Manson in the capital at his usual hotel. Penthouse suite. The Kafka-esque waiting treatment. Curtains drawn. Sunglasses in the afternoon. Business as usual. Only, apparently Manson has just split with his then fiancée, and I'm warned in no uncertain terms that if I was to merely mention the split, Manson would walk. There would be no discussion, no chance to make amends – he would walk, the interview would be over and I could slither back under the stone from which I had crawled.

So you're back in Britain again. How are things going?

"I guess there's something we should talk about first, something I should clear up for the press. Basically, I just split with my girlfriend and lot of papers the have been writing about it. To sum it up, the strain of touring was too much, that's it. It wasn't an ugly break-up and when you know somebody for so long and care about them hopefully those feelings don't change."

Sorry to hear about that. She seemed... you know, um... nice.

"It just got to the point where it wasn't working anymore. So... here I am ladies. Please form an orderly queue."

How have you been dealing with splitting with your girlfriend on the eve of your biggest shows here?

"Last night, I got into London and was obviously jet-lagged, so I headed straight for the absinthe of course, spent a large portion of the evening hanging out with my friend Katie Jane [Garside] from Queen Adreena and spilling my guts out to her. She's a good listener. We were drinking here in the Met Bar, where I'm staying for the duration of my UK visit. I ended up trying to fall asleep amidst the stress and misery of ending a relationship, which kept me awake until about seven. I was forced to wake up about noon and I feel strangely OK, considering everything that has happened in the past 24 hours. I tried to eat breakfast but was unsuccessful. I'm not a breakfast person normally – I usually proceed straight to lunch, because by the time I wake up breakfast time is long gone anyway."

Is touring conducive to your nocturnal lifestyle?

"This past tour around America, I've been going to bed about seven and waking up around four, four-thirty, in time for soundcheck. After soundcheck, we commence the drinking, play the show and start all over again. Some nights I drink more than others before we go on, but I'm not usually completely out of my mind, although there have been a few occasions, which I suppose were down to misery and general self-destruction. Generally, I like to be conscious so that I can enjoy the inter-action between the crowd and myself though. So, yeah, the hours suit me. I like staying in hotels though, probably because I've done it so much. Or maybe it's because if I wake up in the morning and am too lazy or hungover to walk to the bathroom I can always piss on the floor because it's not my house."

Do you have time to do anything else on tour?

"Sometimes I like to read if I have time. Yesterday, I actually did some writing. I'm working on a new piece called 'The Suicide Batteries' that I'm not sure what I'll do with. It's a story that's based on a dream that I had on the plane flying here yesterday and it's about an attempt to return to the womb through a murder-suicide, by eviscerating someone and drowning in their insides."

'Spilling your guts'… 'evisceration'… I'm sure an analyst would be able to read something into that, but fortunately I come a lot cheaper.

"Well, it was a bizarre dream so I thought I'd better write it down, maybe in some sort of an attempt to make some sense of what it all meant. What else have I been doing? Right now I spend a lot of time watching movies, either on the TV or on the tour-bus. At the moment the band have a tradition of watching *The Big Lebowski* every day in the dressing room. It's always playing and for whatever reason we're all familiar with the dialogue so it's often repeated."

Last time we spoke you were talking about this world tour – now it's here, how is it going?

"It's fantastic. I mean, we've got great crowds at every show. When we were finishing up right before New Years, it was good to get a few days break because we were pretty much falling apart at the seams for the usual reasons. I was covered in cuts and bruises, I had a bruised rib that I thought was broken, Ginger had a broken collar-bone which is still troubling him because he's having to play every night. He reconfigured his drum sections so that he could still play, but with less pressure on it so he's still holding it together."

What happened with Ginger's injury?

"What happened was we were in the midst of destroying things as we sometimes do and everyone had left the stage except Ginger. He was pushing his drum-set over and he ended up going through it and falling off the drum-riser, which is about four or five feet high. It was just one of those freak accidents really and, for once, I wasn't responsible this time.

"I've tried to create a stage show that looks like the record sounds, and obviously there's elements of communist imagery because of the revolutionary ideas I talk about on the record, but there's also religious imagery and celebretarian [sic] imagery. It's always very difficult for me to describe because I wish that I could sit down and watch it, something I'll never be able to do. The show is really raw. It's the best – and the longest – set that we've done before. We can now play for an hour and 40 minutes when there used to be a time where we'd struggle to play for 45 minutes because we were so hell-bent on destroying ourselves and everything on stage. That element is still there though. This tour reminds me a lot of the *Smells Like Children* tour, but it still has the grandness, the theatrics and the bombastic qualities of *Antichrist* and *Mechanical Animals*."

How was the last LA show?

"I don't quite remember it. It was a strange and tumultuous evening for me and I don't have a great recollection of anything other than the crowd being fantastic, and at some point I didn't have any clothes on and was in the audience. My parents were there too, sitting next to [Kiss bassist] Gene Simmons. I think they got on quite well with Gene. I don't think he tried to fuck my Mom, although he's welcome to. I also spent a couple of days with Joey Jordison from Slipknot because he doing a remix of 'The Fight Song'."

You're playing Russia soon – have you been there before?

"No, I haven't. I'm looking forward to it. We're thinking about possibly shooting the video for 'The Nobodies' in Russia because the atmosphere, the desolation, the coldness and the architecture would really suit the song."

What got you into metal in the first place?

"The easiest thing to blame for that is Christian School because metal was taboo and I was told I wasn't allowed to listen to it. They used to have these seminars on Friday afternoons where a guest preacher would spin records by Queen, Led Zeppelin and Black Sabbath backwards. It was the Sabbath one that got me."

Were you immediately attracted to the lifestyle too?

"I remember my Mom taking me back to the record store to return *Blizzard of Ozz* by Ozzy Osbourne because she said it funded devil worshippers. I was, like, [wearily] 'Mom…' My parents have became supportive since then, though. To me metal goes back to early rock 'n' roll, to Little Richard or Jerry Lee Lewis setting fire to pianos and having sex with his teenage cousin. That's heavy metal. There needs to be a pageantry, a glamour, a decadence, a danger. And it needs to be loud. Metal attracts the kid that wants to grow up and be like the guy he sees on stage and it attracts the girls who want to grow up and have sex with the guy on stage. Metal and its fans use the fear that their image creates to protect themselves form the fact that they are outsiders. That's why people go for a look that scares people – to shield themselves. It works for me anyway. And when people dress like me it's not because they're sheep but because they're identifying with a world that they feel a part of. Heavy metal music represents the darker side of things and if people like me don't do it things become unbalanced. Perception of what is good and evil is relative – we aren't being bad, we're being ourselves. Look back at The Stones or The Beatles or Frank Sinatra even. They were all considered dangerous whereas now they're just well respected musicians. It's important for me to be remembered. The antics and the scandals are more representative of the media than they are of me. The controversy that surrounds me doesn't define who I am, but I find it to be an essential part of what I do. You can't create music in a vacuum, because even if you have the greatest song in the world no one will hear it. It can only be the greatest song in the world if the world is there to hear it."

What are your memories of your first shows in the UK?

"I remember some Archbishop of something-or-other was trying to stop us from playing and I remember that we ended up having a bigger audience than we originally expected because the venue in London kept changing. It's really unbelievable to go from playing a small club to playing Docklands Arena, because it really shows that if you take every fan in every country as seriously, and treat them as equally as you would in

America, the support and response is fantastic.

"Those first shows gave me a better perspective on what's good and bad about America and it gave me a different outlook on how people respect music and religion. Everything is looked at quite differently here, so Europe gave me a better understanding of my role in the world and in culture, and it enabled me to open my mind. I also learned that wherever you go there is always a McDonald's… I'm just wondering if Mad Cow Disease came about because somebody had sex with a cow. That's how everything bad comes about: somebody fucks something they're not supposed to fuck. But, you know, the support in the UK is probably better than it is in America. A lot of bands don't really appreciate Europe, they think it's a pain in the ass, but I like coming here. I'm more and more tempted to move here."

From what I can gather, European culture seems to be more in line with your own artistic tastes.

"Yeah, nearly all of my influences – whether it's music, literature or cinema – are European. I'm not sure where I'd like to live because I haven't seen all of Europe yet."

Since we talked last time, the American election has been resolved and George W. Bush is now in power. This has prompted many to suggest that the American political climate is going to regress back to that of the conservative Reagan era, or to George Bush Sr, at least. And that doesn't look good for controversial music or someone like you.

"Strangely, it's quite possible that I'm responsible for George W. Bush being in office because he won by such a small amount and particularly because it was in Florida, which if course is where the band started out. Who's to say there wasn't a couple of Marilyn Manson fans who took my sarcasm seriously and voted for Bush? I think it worked out for the best though because the more conservative he is the better because, quite simply, it gives people like me more of a reason to do what we do. They love to take my comments out of context, but what was most amusing was that his press people issued a statement saying that they didn't want Marilyn Manson's support. I thought that was cool."

After the response to *Holy Wood*, do you feel vindicated by the success of this tour so far?

"I don't usually look at things on that scale. I always try and make something that I can be proud of, and I think it's just great that the fans stick behind something and they're always there to learn something new, and if I grow and change they're willing to grow with us. I think with this tour we're back into the ugliness again. There has been a lot of excessiveness but since we became a lot closer as a band and everyone is enjoying themselves, it's not in such a self-destructive way as it has been in the past. It's almost like the last day of school every day for us – there's no care for tomorrow. We're united in our hatred for everything other than our band and our fans.

"As for the album, well… I know that we can't compete with pop bands or even the more mainstream nu metal. If that many people liked us there may be something wrong. I don't want to be competing with Britney Spears, that's not the category I ever wanted to be in."

Aside from both wanting to be famous, your motivations are different. She wants to be loved – or fucked – and you want to be hated. And fucked.

"Yeah, true, true. Everything has become such a product now that angst and heaviness are just as packageable as fake tits and boy bands. Nothing against fake tits of course… Actually, I have a newsflash. A very reliable source tells me that Britney has had her nipples pierced. There's something quite masculine about Britney, don't you think?"

Have you made any new enemies recently? There's usually someone to add to the list.

"It seemed like there was going to be a dispute between Moby and I, but once again it was all the fault of the media. They took an old quote about me out of context and I assumed it was recent so I kinda stood my ground and let him know that he would receive a severe ass-whipping if he needed one, but he sort of cowered in fear and went back to eating vegetables or whatever it is that he does."

How do you feel about these religious protestors who continue to picket your shows? They've been doing it for years, yet are clearly getting nowhere with it.

"It's always amusing to me. Recently the most amusing incident took place in Santa Barbara – which is just outside of LA of all places, so it wasn't like we were in the Bible Belt or anything – where the Christian protestors were handing out pizza to the fans. I found that very odd that they were trying to spread the word of Christ through Domino's pizza."

Ply the culprits with pepperoni.

"Yeah. I thought that it was diabolical that they took communion with pepperoni and tomato sauce rather than wine and wafer, ha, ha!"

What's the most positive thing about what you do?

"I think I'm showing that you can enjoy entertainment, that it's fun, for want of a better word. It's fun to dress the way I like to dress, it's fun to perform. I wouldn't be a happy person if I didn't have this. Probably the most important thing I've done is bring back the rock star in heavy metal, to remind people that the person that you see on stage is not better or different from the crowd. You're in a position where you're supposed to inspire them to reach their heights of their individuality and you can't do that unless you do it in a very explosive way. While there's a lot of anger in heavy metal, it's still an outlet. Critics of this music should be happy that we're exorcising our demons in music at concerts rather than on other people."

Will there ever come a time when you'll stop touring and releasing records?

"Only if I get lazy. The hassle that I get is what makes it good. The best moments we've had were probably towards the end of our last tour when everyone was trying to shut us down. We had something to drive us again. I think everyone needs an adversary, and fortunately for me it's the entire world…"

Notes

1 From *The Guardian*, April 2002.

2 Roman Polanksi's 1968 movie in which Mia Farrow's Rosemary becomes impregnated after being raped in a nightmare sequence in the haunted New York apartment into which she has moved with her husband. Through an anagram of the name of a witch who previously lived in the building and whose followers used the flesh of babies in rituals, Rosemary realises that her friendly neighbour is the son of the witch, her husband has sold his soul and that her unborn baby is the bastard son of Satan, in turn leading to all manner of 'Is God dead?' type arguments that were becoming more widely discussed in the sixties. A year after the film's release, Polanski's pregnant wife Sharon Tate was murdered by followers of Charles Manson. The film was made in New York's Dakota building where John Lennon lived and was shot in December 1980.

3 Aldous Huxley (1894-1963) British author most notable for *Brave New World* ("a prophetic vision of the social impact of genetics and drug-use" – *Cult Fiction,* by Andrew Calcutt and Richard Shephard) and *The Doors of Perception,* from which Jim Morrison took the name of his band. Huxley later appeared on the sleeve of The Beatles' *Sergeant Pepper* album and exited the world tripping his nuts off on a headful of mescaline.

4 Agent Orange was a weed-killing chemical herbicide used by the U.S. military in the Vietnam War, so called because of an orange band that was used to mark the drums it was stored in. Made of a 50-50 mix of the chemicals 2, 4, D and 2, 4, 5T with kerosene or diesel fuel. One of the chemicals in Agent Orange also contained small amounts of dioxin (also known as TCDD), which had been found to cause a variety of illnesses in laboratory animals. Agent Orange was sprayed to remove leaves from trees that enemy troops hid behind, and as a result thousands of square miles of Vietcong tropical canopy was destroyed, but it also led to physical deficiencies and disabilities amongst children born to soldiers exposed to it. Approximately 7,000 veterans have since been compensated by the US government. More recent studies have suggested that dioxin may be related to several types of cancer and other disorders. (Info taken from www.veteranshour.com).

Agent Orange were also a great early US hardcore trio from Fullerton, California.

5 *Portrait of an American Family,* Nothing/Interscope 1994.

6 Over-earnest tree-hugging nu-hippy song from Live's *The Distance to Here* (Radioactive, 2000) album.

7 Black political activist.

Chuck D
public enemy number one

"We're proprietors of ugly music,
the antithesis of superstars…"

IN 1982, graphic designer and part-time college radio DJ Carlton Ridenhour and his friend Hank Shocklee began mixing rap tracks for a show called 'Super Special Show' on Long Island's Adelphi University station, WBAU. They were soon joined by enthusiastic friend William Drayton aka Flavor Flav, who made his mark talking stream-of consciousness raps over the records in the style of the early MCs. Two years later the trio started making demos of their own musical cut-ups and hybrids, and began to pin down a manifesto that would go on to shape the face of not only hip-hop, but white radio rock too, and which would elevate Ridenhour – now operating as Chuck D – to one of black music's most important mouthpieces. Public Enemy was born.

Signing to Russell Simmons's Def Jam Records in 1987, they expanded their ranks to include DJ Terminator X (Norman Lee Rogers to his mother), fellow Nation of Islam member Professor Griff (Richard Griff, vocals, choreography) and the fake Uzi-toting Security of the First World (S1W), a set of 'dancers' whose main role was to provide a sense of tension to the proceedings, to turn the Public Enemy rhymes-and-beats experience into a rock 'n' roll show.

And it worked. Renowned punk rock photographer Glen E. Friedman (whose pictures of artists ranging from Minor Threat to Slayer to skateboarder Tony Alva, are some of the best rock 'n' roll shots ever taken) caught them at their best – mean, moody, subterranean. Just like all those photos of Huey P. Newton, Bobby Seale and Elaine Brown of the Black Panthers. Berets, shades. Leather coats. Badass. People who mean business. Public Enemy's logo of a black man silhouetted against a cross-hair gun sight suggested that they too expected to be gunned down, at least metaphorically, as forefathers Malcolm X and Martin Luther King had been. Even the ever-present clock hanging around Flavor Flav's

neck seemed to scream 'The time is now! Things are changing, bwoy-ee!'

Musically, Public Enemy's early works forged a sample-heavy sound that crucially, was like no other that had gone before, a musical collage that forced issues upon the listener by placing them right in the thick of it – washes or sirens and booming beats, endless dialogue samples dipping into everything from political speeches to racist radio show phone-ins, recycled rock riffs and danceable rhythms. James Brown's 'Funky Drummer' sample alone has appeared on at least seven of their tracks. It's musical journalism from the front-line – or as Chuck D so eloquently put it, "the black CNN". It's music written to precipitate social change, where D bombards listeners with facts, figures, rhymes and commentaries on pretty much everything that's important to the young black American.

Live, Public Enemy took it even further. Yes, they were creating a new music but they loved rock music too. They had seen how Led Zeppelin shook America for a full decade with heavy bass, relentless drums and a big fuck-off stage show. Until then, rap had been about verbal skill and the simplicity of the technology required. Now it was about stepping up and kicking ass with a show that saw Flavor Flav playing the Shakespearean fool to D's tormented protagonist, the pair of them flanked by their unflinching and oh-so-camp security. Now, it was about rousing black people and scaring the shit out of the dumb white people – and this was way before your Wu Tangs and your So Solids.

In a chilling echo of Public Enemy's penchant for playing on the shadowy imagery of the US government's many covert wraparound-wearing departments, in 1990 they featured heavily in an F.B.I. report to congress entitled *Rap Music and Its Effect on National Security*. (Yes, these things actually get written, but whilst mentioned in numerous Public Enemy biographies, the report has never come to light.) Yes, someone thinks two turntables and a microphone can constitute a threat to fat, white America.

As with all great defining acts, things couldn't last. It wouldn't be disrespectful to say that Public Enemy are no longer the musical force they once were, but Chuck D is still a man with many important things to say. As gangsta rap moved from being a commentary on life in those inner city cesspits of America that are the legacy of organised slavery – black people in the US are still consistently bottom of the race ladder when it comes to money spent on education and healthcare, in fact, according to writer/satirist Michael Moore in *Stupid White Men*... the average black American income is 61% less than that of white people, the same percentage difference as it was in 1880 – to a cartoon lifestyle option, the hard-line pro-active politics of Public Enemy and their well-read contemporaries were filtered out. Now gangsta rap is in the suburbs, and its fans wear Nike and boast of drinking Crystal. Even the guns they tote are desirable brand names like Glock or Beretta. There's little room for talk of black separatism or pushing issues pertinent to the community when corporate-spun materialistic peer pressure is on the rise and verbal violence has been deflected away from those in power – racist governments, mass media, exploitative corporations etc – and back into the neighbourhood. So long as rap music is inextricably linked with drive-by shootings and gangsta culture, the real threat (the white establishment) has nothing to worry about while they stay up in their Beverley Hills compounds.

The "black CNN" that Chuck D spoke of is now the black shopping channel and so long as you've got the Benjamins, anyone can get involved. Over two decades, rap music, for the most part, has been carefully contained and controlled, its message of black rage co-opted by white kids who lead comfortable lives but need to feel part of the minority in order to express the usual teenage feelings of rebellion, alienation and anger. Yes, many of the entertainment world's most successful black exponents have come from rap music – for which Chuck D should be acknowledged as a barrier-breaking pioneer – but yet still many of them are on the corporate pay-roll and as tame as Oprah. Characters like Puff Daddy may now be major industry players whose empires extend way behind mere musical production, but still their lack of political content and their ability to play into the hands of white reactionaries through their questionable actions (endless feuds, an on-going fascination with gun culture, a willingness to sell their music down the river for a quick buck) means that hip-hop is bigger than ever, but also less informative than ever. You think Ol' Dirty Bastard is leading by example every time he's arrested on a crack bender? You think Halle Berry really had race politics on her mind when she accepted that Oscar? No, rap music as "the black CNN" that Public Enemy and countless others effectively launched has failed to reach its potential. Once again, it is just more music that has been enveloped by the record companies who have turned it into a fashion-led trend with little room for movement or social change. It's unchallenging fluff. And it's bullshit. The biggest rapper in the world sings about rape, abuse, drug-taking and so forth. There's nothing wrong with that – it's still poetry – but he's white. This immediately prompts one to wonder whether Eminem would have enjoyed success on such a grand scale if he was a black guy singing about forcing himself on various white 'bitches'? I doubt it. When 2 Live Crew did it in the eighties they were effectively shut down.

But what do I know? I'm white too and therefore partly responsible for, amongst other things, slavery, racial inequality and line dancing, for which I can only apologise whole-heartedly (especially the line dancing). Which is why the thoughts and actions of people like Chuck D, now a multi-media mouthpiece for black activism, are more needed than ever.

Ladies and gentlemen: The Incredible D...

This interview took place in a London hotel room, July 1999.

Looking back to your college days in the mid-eighties, when Public Enemy started out, did you ever expect things to turn out the way they have? What are your memories of that time?

"When I was at college, I didn't have any expectations or even any inclination to be an artist, I just wanted to provide service areas to rap music and hip-hop because I thought it was the new rock 'n' roll. I became an artist because it seemed like the only road into the music industry in which I could see myself operating, but then one thing led to another, you know? I knew certain aspects of how to do things, so I did them and I did them right and then I ended up having some free vocal time in the studio and that was it, really. It took X amount of work in the beginning and once we'd created this thing it was very hard to stop it ourselves. Because of that I had to de-emphasise PE in 1995 and take two to three years in order to rebuild myself both professionally and individually as a person."

So you needed to step back from this thing that you had created?

"Yeah, because I started off engineering the locomotive and eventually the locomotive ended up driving me! I've always had good control over my life and that's exactly why I said, you know, my life is falling by the wayside so lets take a time-out so I clean some of the parts and start the loco again."

In your autobiography, *Fight the Power: Rap, Race and Reality[1]*, you talk about how people condemned you when Public Enemy came out because you were considered too old at 26. Was your age really an advantage, as opposed to some teenager who's had little in the way of life experience?

"It wasn't really an advantage that was looked upon by others at the time because nobody had any idea that a higher level of content would even work in rap music, and whether it could be sustained by an audience who may not have been actually ready for us. We thought the audience may not be ready for our weird musical approach too, which was a combination of not just funk and soul, but rock and punk and all those things put together into one big sound. So, our thing was we loved rap music and we were doing it because we liked it – who cares what anybody else thought? There's a rock 'n' roll attitude of 'never repeat yourself twice' and we've never made two albums alike – that was the goal musically. Topic-wise, our point of view was that rappers should talk about things that they know about and that they believe in, so that's what we did and maybe because of our age it worked."

How do you feel when some of your albums are often considered classics and when people call Public Enemy the greatest rock 'n' roll band ever?

"Well, rap-heads and rap fanatics always knew that our music was shitted upon and looked down upon, so we loved being adversaries and rebels and being a part of scapegoat music that never penetrated the mainstream. No rap music penetrated the mainstream at all when we started, but nowadays it's different. There's a certain amount of it that has permeated into popular culture. The greatest rock 'n' roll band? Well, it's not a sleight to anyone else, but we just did what we did and tried to represent rap music as a genre that is a part of rock 'n' roll. It's not like hip-hop embodies all music, but to say that we're an important element of rock 'n' roll might be a fairer assessment. Yeah. Sometimes you've got to watch these journalists, man. A year or two ago, The Prodigy was the greatest rock 'n' roll band all of a sudden."

You famously described rap music as "the black CNN". Does that still stand true today?

"No, not at all. Rap music is a part of black people's lives – it's almost like a worldwide religion for people 25 and under. For all kids, not just black ones. That's my statement for this new millennium: rap music is a worldwide religion for kids. Even though CNN is worldwide, rap music has outgrown that comparison. People get their information from everywhere and, besides, the internet is bigger than rap."

When Public Enemy collaborated with Anthrax on 'Bring the Noise' in 1991, it was probably only the second ever rap/rock crossover record. Nowadays, the sound is all over the TV and radio, but you helped create this sub-genre – how does that make you feel?

"I think we just went along a very unusual time line for a rap group. I don't know if it changed things, but it was a very important piece of our career. I remember seeing a picture of Anthrax in either the *NME* or *Melody Maker* at of one the big straight-up rock festivals – it could have been Donnington – and it was of [Anthrax guitarist] Scott Ian wearing a Public Enemy shirt. Now, Anthrax is a New York City band like we are, so I was, like, 'Oh shit!' It was as plain as that. Ever since then I used to check out what they were doing and we'd correspond through our management at the time. Then in 1991 they wanted to cover 'Bring the Noise', and they wanted us to be down with it. I was, like, 'No, no man' but we tinkered around with it for a while and finally did it.

"Doing 'Bring the Noise' again was a big, big, big move for us because it was already an old-ish song for us , but the fact that it was being covered was a very flattering gesture, particularly as it was being done in another style, another genre. Because of that record we had extended our capabilities way beyond the rap world and it opened up another door for us that we thought we would take advantage of. We had a great time not only at home in our country, but across the entire world. I think that Run DMC and Aerosmith were the first to really break it open with 'Walk This Way', but I also think that they should have toured together at the time."

The general consensus is that 'Walk This Way' was the first true crossover record...

"It was, but Aeromsith didn't take it all the way. To me, they could have shown the utmost respect to hip-hop music and their commitment to mixing up the two genres by doing a tour together, which would have been an awesome spectacle to see back in '86, but they didn't do it. The fact that Anthrax were covering one of our records made things interesting and we realised that it shouldn't just stop at that – we wanted to do the video and the tour. The whole thing. Spread the word."

That song pretty much created a whole new genre in itself through the nineties.

"Uh-huh. You got people like Limp Bizkit, Biohazard, Rage Against the Machine. Rage were the best of the hybrid. They do it like no one else does it; they got the funk, they got Tom Morello's guitar work that sounds like a DJ and then they got Zack on the vocals delivering a whole different cadence than any other rock group. Everything else follows in that vein."

What about other, more metal based bands who've mixed it up and watered it down, but to no less effect – big bands like Korn?

"Yeah, they're good, but Rage had the real combinations. Limp Bizkit's *Significant Other* had it. Everlast too – he's a rap kid who can be a rock kid and he's very strong on vocals. Another thing I like about Everlast is that he always seems like he's not intimidated by shit. That's important for a rock 'n' roller, that he ain't scared. Everlast gives a real good indication that he'll bust that ass, you know? That's admirable."

Do you think enough artists – rap, rock or otherwise – use their platform wisely just as Public Enemy always have?

"People should really say what they really believe in a lot more. I've always had the belief that if you know better, then do and say it better. Don't pretend to be stupid when you're smart. You can either help the people or hurt the people. I try to help the people and leave it at that, then try and move forward onto a topic that might be under-acknowledged and sink myself into it. Simple as that."

Your last album *There's a Poison Goin' On*[2] was first released exclusively on the Internet. Why did you choose to do this?

"Because the conventional, traditional method was tired, old."

So are the record companies and the old major label-led system on the way out for good?

"No, things just have to be adaptable to change. It's a big dinosaur system when you return a record – you do the same promotional and marketing, the same thing over and over again. Soon it starts to become more and more expensive and because of the politics of the majors, when you turn a record in you got accountants and lawyers looking at your shit, you know? Sample clearances, 'is this going to work?', 'is that going to work?'… fuck all that shit. Def Jam used to be a streamlined label but they have changed and become part of the dinosaur and it just so happened that the opportunities of the internet situation fit our vision. It was something that we had been interested in for the past five or six years and we believe that by 2004 it will be distributing at least a third of the world's music. We also got commodities on the internet, such as bringthenoise.com and a rap station that we're building right now. These embody the idea that you can be totally informed and entertained and even get the music through some of these particular super-sites. It all started from the Public Enemy site, so we now say that we are 'internet first'. Not 'internet only', but 'internet first'. Then we do the more traditional stuff, but even that has to run in line with our internet vision now. Being focused, streamlined and looking at micro-targets are things that cannot be part of a big Brontosaurus machine."

Is the Internet's autonomy – its ability to exist self-sufficiently and beyond any one organisation's control – its true strength? The fact that it's the one method of exchange beyond governmental control?

"The difference now is that, yeah, what we do is not controlled and, personally, because I am always on the attack it allows me to continue to do that and still not be controlled by any one body – like a record company."

Professor Griff was famously ejected from Public Enemy over an anti-Semitic remark[3] that he made. Is he back in the band now?

"Well, you know, me and Griff been working together for five years. After I de-emphasised PE in '95 he could have come right back into the ranks, but bridges weren't mended between him and certain other people. Me and him were always cool, but the organisation extends beyond our personalities, so it was just a no-brainer. We'd worked together on my solo record in 1996 and I'd worked with him on his things when we were both living in Atlanta, so last year when we returned to the world with the *He Got Game*[4] soundtrack record, it was a perfect fit, I thought. Yeah, he's back."

Do you have any regrets about anything you've done in your career so far?

"I've said a tonne of times that if I could have handled the Griff thing better, I would have done but maybe I couldn't have done anything differently because you learn as you go along. And the bottom line is I've had bruises, scratches, cuts and scars – more scars on my career than anybody else could handle – from outside adversaries comin' in. There's rust and there's dents in the hull but the boat still floats like a motherfucker. Public Enemy has always been the boat in hip-hop that has comes along to break the iceberg so that all the other pretty boats can float on through. We're proprietors of ugly music and we're the antithesis of superstars. We're totally the opposite. We're the reverse of superstars and we love it back there. I may have regrets over how I've handled a few different things, but that's life you know? I'm pretty sure everybody has looked at their careers and decided that they could have handled some aspects differently, but luckily most of my moves are unregretable."

Is it true you have a rock band side project?

"Yeah, its funk metal with singing, rapping and poetry attack-style vocals all coming at you at once. It's called Confrontation Camp and the name of the album is *Objects in the Mirror Are Closer Than They Appear.*"

I'd like to hear that.

"Yeah, well, the topics roll much deeper in this band. I'm working on some covers for the record now and thinking of using a picture of the Oklahoma City building [reaching for artwork]. Here we go, here's some examples. I've got my lap-top with me so I seem to do a new one every day."

You've never been one for drink or drugs – if you had indulged yourself more do you think it would have held you back creatively?

"Yeah. And I would have been overweight. I think if I'd gone that route I would have been either fucking old and fat or just skinny and depleted.

Either/or. You can be drunk or high and get by singing for years and shit, but you can't do that with rapping. Rapping takes a lot of vocal power – like when we do the power rhyme it would kill you. You can't take breaks, you have to be rhythmic and really strong."

There's also the fact that you take care of all your business yourself – whether it's designing the artwork, releasing the records or giving the interviews.

"We still have a good time though. You can have a good time without drinking or getting high. I mean, shit, we're men! We'll go out and hang-out or dance and be fucking stupid. We got game!"

Who are you listening to at the moment?

"Other than the usual new submissions? When the shit hits the fan, I get stuff from new artists sent to me all the time. I been listening to a lot of Toronto-based rap artists. I've been listening to Limp Bizkit, Muddy Waters's *Electric Mud* – one of my favourite records of all time – the first Funkadelic record. I carry this CD bag around with me all the time, so I have really eclectic sense of listening for a rapper. I don't listen to Geri Halliwell though."

What's your favourite TV show?

"VH1's *Behind the Music*. It informs so many people about the music and the artists that have performed in the past. It's also a good template for an artist to look at when considering his future, especially a young artist who thinks it's all being done for the first time. It's like, [laughing] you're not the first motherfucker that threw a couch out the window! All that type of shit, you know? It's like, you're not the first motherfucker that fell over on stage because you're guaranteed that on *Behind the Music* there'll be a guy before you who fell over so much he fell off his career and now he's… Syd Barrett. Yeah, that's the type of thing I'm talkin' about."

Do you have plans to write other books?

"As a matter of fact, I was going to release another book exactly 365 days after my first one. Then I decided to wait 500 days, then I decided to take the best 500 days before the millennium and call it *Countdown to Armageddon*. It's a day-to-day diary journal. It's crazy. If you could see my schedule, man…"

In *Fight the Power*, you mention Henry Rollins on your recommended reading list…

"Oh yeah. He's an inspiration."

Do you think you and him share the same work ethos that lifts you above many of your contemporaries?

"Yeah, he a renaissance man, he's very focused and regimented. He's good man and he's… intense. Some of the times playing festivals and shows with Rollins just knowing that the energy out there is a good thing. Sometimes you just look at him and think 'Shit, I've gotta get the house all charged up', for sure."

As an artist who's fought his way to the top, do you still encounter racism within the music industry?

"I think rock radio is clearly racist. There's so much rad music that can't get played on soul or R&B radio because it doesn't follow their classification… I mean, I dig Led Zeppelin, The Yardbirds, Aerosmith, Boston, Meatloaf, Black Sabbath and people like that, but how can you play Pearl Jam and Nirvana but not rap/rock hybrid songs that lean towards the rap side? In response to this I recently turned around and did a record of rock versions, one of them strangely enough with Sean 'Puffy' Combs called 'P.E. 2000' which is so fucking rough, it's really good. That's my problem: I'm saying that there's no way that rock radio can't play this song. It's not like the *Godzilla* song that he did ['Come with Me'] all heavy riffs and stuff – this is really original and organic.

"That's my major problem with the United States right now – rock radio is still musically racist. As a black person, if you're perceptive you can see racism as a whole every day. I can turn your head to some of the subjects and situations that get asinine – 'cos you know I've never been one to bite my tongue – so I'll call it out. But the realisation is with racism at that level is that it dissipates. This next century is probably going to bring about the strongest class struggle ever. Not just in America, but all over the world. It's already taking place now. Racism is a tool to keep people sub-divided so that the powers that be can then control those divisions. The race card has kinda played itself out because kids are coming together and thinking, 'Fuck it, we gotta figure out what's going to happen next because this division ain't working'. But if you're black coming up in America there's always going to be that sort of bullshit coming from the establishment and there's always going to be racist people running major institutions in the US, but the more that certain areas of society get side-stepped or ignored, the more they come up with something else. It's happening right now all around us. People just need to open their eyes to it."

Notes

1 According to www.amazon.com, *Fight the Power: Rap, Race and Reality* by Chuck D with Yusuf Jah, "examines a multitude of complex social, racial and artistic issues. In his unmistakable voice, Chuck discusses the role of heroes and role models in the black community, Hollywood's negative images of blacks, the effect of gangsta rap, its images on the country's youth and the war between east and west coast rappers that may have spawned the murder of Tupac Shakur, the role of athletes and entertainers in eroding and strengthening values, and other vital contemporary concerns."

2 Play It Again Sam Recordings, 1999.

3 Shortly before the release of *It Takes a Nation of Millions to Hold Us Back* in June 1988, Public Enemy's Professor Griff was quoted in the *Washington Times,* May 1988, as saying, "There's no place for gays. When God destroyed Sodom and Gomorrah, it was for that sort of behaviour." And, "If the Palestinians took up arms, went into Israel and killed all the Jews, it'd be alright... the Jews finance these experiments on AIDS with black people in South Africa..."

Writes *Village Voice* music critic and New Yorker Robert Christgau on his coverage of the event: "Odious as these sentiments are, the fact remains that there's no discernible homophobia or anti-Semitism (and only a touch of reverse racism) in the crew's recorded work. Furthermore, the offending bigmouth was PE's designated Minister of Information, Professor Griff, reputedly a Black Muslim, though one hears that Muslims don't trust Griff because he declines to observe Nation of Islam tenets."

Chuck D was reported as responding with the following in the *Los Angeles Times,* June 1988, "We are not anti-Jewish, we are not anti-anybody – we are pro-black, pro-black culture, pro-human race. Professor Griff's responsibility as Minister of Information for Public Enemy was to faithfully transmit those values – to everybody. In practice he sabotaged these values."

4 Released by Def Jam in 1998, *He Got Game* was the first entire soundtrack album by a single rap act.

Jello Biafra
situationist shit-stirring, American-style

"We helped annihilate the seventies. We burned down the 'Hotel California', and not a moment too soon…"

Why did you decide to call yourself Jello Biafra?
"I figured it had more staying power than 'Smegma Pigvomit' "

Online interview with Jello Biafra

PUNK ROCK. I want to talk about punk rock. I want to tell you why I think it will always exist as a philosophy, a question mark to brandish like a blade when a situation demands it. Punk rock. It's way beyond music now. It's a political lifestyle option, an adaptable, pliable set of ethics through which to view all forms of culture, art and beyond. And maybe one day the punk rock spirit will be running the planet. Commerce, economics, formation of treaties, laws, wars, space travel – it'll all be run by angel-faced punk rockers with compassionate hearts and awesome record collections. Well, maybe…

I interviewed Jello Biafra at a perfect time. George W. Bush had just dubiously bluffed his way into power in what had been the closest American presidential election in history, with all signs suggesting the country would see

a return to the conservative, holier-than-thou Reaganomics of the eighties that had flourished in tandem with Thatcherism in the UK. But, hey, it didn't matter to me. I don't live there. But then a bunch of terrorists, drunk on the word of Allah, crashed a plane into those great phallic symbols of the nation's economic superiority, the World Trade Center's twin towers in New York and the entire world was plunged into a fresh moral hell. Knees jerked all over the place. Xenophobia, racism and intolerance of other cultures – the very things which the Clintonian political correctness of the nineties sought to repress – were suddenly back on the agenda, in the media and in the vacant glint of the proud President's eyes. Suddenly, it was uncool and definitely unpatriotic to criticise any symbol of the establishment, and close to treasonous to question the blank-bombing response – even here in the UK where the maxim of "you're either with us or you're with the terrorists" had been relayed across the water, loud and clear in Texan tones. The appearance of anthrax pointed to a future in which no one will be safe, although the likeable, pioneering New York thrash band of the same name suddenly enjoyed renewed interest when they least expected it, so every cloud etc etc. For the most part the Western world was paranoid and secretly taking sides. Even many of those we rely on to consistently speak out on such occasions – those artists impartial to traditional party politics – were either out recording lame charity records or cancelling tours and dropping contentiously-titled songs from their records in order to hole up in their homes with a six-pack, a crack pipe and some young boys or whatever it is rich, disaffected rock stars do.

Two short months after the attacks, and Jello Biafra was in King's Cross, London to speak at an anarchists' book fair, a generally entertaining affair, save for the bad hygiene on display. Clearly deodorant is not a vital part of the revolution. Biafra's set was sabotaged by a crazed Italian Anarchist stereotype barking random slogans. Biafra talked right on over him. He's not someone you can interrupt.

Even if you're not familiar with his work, the chances are you've been affected in one way or another by the man previously known as Eric Boucher. If you've ever engaged in a debate about what constitutes artists 'selling out', you may have used him as your trump card to show that punk rock is a state of mind, a way of life that is wholly disconnected from the fashion-led entity that it has become today, and that a non-corporate funded life of independent thought and action is still attainable in the face of growing globalisation. If you've ever bought a record in the past 20 years that's deemed subversive in any way or is just plain addled with expletives, then you've got this ex-drama student motormouth to thank for allowing such music to make it to the record racks in the first place. Or maybe you've just punched the air to 'Holiday in Cambodia' or pinned the 'Nazi Punks Fuck Off' patch to your arm.

Either way, it's safe to say that the portly 43 year old arch punk prankster and Green Party candidate is one human-sized middle finger, proudly standing tall against opposition from all angles, consistently fighting the corner for artists and activists the world over. You probably know him as Jello Biafra, leader of the Dead Kennedys ("the definitive Punk name", according to author Jon Savage in *England's Dreaming)* singer with Lard, political campaigner, chat show guest, American heretic and inventor of hardcore as we know it.

The interview took place October 2001 on an empty stairwell, tribal drums banging away down empty corridors somewhere in the distance.

I'd like to find out a little about your early years and what prepares someone for the type of career that you have heard.

"Well, I was born in Denver, Colorado in 1958, on the same date that later saw the Watergate break-in and the OJ Simpson car chase, amongst other things. I actually grew up 20 miles away in Boulder, which is right up against the Rocky Mountains, so I guess that makes me something of a mountain guy. Later, after getting to California, I realised that there was still very much a Wild West thing going on in Colorado, far more than I had originally realised. There was a bunch of ranchers on my father's side of the family who I've never met and his father was the first one to leave the farm and go to college. But that's all immaterial. My mother was a librarian and my father was what you call a psychiatric social worker, which meant doing everything from trying to reform the mental health system to flying off in a prop plane to treat people in smaller Colorado towns. Later, he worked with another group trying to set up adult education centres in slums and Indian reservations across the States. He had a lot of interesting friends, although a lot of that wasn't shared at home. For people their age, my parents are borderline radical, although I've always been a much blacker sheep than they have ever been."

What was your first exposure to music? Who inspired you early on?

"Most of the music that I heard at home was classical music or the occasional ethnic record that my Dad would bring home. One that I particularly liked was a Japanese kabuki[1] music piece which later inspired the chorus and vibe of 'California Uber Alles'. I first heard rock music in late 1965 when my Dad was blundering around with a radio in order to get me to shut up and go to sleep, and I immediately thought 'Now, this is for me'. Beatle-mania and the British Invasion was still going full-on but I quickly graduated to the wilder, heavier sounds of early Stones, Music Machines and the great unacknowledged godfathers of the

American garage punk era, Paul Revere & The Raiders. That band was on TV five days a week at one point in the sixties, which enabled them to reach all those teenagers in small towns in Texas and places like that, but yet still their influence is barely recognised. In those days even the big commercial stations played local bands, so some of my favourites were Colorado bands like The Moonrakers, whose singles were great but whose later Christian rock album is not quite the great work that it's hyped up to be. As soon as I heard 'Born to Be Wild' by Steppenwolf, I thought it was great, but pretty soon a lot of this so-called harder music began wimping out and getting really adult. All of a sudden people were into 'soft rock' or 'adult-orientated rock' and Boulder in particular became a mecca for the most horrible kind of country rock imaginable. The Eagles lived in Aspen for a while, Elton John bought a place in Boulder, as did Stephen Stills, Joni Mitchell and Joe Walsh. In other words, it was total hell for me as a teenager.

"This also meant that by the time I discovered the second hand record shops and bid farewell to the radio once and for all, a lot of the music that I liked was already in the 50 cent or 25 cent bins, or even thrown out of the door for free sometimes. I got all The Doors albums within a few weeks and then I began picking up anything that was interesting. I'd go to the store once or twice a day from high school and pick up things for free. I wound up with records by 13th Floor Elevators, I got *Kick Out the Jams* by MC5 for a quarter and a copy of *Fun House* by The Stooges for a dime. That was the only good thing about living in country-rock/jazz fusion hell, because to this day Boulder is still a magnet for really snooty, high-brow yuppies and new age cults, and that had already started back then, hence songs like 'California Uber Alles'.

"I was guided in this musical direction by a critic on the local paper, *The Denver Post,* who said that Paul Simon and the Bee Gees were the greatest composers of the twentieth century, but went way out of his way to bash things he didn't like. So when he said Alice Cooper was almost as bad as the New York Dolls or that Black Sabbath was as bad as MC5, I knew exactly which records to buy. In fact I bought an MC5 record that very afternoon. Unfortunately, the few friends who I knew who played instruments started getting into Yes and Emerson, Lake & Palmer and all that fairy-poo prog-rock shit. I mean, I like some progressive rock, but not anything fronted by a classically-trained Donny Osmond."

So when were you first aware of punk rock?

"When the term 'punk rock' began creeping in to describe some of those sixties bands that I liked – The Flamin' Groovies, The Stooges, The Dolls

– I blundered into a pre-release copy of the first album by The Ramones and… well, they certainly didn't look like Styx. At first I thought it was funny – no guitar solos and succinct lyrics. But then, lo and behold, The Ramones came to Denver opening for some long-forgotten major label FM rock 'flavour of the week' band and the few of us who actually knew who The Ramones were got in early and lined the front row. Not only was it the most powerful thing I'd ever seen, it was also great fun being able to turn around and see the look of utter horror on the faces of the assembled country-rock glitterati who just didn't understand these four guys in leather jackets playing a hundred times louder than anyone could ever have imagined. This was January 1977. Not only were The Ramones powerful they were also very simple – that's when it dawned on me that even I could do something like that. They even talked to teenage dorks like me backstage, something I never previously thought possible. Other people who were there in the front row went on to form the Wax Tracks label, the band Ministry… all sorts of things. Wax Tracks was a label that had a used record store in Denver around then, and the first time I went there I saw they had a John Denver album on the door with nails driven through his eyes and blood coming out, so I knew it was going to be the store for me. It was another pipeline through which to hear this new punk rock music. In fact they could well have been the first people in the States to stock a copy of *Anarchy in the UK* by the Sex Pistols. We realised right away that something important was going on."

So were you instantly smitten by punk rock as a sound and ideology?
"Yeah, because that summer – 1977 – I went to England and saw The Saints, Wire, Count Bishops, all sorts of groups. When I returned it was time to go to college, so I moved from Boulder, Colorado to go to school at the University of California in Santa Cruz, thinking that at least it wouldn't have fraternities and a big athletic programme and would do evaluations instead of grades, but to my horror it was just another Boulder filled with trust fund deadheads who didn't want to learn anything. So I gravitated up to San Francisco on weekends and started seeing early punk bands like The Avengers, The Dils, Crime and The Nuns and I plotted my big move to the city. First though, I had to go back home to get money together and my parents were most displeased because they'd just finally got me off to school and there I was back again after a mere two months."

What had you been studying at college?
"Unfortunately, you couldn't just choose what you wanted to do then,

you almost had to audition for courses. For example, I wanted to do Film-making but in order to get in you had to already have made a film, which made no sense, so I wound up taking Acting and the History of Paraguay."

Nice mix.

"If you think Idi Amin was out of his mind, study Paraguay sometime! They've had dozens of them. So anyway, I got a job doing dirty laundry in a nursing home until I could get the money together to move from Boulder to San Francisco. I got there the last day of January 1978. I drove from 6am until I got there, dumped my stuff off at the house of a friend who played in a Colorado punk band, and then went straight to a show to see The Nuns and Negative Trend."

How long was it before you formed the Dead Kennedys?

"We played our first gig on July 19th 1978 after being together for a week. Me, [guitarist East Bay] Ray and Klaus [Fluoride, bass] had been at it for a little longer but we lucked out when we met Bruce [Slesinger, drummer] who also went by the name of Ted, a week before our first show. He was a little straighter than the rest of the band – the Glen Matlock[2] figure, complete with the eventual ejection for the same reason – and we also had a second guitarist who went by the name of 6025. He was a fellow Captain Beefheart fan who I had met at various shows so when his band split up I just said, 'Why don't you come join ours instead?'"

Was there a set goal for the band from the beginning?

"I was aware that I was in the midst of the biggest explosion of talent since the British invasion of the mid-sixties. I thought that even if I didn't get things done, I could always tell my grandchildren that I was there. My real dream of dreams was to get a single out and finally accomplish something that I did for me instead of because somebody else told me to. Plus, one thing that has probably been lost since that original explosion of punk bands was that we were not out there to please anyone, we – and I in particular – were there to provoke the audience, annoy them and mind-fuck them as much as possible. There weren't all these formulas and stupid sub-genres with everybody eager to please like it is now, it was quite the opposite."

You achieved a lot in a relatively short space of time. What would you say was the band's greatest achievement?

"There were a lot. I was the one who drove the band and who had to crack the whip while East Bay Ray looked at his watch and bitched; I was the one who wanted to make the music sound as good as it possibly could. I guess one of the main accomplishments would be helping to get not only the American punk and hardcore scenes off the ground, but also lighting a lot of fires on the continent too. The *Let Them Eat Jellybeans*[3] compilation was quite big across Europe and all of a sudden there was an explosion of hardcore bands and experimental bands who were tapping into that energy, as far flung as Finland and Italy. We also combined thought-provoking lyrics with good music. Some of the best bands have the worst lyrics and attitudes and some of the coolest people are in the weakest bands, but I think we managed to combine both.

"Being a fanatic record collector, I wanted to leave behind things that would blow people's minds, so I put in a lot of extra work into the packaging concepts, not to mention all the music I came up with. It was then that my early acting training came in very handy, because in high school I had really demanding method directors, which is where you have to build the character from within. I was never much in for technique acting, but with method it was like a spiritual thing that worked all the way until your own creation takes over your body. It built my skills so that I could imagine myself in other people's minds or place myself in other situations in order to write the lyrics from a you-are-there perspective, so instead of writing another song saying that nuclear war is bad, you've got a song like 'Kill the Poor' written from the military crackpot's point of view. In a nutshell though, the proudest thing the Dead Kennedys achieved is that we helped annihilate the seventies. We burned down the 'Hotel California', and not a moment too soon."

What prompted you to stand for mayor of San Francisco in 1979? Was it a long-term ambition of yours or did you do it because of the exposure Dead Kennedys had gained?

"We didn't have that much exposure at that point, we were still playing second on the bill to bands like The Dils or The Mutants, or whoever else helped us out at that time. I basically did it for a dare. I was folded into the back of a Volkswagon Beetle on my way to a Pere Ubu show and everyone said that because I had such a big mouth I should run for president, or better still, mayor. So I thought 'OK, I will'. I had no idea what that decision was going to cause, but immediately started telling people at that night's show that I was going to run for mayor and promptly spent the rest of night writing out my platform on a napkin at a table while Pere Ubu were playing five feet away. I've kept some of those very proposals in my spoken word show today. One of those ideas

I'm trying to get into the Green Party, is that police officers should be an elected office, therefore the cops would have to live in the neighbourhood and be accountable to the community. You'd see a lot less beatings like that of Rodney King and you might get professionals for once. Granted, anyone could run but it might be like running for coroner or something – someone who is a funeral home director is going to be a lot more effective than a used car salesman who wouldn't know the first thing about cutting up bodies. Someone who is accountable to the neighbourhood would make people far less likely to abuse their position."

Having had that insight into mainstream party politics, would you recommend it to other musicians or artists who already have a captive audience or an established platform from which to be heard?

"Krist Novoselic, formerly of Nirvana, took a serious look into running for Washington State Legislature as a Green Party member from his native town of Aberdeen, Washington, but soon realised that he would have to moth-ball his bass for good, so decided against it. And he's someone who gets along with the mainstream a lot better than I do, so he could well have got elected. But, yeah, I'm hoping that more musicians will inspire people to get off their asses and participate, particularly in something like the Green Party, which is really the best option for people in America right now. Recently some Germans were telling me to shut up about the Green Party because apparently, they've screwed up and betrayed their ideals, but in America it is the only electoral outlet for the 'Spirit of Seattle'. I mean, I love insurrection on the streets – I think it's great fun and participate whenever I can – but it's not going to get much done without insurrection in the voting booth, which is where the party comes in. And right now, the mainstream corporate Democrats are jumping down the throats of Greens, even before the post-September 11th patriotism uber alles took over, and are trying to bully Greens into not running in case they tipped the vote towards conservative Republicans."

Do you think the leading political parties in America have moved on at all since you first came into contact with mainstream politics – and if not, is that why events like September 11th inevitably occur?

"My attitude is that these corporate Democrats sold their best principles down the river to corporations – the exact same thing Labour is doing in the UK. I mean, Jack Straw is an embarrassment to the human race enough, but Gore's vice-president, Joseph Lieberman, who plans to run against Bush in 2004, is like Tipper Gore on crack when it comes to music. He's organised not one, but three Senate committee meanings investigating the evil, wicked effects of rock music and quite recently proposed black-balling Marilyn Manson as a solution to high school shootings. I mean, the guy's got some serious screws loose. He's also pals with the extreme right-wing televangelist Pat Robertson, a man who believes that we should have biblical Old Testament law – just like the way the Mullahs run Iran, where people have been punished for homosexuality and witchcraft. Yet Lieberman is down with the guy, as is Tipper Gore. Unbelievable. It was Joseph Lieberman who said that the Constitution only applies to moral and religious people, yet the same day said the Constitution guarantees freedom of religion, but not freedom from religion – thus adding more fuel to the fire to illuminate the reasons to abandon the Democrats and go Green.

"What might happen soon is that the Green Party will be acting as a spearhead for the movement against the war on terrorism, something which right now seems to be growing in Europe and the States. We're still a vocal minority, but vocal minorities often get a lot of things done, such as stopping the Vietnam war and shortening the first Gulf War. Only a decade ago King George Bush the First was all set to storm into Baghdad and [US army General and Commander] Stormin' Norman Schwarzkopf was all set to go too, but the protest against the war had gotten so large and so fierce very quickly – bigger in two or three weeks than anti-Vietnam protests were in America in the 1960s – that public pressure kept Bush from expanding the war. I doubt Margaret Thatcher or Helmut Kohl gave two shits whether Bush went in and took British and German troops with him, but they knew their people wouldn't stand for that. Basically, public pressure shortened that war and that's what I'm urging now: people should work towards shortening this war on terrorism. I'm no fan of Osama Bin Laden either – he's just one more example of why religious fundamentalism should be completely eradicated. Bush says 'you're either with us or with the terrorists', but I say it's possible to be with neither."

It's really not as black and white as President Bush makes out, is it?
"That's what they're trying to blot out of public discussion and I say that's wrong. You're right, it's not as clear-cut as that. It is perfectly possible to be against blowing up the World Trade Center and killing thousands of people yet still not be for Bush and his administration either."

What did you learn from the lengthy obscenity trial that you went through with the Dead Kennedys over your use of Giger's 'Penis Landscape' artwork for *Frankenchrist*?
"Well, the net effect in America was the Tipper sticker. Yes, she's reached

across the ocean and fucked with you too. Those 'Explicit Lyrics: Parental Advisory' stickers were Tipper stickers. Of course, she originally wanted a separate rating for sexual content, violence, the occult – which some of her associates defined as 'Jews' – and for homosexual content, which is exactly what the likes of Jack Straw and David Blunkett are trying to do with you now. I guess the result of it all was that it set an example that if you try to bust somebody they are going to fight back. The attorney at the time, a second or third generation politician rich guy who has unfortunately just been elected mayor of LA, was hoping that I would plead guilty due to poverty so they could then go and bust the other people in the prosecutor's file. I suspect they were looking to bust Ozzy, Judas Priest, Prince and the rest of the targets provided to them by Tipper and her society-lady friends. We put a stop to that, but there was enormous pressure at the time. I felt that if I blew the case then the whole music industry would go down, although with the exception of Frank Zappa, Todd Rungren and [Bruce Springsteen guitarist and later actor in *The Sopranos*] Stevie Van Zandt most major label people weren't exactly supportive. So it was a very nerve-wracking experience for me. Any time you're facing a jail term over a piece of artwork or walking around with a cloud over your head as the person who lost the *Frankenchrist* case, well, that can really fuck with you.

"I should also mention at this stage that none of the other Dead Kennedys band members helped in any way – they didn't even lick a postage stamp – yet are now claiming credit for fighting censorship."

So how do you feel about the Dead Kennedys recently reforming without you?

"Their motive is sheer greed. I mean, it's not as if Klaus or Ray has had a single good thing to say about punk music in years; it's all a scam. They also went ballistic when I wouldn't put 'Holiday in Cambodia' on a Levi's commercial and promptly brought a law-suit against me. To me it was a no-brainer decision and not just for political reasons. I mean, talk about being on the wrong side of an issue! Selling out to Levi's right before the Seattle demonstrations? Klaus was trying to tell me that Levi's were a good socially-conscious company the very week they laid off almost 7,000 people in Texas, whilst at the same time giving a retiring executive a one hundred million dollar bonus.

"Yes, there were other disputes amongst the former Dead Kennedys at the time, but we were trying to resolve them like adults. As soon as I wouldn't do Levi's, Klaus fell into the East Bay Ray greed brigade and I guess they decided they wanted revenge. I pleaded with Klaus and tried to tell him that this was not such a good idea and he told me that I should go to the press and tell them that we were donating our Levi's money to charity and then only donate 5% and keep the rest for ourselves. I was sick to my stomach when I heard that."

How did Alternative Tentacles, the label the Dead Kennedys founded, feature in all this?

"What they cooked it up into was a claim that I had stolen all this money from them, which was just untrue. There was indeed an accounting mistake that we were trying to get to the bottom of, but Ray was so abusive to the whole Alternative Tentacles staff that we couldn't get together to clear it up ourselves. He wouldn't show up for meetings, then the threat letters began to arrive. They claimed that all the money that our label put back into the community to help out bands like No Means No, Butthole Surfers, D.O.A., Neurosis or newer bands on our roster like Iowaska, The Phantom Limbs, the Fleshies, should really have gone to the former Dead Kennedys members. No label operates that way, but they genuinely seemed to think they'd been ripped off, even though a good chunk of money also went into their non-DK's projects that no other label would put out.

"So you can imagine how sick I felt to see Ray, Klaus and DH [Peligro, drums] put me through a much more nerve-wracking trial than the obscenity one by trying to tear apart my personal life, something that they're still doing to this day. I had to sit and watch them go up to the witness stand one by one and lie by claiming that they wrote all the music to the songs because – and I quote you here – 'Jello Biafra doesn't play an instrument and doesn't read sheet music.' I mean, there are plenty of people who have sung their parts to other musicians, ranging from Charlie Chaplin to George Clinton to Captain Beefheart, but they were having none of it.

"My former band members also claimed that there was a huge plot to hide money from them before bringing out an expert witness from Grateful Dead Records of all places, another fine bastion of grass roots punk consciousness. He claimed that I should be forced to pay them half a million dollars in damages because the Dead Kennedys weren't regularly on MTV and VH1 or in *Rolling Stone* or *Billboard* magazines. Sadly the jury fell for it, so the result is they've stolen my name, stolen my face, stolen my songs, stolen my lyrics and stolen the artwork that myself and the artist Winston Smith did, and can now pimp it out anyway they want, all ethics and honesty be damned. I thought they'd at least keep the books straight after what they accused me of doing, but I now get paid a third or less of what they get and I'm only allowed limited access to the books. What we've basically seen is an attempt to cut the heart out of something that means a great deal to many people and then chop up the body and sell the parts down the river."

I'm actually meant to be talking to East Bay Ray this week too[4].

"Well, I hope I get the right of reply because he's an extremely dishonest person. Ray has openly admitted to mutual friends that he wants to destroy Alternative Tentacles, which would cost people jobs and screw over dozens of other artists, but it doesn't seem to bother him."

How have the events of September 11 affected you and your career? As someone who is now predominantly a cultural commentator and activist, I imagine you've now got a lot more to talk about. Not that you needed it, of course.

"I had a tour booked at the time but nearly didn't make it out there because they shut the airports down, so now obviously the war on terrorism plays a huge part of my spoken word shows. Hopefully, I'll be able to squeeze out some music on the recent developments.

"Well, hopefully there'll be some music projects, but I don't want to curse them by talking about them. Hopefully, there'll be some noise and it'll be a bit more original than reforming an old band."

Having been viciously beaten up for supposedly being a 'sell-out', do you get bored with the usual 'punk rock sell-out' argument which inevitably rear its head.

"For the most part I avoid anything retrogressive like the plague. I have no objections to other people getting back together to play new material and have fun, but when it's done cynically I'm not interested. Most of those bands were boring cartoon punk bands the first time around anyway, so it's not like I feel any allegiance to them. I still love punk when it's something fresh, something that hasn't been done to death – everything from Turbo Negro and the Scandinavian explosion, to people like No Means No and other bands who we release that have that punk energy but are pretty much unclassifiable. I'm not into the kissy-ass, genre-conscious, formulaic bullshit that plagues punk rock today."

Which bands are you talking about?

"I'm talking about people who form Oi! revival bands and who only acknowledge earlier Oi! bands. Or you've got your goth-punk and horror-punk and pop-punk and street-punk and drunk-punk – and all of this gets called 'old school'. I mean, punk freed me from school. I liked blowing up the old school, but even then that was nearly 25 years ago. All those awful bands like ELO and Journey…"

Do you think teenagers have it easier or tougher these days?

"One thing I feel particularly strongly about, is the war against teenagers that is going on in America at the moment as a backlash to the Columbine High School shootings. Now they're making kids wear ID badges with barcodes on them, suspending them from school for wearing clothes that are the wrong colour or have something like 'Korn' written on them, arresting kids for wearing Marilyn Manson or Dead Kennedys T-shirts or for wearing trench coats, and are now urging that more and more kids be put on Ritalin and Prozac. I mean, guess who else was being doped up before they picked up the guns and pipe-bombs?"

As well as forming Lard, you've also collaborated with a lot of people over the years.

"Lard did four records, the last one of which was called *70's Rock Must Die*. Al [Jourgensen, Lard collaborator] insisted that I sung like Brian Johnston from AC/DC, but I think I'd burned that octave away smoking too much pot in my pre-punk teenage years. I couldn't talk for two days after that, and I think some people missed the humour involved, especially in Germany where they thought it was a serious change of direction. That's Lard humour though. That's what we're about. Al Jourgensen is like the Jerry Lee Lewis of our generation. He has a sense of humour and mischief that is cranked up to a new level. Lard came about when we were working on remixing a band and we had some spare studio time so decided to do something ourselves. So we said 'what should we call ourselves?' and the first name that I could think of was Lard. Al fell about laughing and Lard was born."

What about the other bands you've worked with – people like The Offspring who represent a mainstream, pop version of punk?

"They're old friends. I've actually got a demo of Dexter Holland's pre-Offspring band, Manic Subsidal somewhere. To keep up with all the cool punk bands at the time, I used to write to all those featured in *Maximum Rock 'n' Roll* if I couldn't find their record in the shop. So that's how I met that band and we kept in touch. I knew them for years as a smaller band on the DIY circuit, so when they asked me to appear on their record, I thought 'What the hell…'

"Pitchshifter were a politically-minded band who I knew about all along and they originally wanted me to do some remixes for them, but it probably would have helped if I knew how to remix songs... So they came back and asked me to do some improvised spoken word, which was a lot of fun. One thing I don't have to worry about is that I'm so good at imitating other people's voices, I can pretty much sample them directly without worrying about copyright laws.

"Sepultura were a band who I first met in Brazil when we performed together for an encore. Later they wanted a lyric, so I whipped something out real quick by singing along into a tape recorder because I had to fly back the very next day. To my horror they sampled me off that and put me on a song. They used my annoying little nasal voice instead of the death metal voice that it deserved. Since it was a Brazilian band, I wanted something relevant. This was in 1992 when George Bush Sr had sent Dan Quayle down there to try and fuck the whole Big Earth Treaty up, in order to give American corporations more rights to go into the Amazon and take people's plants and crops and patent them, which we are now doing. Some corporations even went over to India, pulled up some rice, took it back to America, patented it and is now using the World Trade Organisation to try and extort sanctions out of poor subsistence farmers to pay to use the rice that they've being growing for hundreds of years. You should ask Tony Blair about this subject as he's pretty big on it. This is what happens when the market place runs the world, and it is the topic that I addressed on the Sepultura collaboration."

How did you hook up with Ice-T? Is he someone who you have also had an affinity with?

"Well, we didn't really work together as such – it was a collaboration by mail using a four minute sample from my first spoken word album, *No More Cocoons*. I just got word that I was on Ice-T's album and it worked out well. Whether you agree with what Ice-T says or not, he's definitely one of the most intelligent people I've met in my life and no matter what he does he's always looking for something more. He has a much deeper insight than other people who are stereotyped as gangsta rappers. I even got paid too, which I appreciated because I was able to use the money to fund the album we did with Tumor Circus, who featured myself and members of the band Steel Pole Bath Tub. It was one of the worst selling albums we've put out, but it is one my favourite albums that I've been on. If I want to rock to my own work, that's the album that I'll listen to. So effectively, a sample on an Ice-T record paid for the entire recording."

Let's talk about your spoken word work. How did you get into that?

"You know, in some ways I'm disappointed that I never got it together to form another proper band after Dead Kennedys, part of which was down to undue legal harassment from born-again greed-heads and also because I wound up having this other skill, this other livelihood known as spoken word. The more I worked at it the more important it became to me. I started out at little poetry readings run by a guy called Harvey Kubernick[5]. He's the same guy who got Henry Rollins into it and he's still on a mission to get musicians to push themselves as poets and to combine the music and poetry scenes so that people can get to know each other and exchange ideas – brain food, if you like. I was nervous as hell when I started but it took off like a rocket. I sensed that the things people were getting off on was my warped sense of humour and the buried information that I was weaving into my work, such as why I was glad the space shuttle blew up, so I went further in those directions. Then after the *Frankenchrist* bust I was suddenly taken seriously as an anti-censorship advocate by people who had labelled me a paranoid lunatic two weeks earlier for saying that Tipper Gore was a front for right-wing Christian supremacists. Suddenly these people were listening to me, and it meant that interviews evolved from boring punk-type questions to talking about real issues and it's something that has remained to this day. I had a very long story to tell about the obscenity trial and that vaulted me into the college lecturing circuit as a supposed speaker against censorship.

"Spoken word today is basically a catch-all term for everything from poetry to comedy, commentary, performance art, theatre. Like, when Ice-T sampled me he used a piece called 'Message from Our Sponsor' which I had originally conceived as a radio play. I wanted it to be like HG Wells's *War of the Worlds,* where instead of broadcasting a real Martian attack I wanted it to be broadcast as a real military coup at a time when Reagan and Bush were running amok with more and more excess law enforcements. I wrote it really fast backstage before a spoken word show and quickly realised that I could deliver it onstage instead of on the radio, secretly knowing that I'd probably never get it broadcast anyway."

What do you gain from doing endless spoken word shows?

"Spoken word is a different thing as it doesn't have the primal energy of working with a band, but at the same time I can penetrate deeper into people and do a more thorough job of infecting their brains with positive disease. That's what it's about – cultural terrorism and positive disease. In the early days when I was doing university shows, I'd get one third Dead Kennedys fans, one third activists ranging in age from eight to eighty who'd heard about the *Frankenchrist* case, and the rest was people in these towns who had nothing else to do that night. Of course, these were the people I was most interested in mind-fucking. Spoken word has dragged me kicking and screaming over the years into a position of leadership. There's far more pressure on an artist when people are actually listening to them and taking them seriously. I had to be conscious of this when the religious right and the Crass-type punks both misinterpreted 'I Kill Children'[6] at the same time."

Tell me about your latest spoken word album. How did your experiences in mainstream politics inform the content?

"The last spoken word album, *Become the Media,* was much more of a story-telling of recent events than earlier albums, which may make it obsolete quicker or it may become an important part of recent history that is already being rewritten as we speak. It includes my experiences in Seattle and at Democratic and Republican conventions, including my nausea and horror when I actually got into the Democratic convention with, shall we say, a 'borrowed' press pass and saw 5,000 previously comatose *Truman Show*-calibre delegates erupting in Nuremberg Rally-fervour, all waving signs saying "Tipper Rocks!' I couldn't believe that they'd actually be that cynical at trying to rewrite history and insult the intelligence of the American people.

"You know, a lot of people point the fingers at the Green Party for costing Al Gore that election, but I say no way, Gore cost himself the election. Those of us who voted for Ralph Nader and the Green Party refused to vote for somebody who, like Bush, supported the death penalty, globalisation, the drug war, putting nuclear missiles in outer space, dismantling the welfare system and throwing poor people – especially single mothers – out on the street... The list goes on. Al Gore picked Joseph Lieberman as his right-hand man and suddenly out come the 'Tipper Rocks' signs and everyone conveniently forgets the hell they put us through in the eighties. Nobody in the American media has ever acknowledged the role of Gore's wife in costing him that election. Granted, my audience has a high percentage of people who know just how evil that bitch really is, but it amazes me that after ten years of make-overs people haven't forgotten a damn thing. It's extremely important for people to hang onto their memories as history seems to be rewritten at warp speed these days."

You've also done some acting which seemed to combine your earlier acting school training with your spoken word shows...

'Yeah, *Terminal City Ricochet* was a movie that I made and which a lot of people still ask me about. Unfortunately, that too was in litigation after a fall-out between producers and backers, but I hope it gets out the bag because it was a great statement on the use of tabloid media to herd society into supporting dictators. It was made in 1989 and the basic plot was that this dictator of Terminal City – one of the last liveable places on the earth and the real name of Vancouver, which is where it was shot – runs over an innocent person in his limo and then spots a newspaper delivery man nearby and decides to blame it on him. They call this guy the 'Rock 'n' Roll Terrorist' and the dictator sets about telling everyone that they must re-elect him in order to save themselves from this threat. I played an Oliver North-type figure, which was intimidating as my acting experience is still pretty limited, plus I was trying to write the soundtrack with No Means No and D.O.A. I'm hoping the film will come out some time."

How did you come to be so involved with the Green Party in the first place?

"It was a complete shock that the New York State Green Party nominated me for president at the primary elections, along with Ralph Nader. I certainly did not intend to run, although the thought of running for Governor of California had occurred to me because I couldn't stand to see Democrat and Republican corporate lackeys arguing over who hated immigrants more and who would execute more people. I'm a little reluctant to do something like that for real as it would completely decapitate me as an artist, but at the same time, being involved with the Green Party is a good way to use my position as someone who people listen, in order to steer their thoughts and their anger in a positive direction. In America, less than half the people in the country ever vote, so there's really room for a new party to unite all these disillusioned people. It's not because they're apathetic, it's because they're so heartbroken and so fed up with our one party state masquerading as a two party state that they're desperate enough to elect a wrestler, Jesse Ventura, as Governor of Minnesota. A wrestler! The Ventura people are ripe for the Green's if they can only learn to talk to each other. The same needs to be done by branching the Green Party out into something more than the white eco party, by making better relationships with low-income people and more people of colour."

When the WTO demonstrations occurred in Seattle you were there on the front-line – how important was it for you to make an appearance?

"My mere act of showing up and being visible meant a lot to people. I was running around like a chicken with my head cut off causing trouble in the streets by day, and speaking to groups of people ranging in size from 200 to 8,000 by night, and then running off to rehearse with Krist Novoselic and Kim Thayil [Soundgarden] and Gina Mainwal [Sweet 75] to form The No WTO Combo. Yes, I was in a band again, although only for four days."

What was your agenda behind The No WTO Combo?

"Originally Krist and I had done a joint spoken word show as part of something called The Spitfire Tour which was hosted by Michael Franti [Disposable Heroes of Hiphoprisy]. We were trying to figure out who we could get to play in order to get more people to attend the Seattle demonstrations – people like Rage Against the Machine and Pearl Jam who proved to be, shall we say, unavailable – so finally Krist said, 'Hell, let's do our own band instead'. We hardly had any time to prepare but somehow it came together, although I had my doubts when Krist wanted to release our 24-track recordings. But with some clever computer editing on his part and a kick-ass mix by Jack Endino it turned out to be a pretty good album[7].

"One of the songs The No WTO Combo recorded was 'Full Metal Jack-off', which I had originally done with D.O.A., was originally my expression of horror at the ascension of the first George Bush to the American throne and I was surprised how few lyrics I had to change when I rewrote it about Clinton for the Seattle demonstrations. I sometimes think maybe I should quit writing stuff like this because my worst paranoid nightmares keep coming true.

"One other No WTO story for you: the first day of the really big demo's there was so much energy in the air. Over here in the UK they call it the 'Spirit of Seattle' but to me it was the spirit of Europe. To me, the poll-tax riots had come to America, although they weren't really riots until the cops went crazy later on. It was a peaceful march uniting everyone from anarcho-eco freaks to labour unions who had been there during the anti-Vietnam war protests, so never have I wanted to get onstage and rock so badly as that day. But then the curfew came down, so I called Krist on his cell phone: 'Are we going to play?' 'I don't know, I'm running from the police! I gotta call you back!'

"He got to the venue and got the equipment in but then the raging, running battle between the protestors and the police ended up taking place right outside the venue, The Showbox. So Krist had the surreal experience of watching the police battling the demonstrators on TV while it was going on right outside the door of the club. Weird."

Notes

1 Classical Japanese theatre.

2 Later replaced by Sid Vicious, the original bassist/songwriter for the Sex Pistols was ejected from the band on the grounds that he washed his hair too often.

3 Alternative Tentacles compilation album (1981) featuring the likes of Dead Kennedys, Black Flag, Flipper, Circle Jerks and Bad Brains.

4 Excerpt from an interview with Dead Kennedys guitarist and founder member East Bay Ray, November 2001.

Why did you decide to reform the Dead Kennedys?

"Well, we're not actually forming the Dead Kennedys per se, but we are playing together with Brandon Cruz from the band Dr Know on vocals. The reason it came about was because we had a record release party in LA for the new live album and for a laugh we thought we'd get up and play after the other bands. Actually, it wasn't totally unannounced because we had rehearsed so the place was sold out weeks in advance and it basically turned into a big love-in. People were singing along and the promoter said he's never seen so many smiling faces at a punk show. We're hoping to organise some more shows soon."

Isn't the Dead Kennedys without Jello Biafra a rather strange concept?

"Everyone knew Biafra wasn't going to be there but it worked out pretty good and Brandon did a great job – just hearing that Dead Kennedys sound live through a big PA was amazing. So, we thought we'd do it some more, although we haven't figured out what to call ourselves – maybe Decay Kennedys. Something that lets people know it's different. To everyone, Dead Kennedys would be with Biafra, but this is without him. People have the choice of coming to see us – it's up to them."

Why did you and the other band members decide to take him to court last year?

"The court case? Oh, he did wrong. There was royalties owed to us and it wasn't until a whistle-blower at the label told us we were owed money unconditionally that we found out about it. His story has changed over time, but basically we were owed $76,000 – it wasn't small change. He'd been paying himself and the label more per CD than the rest of us."

But, to be fair, he does run Alternative Tentacles.

"Well, I was one of the co-founders of Alternative Tentacles. I financed and produced the first single 'California Uber Alles' and sold it out of the back of my trunk. Then later, in '83, we set up a more formal label, which I was involved in until 1986 when it was turned over to Biafra. Dead Kennedys pretty much financed the operation, yet when the albums came out on CD I found out we were getting paid less than everybody else on the label. We asked him what was up and he stonewalled us. The jury thought what he had to say was all bunch of junk and he was found guilty of Fraud With Malice, which means he did it on purpose."

Hearing all this makes Dead Kennedys sound like just another band – something you clearly weren't. Given your watertight convictions did you ever envisage falling out so acrimoniously?

"When I was told about the money thing I didn't believe it, because this was a band-mate who I'd known for twenty years, someone I'd toured and recorded with.

When I found out it was all true it was very sad to realise that he could get his priorities so mixed up. But, hey, he's only human!"

If this fall-out was merely down to human error, then surely it could have been resolved without such a costly court case?

"But he did something wrong and I'm concerned because he's never admitted that. If you make a mistake, you try and avoid doing it in the future, but instead he's gotten very spiteful and bitter and is saying lots of nasty things about us. We're sad that he's reacted in such a way. I mean, sometimes the deeds don't always match the words – everyone is human. Even Biafra..."

5 Through journalism, A&R, production and promotion Harvey Kubernick was well-connected in LA's thriving subculture, from the sixties onwards. Recognising the obvious link between subversive music and non-academic poetry, Kubernick has also encouraged numerous performers to cross over and is a key figure in the development of the Californian poetry and spoken word scenes – the latter is a phrase for which he is responsible. "I didn't want to put on poetry readings, so I coined this term Spoken Word," Kubernick explains in *Turned On: A Biography of Henry Rollins* by James Parker. "I wanted it to be diary rants, improv, fragments of song lyrics, some traditional poetry, excerpts from in-progress books – I wanted it to be narratives, but I took off the strait-jacket." Other people Kubernick encouraged to do spoken word included Jim Morrison and the premier poet laureate of LA's low-life, Charles Bukowski.

6 From *Fresh Fruit for Rotting Vegetables,* Alternative Tentacles, 1980.

7 *Live from the Battle in Seattle,* Alternative Tentacles, 2001.

At the Drive-In
the politics of the pit

"It's not contrived, it's 100% real..."

"A heaving sea of air hammers in the purple brown dusk tainted with rotten metal smell of sewer gas... young worker faces vibrating out of focus in yellow halos of carbide lanterns... broken pipes exposed..."

William Burroughs, *Naked Lunch*, 1959

AT THE DRIVE-IN have the best hair of any band I have ever encountered. Looking good while starting a revolution, however small, is always important. Just look at Fidel and Che, Jimi and Johnny (Rotten or Thunders). These five skinny young men from El Paso, deep down in Texas near the hot Mexican border, are one of the hardest working bands around. Their agenda, if it can be pinned down on paper, is to make real, truthful, honest music on their own terms. Music that kicks against the tawdry blandola of the charts. Music you can dance to without a routine.

Formed in 1994 by guitarists Jim Ward and Omar Rodriguez and acrobatic – both vocally and physically – frontman Cedric Bixler, they released a series of excellent records, and built a solid underground reputation through the kind of relentless touring at a grass-roots level that is so essential to bands with no external support (10,000 miles in 40 days in an old '81 Ford Econoline, anyone?) before being joined by Paul Hinojos (bass) and Tony Hajjar (drums) in

1996. With a solid line-up in place, they released the mini-album *El Gran Orgo* (One Foor, 1997) and sophomore album *In/Casino/Out* (Fearless, 1998) between more sparsely-attended road stints.

At the Drive-In are the very type of band that show that hardcore and punk rock are still relevant sub-cultures, at least philosophically. Like so many people initially attracted to hardcore's abrasive delivery and personal-political content, the five members were smart enough to take in other disparate sounds (although the likes of their beloved Can, Captain Beefheart and Kraftwerk are all punk rockers in spirit too). They also took a stance wherever necessary – in this case against the 'macho bullshit' or the politics of the pit that have been turning this form of music into just another dumb, boyish self-perpetuating rock 'n' roll pigeon-hole for some time now. Which is why when a band like At the Drive-In come along you pay attention. You know greatness will follow. You know that at the very least, a clutch of great new bands will appear in their wake.

The way At the Drive-In operate is punk rock to the core, remaining both politicised and intelligent whilst also being totally rock 'n' roll in a classic style – right down to the tightness of their trousers. In half a decade they moved from releases on their own Western Breed label to Flipside Records then on to Fearless, and by the time Beastie Boy Mike Diamond signed them to his Grand Royal imprint (itself a subsidiary of Virgin) and turned on top metal producer Ross Robinson enough to offer his services, At the Drive-In were ready to step up a level. A number of releases on numerous smaller labels had alerted the ever-hip underground, now it was time to go global.

The result was *Relationship of Command* (Grand Royal, 2000), an album that saw them swiftly move up, in the space of 12 months, from the sticky-floored clubs of the punk rock hinterlands to larger venues and festival bills the world over. Although a product of the burgeoning emo movement, the album's sound is far more complex than that of the usual wimpy navel-gazing punk-lite that so far has been the defining rock sound of the early millennium. Taut like all the best hardcore, raw, pure and genuinely vexed like early Nirvana, and with enough pop hooks and up-at-'em guitars to bring in some of the metal kids, it was an album that arrived at a time when big-selling alternative music was limited to pay-roll production line chumps like Papa Roach, Disturbed and a popular boy band too ugly to package to the pre-teens, who go by the name of Linkin Park.

Playing supercharged, diverse, electrified and thought-provoking shows which, like some of the jazz-improv greats, tended to vary greatly from night to night (depending on audience reaction, instinct, mood and sound quality) took At the Drive-In to the peripherals of the mainstream rock arena. TV appearances, press hyperbole, magazine covers, cynical piss taking – the usual type of thing.

It felt awesome just imagining a band like them on *Top of the Pops*. Or even better, a band like them turning down that dusty institution like The Clash and The Prodigy did.

But it wasn't to be...

By the time the five members convened in the scummy surroundings of the upstairs Keith Moon bar at The Astoria theatre on a cold London evening, tour fatigue had clearly set in and thoughts seemed to be turning inwards. While spirits were generally high, it was clear that road psychosis was in the post. Still, at least Cedric still looked cool shivering beneath a ridiculously long scarf. Talking to each member individually, it became clear to me that At the Drive-In were no average thrill-seeking hedonistic Yankee band on a JD-and-coke death trip. Articulate, incisive and refreshingly humble, their stance was resolutely against everything the vacuous mainstream pop world stands for. A short while later they cancelled the remaining dates of their tour and went home to El Paso for "an extended hiatus." In reality, At the Drive-In were burnt out and no more.

Which is not necessarily a bad thing. Rock music is littered with the corpses of wide-eyed young things who have seen their stars briefly burn bright, before crashing spectacularly. With each passing decade, new names join the roll-call of the great jam session in the sky. For some, death has merely served to enhance their reputations (Jim Morrison, Janis Joplin), others have been martyred as angelic beauties too sensitive for this world (Kurt Cobain, Nick Drake, Richey Edwards from Manic Street Preachers) while others are posthumously turned into false icons whose public profile far exceeds their creative talent (Sid Vicious, Elvis Presley). Yet, still the music business threshing machine continues to creek forward, sucking in, tearing apart and coughing out anything that gets in its way – anyone who thinks they can bring it down with a hastily lobbed spanner. The fact is, you either ride the machine and risk, at the very least, losing some limbs or you go plough another field for a pittance and eternal happiness.

Luckily there are some for whom fame is just not worth it. It neither makes their lives particularly better nor validates them as credible artists. The money may be good... but good enough to sell your soul for?

This is where At the Drive-In were headed – right down to the lazy Nirvana comparisons – before punk rock providence prevailed. They got out before the bone-crunching, spirit-sapping death machine conveyor belts labelled 'marketing', 'publicity' and 'product management' whisked them ever-closer to the mincer that would turn them into reconstituted rock 'n' roll offal, ready to be served up for nostalgia-hungry, death-trip fixated music fans of future generations.

At the Drive-In split while they could. As more bands should.

Jim, Tony and Paul swiftly put together the promising Sparta (who, perhaps somewhat surprisingly, swiftly signed to another major label) while Omar and

Cedric continued with their dub band De Facto and formed the awkward, explosive and angular-sounding The Mars Volta. At the time of writing, the signs for all these bands are looking good. I suspect we have not heard the last of these heretics.

This is a chapter we can subtitle: 'Survival of the Heretic'.

Here are the highlights of their final UK interview, which took place February 2001 at the Astoria Theatre, London.

Interview 1: Cedric Bixler (vocals, dancing)

What is your non-musical role in the band?

Cedric: "Between Jim and I it's crowd control. We make sure people don't get beat up. For me it's also about trying to shed a bit of light as to the meaning of the lyrics because I understand that a lot of people don't always understand what I'm saying. I also try to provide a bit of dancing. Maybe people can take a lead from what we do and see that we do technically dance, and hopefully they'll then invent some new moves. We just played Melbourne and we did one song that's inspired by Roni Size and there was all these women dancing round the side of the stage. We made eye contact, it was all going off and I was, like, 'Fuck yes!' That's exactly what I like to see people doing."

Despite increasing numbers of crowd fatalities at rock shows you've been criticised for your anti-stage-diving stance – particularly by the less sympathetic mainstream press. How do you explain it to fans who just want to appreciate the physical aspect of an At the Drive-In show?

Cedric: "The other day this guy was complaining to us about where we stand on these things and that's cool, so I gave him the microphone because I don't want us to be like some fascists or something. In a sense, with the struggle that we're leading, there does have to be an element of fascism about it, but it's a fascist form of pacifism. I really don't think it's bad to be hard-line about being nice to each other. Some people just don't get it though because they've been force-fed their information through TV, newspapers and what-not about how to act at a show, whereas we come from a different world altogether."

The hardcore scene is notoriously critical of bands who try to reach bigger audiences, as you have. How do you handle this criticism?

Cedric: "Yeah, we grew up listening to hardcore and punk, but this is what we have become today. Don't get me wrong, slam-dancing, mohawks... they had their time and place. I mean, if you take a look at how I acted and how I looked six or seven years ago you'd be pretty amazed – I was just as brutal as a lot of those kids who come to our shows. But now it's our choice to be on a major label. We do get attention from bigger bands – whether it's Placebo or No Doubt – but we don't come from the same world as them. We can respect other musicians because we're from an underground scene, but I believe that we have to personally pump new blood into that scene – punk and hardcore – because there's still a lot of snootiness and elitism there. It's like in the movie *High Fidelity* there's that scene where the record store owner won't sell a kid a Captain Beefheart CD because he's not cool enough... [laughing] that's really not much different to the scene we come from! We're fighting against that and we're fighting the chauvinistic macho brutality at shows that a lot of other bands think is OK."

One of the things that grabbed me about the band were your unique lyrics. Although often abstract, they seem to paint a bigger picture of the world. Who influences you?

Cedric: "I'm really into William S. Burroughs. I'm also into a writer called Oscar Zeta Acosta who is better known as The Samoan in Hunter S. Thompson's *Fear and Loathing in Las Vegas*. He's from El Paso and he's written books called *The Autobiography of a Brown Buffalo* and *The Revolt of the Cockroach People,* the way he writes is a lot like Thompson, who I'm also a fan of. I watch a lot of movies too, so Federico Fellini influences me a lot. I keep watching his movie *Satyricon* over and over because it inspires me to write lyrics. I also like a lot of the phrasing that Mark E. Smith from The Fall uses. People say I try to sound like Zack de la Rocha from Rage Against the Machine – probably because I try and cram a lot of words in – but I'm really just trying to do my best Kathleen Hannah/Mark E. Smith impersonation."

Where do you see At the Drive-In in five years time?

Cedric: "I think we'll still be doing the same thing, maybe minus the tour bus. Things might get stripped down and we could be back to where we started, but it'll be OK. We're always criticising our music and we're sick of playing some of the songs so we totally want to experiment with melodies and with mellower songs. I don't want to be 30 or 40 years old and have to rely on my jumping off things to get people's attention – hopefully they'll see that there's actual music there. Some of our stuff is very influenced by bands like Drive Like Jehu, but we'd also like to be able to showcase our Nick Drake aspect. Sometimes we come offstage and we just want things to be mellow, no rock music. It's totally necessary sometimes."

What has been your most embarrassing on-stage moment?

Cedric: "There are some nights when our equipment doesn't work – and that happens a lot. It just goes to show that we are not saving rock 'n' roll in any way, we're just kids who don't always know what we're doing. Every day there can be an embarrassment, like when we were on *Later... With Jools Holland*. Omar dropped his guitar in the opening song, but we can now look back on it as a little bit of musical history. It's not contrived, it's 100% real. He dropped his guitar, but that's what makes rock 'n' roll real, I think."

Interview 2: Jim Ward (guitar/keyboards).

What is your earliest childhood memory?

Jim: "I remember we had hard wood floors in our house and I used to slide around them in my socks. There are fragments of little memories here and there, like my great-grandfather's 80th birthday. He was a really old man who kinda looked like William Burroughs, like his body hung on his bones. I guess I was about four years old.

"I also remember being a kid and reading about an airplane that had crashed, killed everyone on it and wiped out six blocks of the city. That was the first night that I couldn't sleep. It was weird, like I could feel the pain. I was just laying there and thinking about everybody who would have got the call that day – I was fucking ten years old then but it's still with me to this day. When earthquakes happen I can't sleep because I'm fucking miserable. I can't imagine what that must feel like. It's almost better when it happens to you – when one of your friends dies – because you're not worried about other people. Just thinking about kids whose parents have died brings me down. I'm actually a very optimistic person, but you get bummed out, you know?"

What did you do before the band took off?

Jim: "I used my college savings to fund a lot of the early At the Drive-In seven inch singles and to run the van. I worked shitty jobs in diners and I worked for Kodak developing micro-film. I also went to college, on and off for a couple of years. It never really clicked because I was always just hanging out and slacking off. Yeah, I was definitely a slacker but if I wasn't in the band I think maybe I would still have finished a degree in civil engineering."

What is your non-musical role in the band?

Jim: "I sorta ride the middle of the highway a lot. Like when there are decisions to be made I find myself in the middle – it's not fair to say 'mediator', because it's never about negative shit. I think, more than anything I also bring a pop element to the band. One of my favourite records recently was *Parachutes* by Coldplay, would you believe. Yeah, I hung out with them recently and they're really nice guys. I like pop songs. Aside from that, I don't think I'm the most creative person in the world, but I work pretty hard."

What is your key to survival on this never-ending tour?

Jim: "I'm really starting to wonder, man. One thing for me is I have probably the greatest girl in the world and we're getting married in a couple of months, so it's frustrating for me being gone because there's so much to be done. I really want to be there, you know? I spent three weeks at home at Christmas, but now it's getting harder and harder to leave. I think maybe I'm settling down and becoming a different person. Part of it is because of this – the band. It changes you. Right now, I'm at the point where you question everything, I've been doing a lot of deep, deep questioning as to what I'm contributing to the world. It's just typical mid-twenties bullshit, but I think it's harder because we're in such a narcissistic field. I mean, music is such a me-me-me thing because you talk about yourself all the time. I'm not taking it for granted because I love the opportunities we've had, it's just that I've never really thought about these things much until now, when we're finally getting some recognition."

Is it hard for a band to come from the underground scene and find yourselves having to do endless, mainstream-orientated promotion – given that punk rock generally tends to be a word-of-mouth thing?

Jim: "No one ever believes us when we say that fame was never a goal. Maybe when you're a kid it seems cool to be a rock star, but that's one of my most despised words. I hate when I go back home and friends say 'What's up, rock star?' I get so mad because I'm definitely not one and I don't want to be considered one. I'm a normal person and we're a normal band. It's a double-edged sword though because you say it so much that it becomes your shtick – not having an image becomes your image. That's where I'm at right now. I can't win with this shit. I just want to make records, but it seems like so much comes along with that. It's still definitely worth it though – the stress, I mean."

Who is your all-time hero and heroine?

Jim: "My mom and dad. It's true. They're the shit because they're the ones who turned me onto my heroes – people like The Beatles or Jack Kerouac. I'm a pretty religious person and grew up in a household where Christianity was a very liberal thing. I remember when I was young I said to my mom, you know, 'Give me the fucking technical definition of Jesus because I question him,' and she said, 'There isn't one, man! It's spirituality – it's your soul.' She told me how we call him Jesus, but some people call him Buddha and then went off on a whole tangent of middle Eastern religions and shit – I was only nine years old! So, honestly, my heroes are my parents because they really kick ass."

What do your family think of At the Drive-In?

Jim: "They've always been supportive. We used to practice in their den and they've listened to the shitty band for years, but now they love it and keep all the articles and watch the TV shows. It seems like every decade in your life you reach a point where you question what you're doing and whether you want the responsibility, and luckily I can go home and talk to my parents about it. I think maybe they're a bit worried because they're parents and they see me struggling with my own inner shit while I try to figure it all out. Our generation is a weird one. We remember being 13 or 14 and seeing what happened to Nirvana. Like when he [Kurt Cobain] died, it impacted me a lot. It changed the way I think about big rock bands because I felt sorry for him. I got tired of people saying it's a choice to be in a band because you can still get pushed into a corner. I could quit today if I wanted to, but I feel like I want to be the loudest fucking megaphone that's speaking common sense and telling people that homophobia is stupid and sexism is stupid. I've always wanted to do that and this is a great vehicle for it, but the tricky part of it is I'm also an artist – we're artists before we're politicians, that's why we don't care to be a political band. It's not a choice of being in the band, it's a choice between the music and the whole interview and touring process. I'm stoked to be asking these questions of my self because few people have the opportunity to do even that. I'm in a great position. I have tons of choices. I can live my life pretty carefree. Going all over the world and touring six or seven hundred shows in the last five years, you meet people and they bring up issues to you."

What has been the highlight of the band's career so far?

Jim: "There's been shows where you walk off and everybody looks at each other and you just know. The best thing is when the five of us connect without talking, when we can understand each other without saying a word. I'm closer to these guys than most people in the world. Being in a band there's some heavy shit that goes on and we've shared a lot of things along the way."

So what has been the lowest point – the point where you really feel like it's not worth it?

Jim: "The Big Day Out festival in Sydney. That was one of the worst feelings that I have had – I felt the pain of the people down the front who were getting kicked in the head by these guys who kept coming over the front into the crowd. On the Gold Coast, I watched a 16-year-old girl come over the crowd and they were fucking trying to take her pants off, man. I've seen that so many times. I only ever went to one festival before I was in the band and I said 'I'm never going to this shit again'. Too many bands encourage that kind of behaviour."

Interview 3: Tony Hajjar (drums).

What are your memories of living in Beirut?

Tony: "I was born there in 1974 and then moved to the states in '79 when things in Lebanon were getting really, really bad. The civil war was getting more and more dangerous and there was a feeling that you couldn't go anywhere for fear of a missile hit or a grenade being thrown. I don't remember a lot of the details from the time, but we moved straight to El Paso, Texas of all places because we had some family around there. I've lived there most of my life, until 1999 when I moved to LA. Omar and Cedric live in Long Beach, I live in Hollywood, Paul lives in Silverlake and Jim still lives in El Paso."

What would you say is your non-musical role in the band?

Tony: "I think maybe I bring a business sense to proceedings – Jim and I tend to take care of those things. I bring in a 'don't quit' attitude. I have no other discernible skills, that's for sure. My personality is weird because I always get scared to stop doing anything that I feel is productive. If we're on a break, I always want to get back on tour, do business, start writing music – anything as long as I'm not stagnant."

Do you have any tips as to how to keep it together when you're touring for months at a time?

Tony: "Definitely: try and forget how long the tour is. Don't think about the date, don't think too far ahead. I often don't know what city we're in until we show up there, then I ask someone. I'm a very analytical type of person so if I knew that there was, say, 26 shows between us and a couple of days off, I'd probably wind up killing myself."

What were you doing before the band?

Tony: "When I joined the band I was going to college to study chemistry and math. I had two semesters left, so I was practising during the day and finishing my research at night. After our first tour with this line-up I finished my degree and was teaching students as well as high school teachers. It was the last job I did before I became a full-time member of At the Drive-In. Chemistry is my second love – it doesn't compare to music, but I enjoy it, so I guess I'd probably be continuing my education and research if I wasn't here in the band."

At what point did you realise things might happen for the band?

Tony: "There was a time when no one gave a crap about this band – no one would even give us $500 to make a record. Then one time we played in front of 20 people in Costa Mesa, California and Fearless Records saw us and gave us a chance. The result was our record *In/Casino/Out,* and I think it's safe to say that four day period of writing and recording is one of the most beautiful times I have ever had."

What, for you, has been the lowest point in the band's career?

Tony: "There has been one real low point as a musician in this band and it was not so long ago in Australia. We were in one of the most beautiful places in the world and we were about to play a big TV show. We were all feeling tense and starting to feel recent pressures a lot more, and it was the first time that I have ever wanted to leave the band. I remember, we were sitting in the green room beforehand trying to work out which songs to play and I just broke down, started crying and walked outside. Jim followed me and I told him that I had never felt so much pressure before. For the first time in my life I couldn't fight it. After talking to everyone though, things felt better and we played a great show."

What goals do the band have for the future?

Tony: "I think we've achieved all our goals and now we have to push ourselves musically. Some bands' achievements are about selling tonnes of records and that's all that they think about, but with us our goals are different. Obviously ,we like to sell records, but as long as our audience and the press don't suddenly turn on us, my only goal is to push ourselves musically. I want to write music that will drive us crazy because we're pushing each other so much."

One of the recent TV highlights was undoubtedly At the Drive-In blowing Robbie Williams away on the BBC's *Later... With Jools Holland* – what are your recollections of that performance?

Tony: "Well, we really went for it that day! There was certainly a lot of fear and uneasiness before we started. I was sitting on my drum stool and looking out at Van Morrison and Robbie Williams and it was strange... but nice, you know? We're all musicians and we're all doing the same thing – that was the beauty of it. I don't really like Robbie Williams's music and he probably doesn't like ours, but you know what? He watched us and we watched him. It's all music."

Who has been your biggest single influence?

Tony: "My brother. He pretty much raised me and my sister since he was 23 years old. My mom died of cancer in 1988 and he gave up everything for me and our sister. He dropped out of college, worked two jobs and was raising both of us. When my mom died, he became my legal guardian and has raised me ever since then. To this day, I look up to him more than any supposed famous person out there. He's a true hero. My mom is my heroine. She told me the only reason she stopped fighting cancer was because we were old enough to take care of ourselves. She held out until then."

Interview 4: Paul Hinojos (bass).

What did you do before the band?

Paul: "I worked with a friend at a sheet metal cutting place. I cut slabs of sheet metal and was always afraid that something would happen to me – there was a lot of people with half-fingers and stuff. I'd work 12 hour days to save money to fix the van so that we could go on tour again."

Was there a point where you decided to turn professional?

Paul: "When Tony and I joined at the same time in late 1996, we all sat down and talked about how this band was going to be. We were all pretty serious after various member changes and it was then that we realised that we had to sacrifice everything for At the Drive-In."

Had you played in many bands previously?

Paul: "I was in maybe four other bands. In El Paso there's only a few bands, so you would wind up playing with the same guys in different line-ups. I was in a metal band with Tony and then later I was in a pop band that he ended up playing drums for. What was the name of the metal band? It's too embarrassing. We were a total Pantera-style power metal band."

What is your non-musical contribution to the At the Drive-In?

Paul: "When we sat down and had a talk we assumed different responsibilities. Back then, I would do all the transportation stuff. I was like the tour manager because I'd read maps and navigate. I'd wake people up, I'd let them know where we had to be – that was like a full-time occupation in itself. Then we'd each take it in turns making sure we got paid our $40 or whatever. It was cool, I got into it."

What would you say is your greatest extravagance?

Paul: "I keep buying stereo equipment and I can't seem to stop. I'm obsessed with speakers, computers and technology in general. I'm amazed at how small everything is becoming. In the States we got totally out of control with our cell phones – it's like a constant battle to see who can get the smallest one."

What has been the lowest point in At the Drive-In's career?

Paul: "My first tour with the band was 100 dates and there was about five people coming to see us each night. One night in New Orleans, right before we were due onstage, the bartender said there was an emergency call for us, so Cedric went down and took it. Some friends of ours had just been killed in a car accident. Cedric didn't say anything because we were about to play but we knew something was up. After the show he told us: two of our good friends were coming back from Austin, Texas and fell asleep at the wheel. They were 17 years old. The song 'Napoleon Solo' from *In/Casino/Out* is about them, and we always close the show with it because we know that they're around us somewhere. That was a very sombre week for all of us."

What has been the highlight of the band's career so far?

Paul: "For me it's a combination of moments. The first time was came to Europe in March 1998 it felt like a big accomplishment because we did it on our own dime. I remember on the plane over here we were looking at each other and nodding like we could hardly believe that we'd finally done it. Being able to see the world is a definite highlight – I get to do the best job in the world with my best friends in the world. I wake up, they're there and we're somewhere cool like here in London. Our first UK tour was very DIY."

Where was the first UK show?

Paul: "It was upstairs at The Monarch[1] in London. We got paid, like $100. It was cool. I remember there was only one key for the dressing room and, sure enough, we locked it in there with all our guitars right before we were meant to play, so some guy had to come and kick the door down for us. The usual shit…"

Interview 5: Omar Rodriguez (guitar).

What is your non-musical role in the band?

Omar: "You mean, since I have so few musical skills? I probably provide comedy relief – I'm always joking around and trying to cheer everybody up. The other day, everyone was loading gear except me and Cedric, who were just hanging around making everybody laugh. Jim said that's what he loves about our band – the fact that nothing has changed. While they're loading the gear and doing the hard work, I'm telling jokes. I'm pretty irresponsible and I'm not very good at dealing with business stuff so besides creative input I tell jokes and have an all-round good time."

Who made you want to pick up a guitar in the first place?

Omar: "Definitely my father. He was my biggest inspiration because he's a musician and I would always go with him to band practice. He plays our traditional music, which is salsa. I always wanted to be a salsa performer. The salsa groups of Cuba and Puerto Rico influenced me because I was 11 when I started playing – a relatively impressionable age. It was right before I found punk rock. That came later."

Having toured heavily, do you have any tips for survival on the road?

Omar: "Try and stay focused on the goal: the music. Remember never to take yourself too seriously – it's not that important – and remember how fortunate you are because there are probably hundreds of bands who deserve opportunities and recognition more than you do. If I'm feeling bitter I remind myself of what I'm doing, from being in the band to being grateful that I have both arms and both legs. A lot of good friends have illnesses that don't make it possible for them to live out their dreams."

What were you doing before the band took off?

Omar: "I had day jobs between tours. I've been a telemarketer; I've worked in a pizza shop… dull stuff. Telemarketing was the worst. I sold AT&T to people and could barely live with myself because I was basically ripping them off. It was a sacrifice I had to make for art. Now when people call me up and bother me I can sympathise with them – they're just doing their job."

What has been the highlight of being in At the Drive-In so far?

Omar: "It's all so good. I'm a big history freak so being able to come to England, a place of great musical importance to me, is a highlight. I love Syd Barrett and the Gang of Four. But also to be able to go to places like Poland or Slovenia where so much has happened historically compared to back home in the States. Getting to work with Iggy Pop[2] and four of my closest friends was also amazing. To me it seems absurd to be in a band with people whose company you don't like. These guys are my core group of friends."

Do you have any time to pursue other things outside of the band?

Omar: "I've been painting since I was about 13, I keep a journal every day, I take photographs and I'm working on some short films with Cedric. When we do have any free time, Cedric and I work on our dub band, De Facto[3]. When our current tour ends we're doing our second European tour with De Facto because we've got a record out on Jim's label and we're in the process of writing one for Grand Royal. Cedric and I live together and are in two bands together."

It's a good job you get on. What is yours and Cedric's house like?

Omar: "We've got a little home studio there, so last Christmas was spent working on a new De Facto record. I also collect TVs and second-hand stereo pieces. I have a wall of 16 TVs that I've collected from all over the place and I have them all tuned in at once. I've also got 26 old seventies stereo pieces, silver retro-style. I've got reel-to-reel machines and all sorts of stuff. I've also got thousands of records. Right now I'm listening to all sorts: OutKast, Captain Beefheart, Can and Kraftwerk. I just like music. How can you only obsess over one field or genre? There's so much out there to be taken on as an inspiration. You know, recently some people have been telling us that we need to slow down, but there's really no reason to. Why slow down when you're in full-flow…?"

Notes

1 Situated just past Camden Lock and the infamous outdoor market on Camden High Street, The Monarch is London's premier venue for up-and-coming bands – most who make it will have played there at some point or another. It is currently home of The Barfly club. Like every other 'toilet venue' in the UK – particularly London – it is a fetid little grief-hole with basic, barely functioning amenities. This author has had many a good night there.

2 Pop provided guest vocals (albeit the typically Iggy-esque two-word mantra of "manuscript replica!") on the excellent 'Rolodex Propaganda' single from 2000's *Relationship of Command* album.

3 With Rodriguez on bass and Bixler on drums, De Facto also feature Jeremy Ward (vocals/FX) and former Sublime/Long Beach Dub Allstars member Isaiah Ikey Owens (keyboards). Playing traditional dub music as inspired by Lee 'Scratch' Perry and King Tubby – but with a distinctly Mexican/Spanish influence – although hardly ground-breaking, De Facto are authentic and genuine enough to contribute to a genre whose roots are inextricably tangled with that of punk. "Given that back in 1977, before much punk rock had made it to vinyl, such similar dark, smoky bass-heavy rhythms and twisted keyboard FX were a big influence on the genre in the first place, it begins to make sense," I wrote in a January 2002 review of *Legende du Scorpion à Quatre Queues,* "Hardcore circle-pit dwelling youths will probably hate it, but perhaps that's the point..."

Releases include *How Do You Dub? You Fight for Dub. You Plug Dub In* (album, Headquarter, 1999, re-released by ReStart 2001), '456132015' (12 inch single, Grand Royal, 2001), *Megaton Shotblast* (double album, Gold Standard Laboratories, 2001) and *Legende du Scorpion à Quatre Queues* (album, Modern City Records, 2002).

Slipknot
masks, maggots & minorities

"We're nothing but a bunch of filthy fucking viruses that consume beauty and shit it out…"

FEBRUARY 2001. The phone rings. I pick it up.

"Do you want to go on tour with Slipknot?"

Slipknot. The much-talked about nu metal band whose nine members only appear in public in customised horror masks and old coveralls, who each prefer to be identified by numbers rather than their names[1], each of them a mad bastard to a T. Slipknot. The band whose chaotic live shows transcend rock music and move into the realms of a religious experience. Slipknot. The band taking metal back from the grubby hands of fake-angst merchants like Fred Durst (Limp Bizkit) and Korn. Slipknot. The band who have put the gentle farming state of Iowa on the musical map. Slipknot. The band who boast the biggest following of freaks, rejects and maniacs since Charles Manson declared an open house. Slipknot. The band who, if the rumours are to be believed, routinely punch each other in the face before they go onstage. Slipknot. The most ludicrous and laughable band on the planet.

Do I want to go on tour with them? Yeah, I laughed when I saw them too. Still do.

It takes a split-second of thought before replying with a solid a two word affirmative. Fuck yes. Give me the details and I shall be there.

The success of such an anti-social – though highly profitable – operation as this volatile nontet is not a new phenomenon. Their tribal approach, Neanderthal delivery, honest artistic intentions and vague social agenda (some sort of 'change' through confrontation and chaos) suggests that Slipknot are out to

confront mainstream music's soft sensibilities via the age old method of over-the-top theatrics and the thick, roaring tones of base metal. However, as Marshall McLuhan put it, Slipknot's medium is their only real message. If Slipknot's medium (a colourful cross between orchestrated WWF wrestling, ballet and bar room brawling) really is their message, then this being the consumer age, their image is their product. People who buy into Slipknot buy into the whole angst-ridden aesthetic of America's growing nu metal movement of the late nineties and early zeroes, of which the band are leading lights.

Throw in a heavy splatter-core cinema influence, the morbid appeal of society's ultimate transgressor, the serial killer, an easy to ape and appropriately colourful group uniformity, a geographical outsider's approach to the world – coming from Des Moines, Iowa in the mid-West has always been a big talking point – and a dearth of ideas to share, and you've got one of the most entertaining and ambitious bands to come out of American in recent years. Right from the outset, Slipknot couldn't really fail.

But do they really mean anything? Does their willingness to write semi-hummable, radio adaptable songs like 'Wait and Bleed' and 'Left Behind' detract from their sterling work offending the sensibilities of the many English local councillors who attempted to have the group banned from their particular tawdry Middle England grief-hole's – because of the band's penchant for pissing and shitting and setting fire to each other onstage – or, like the Sex Pistols before them, does it reflect their genuine desire to destroy the music industry from the inside? Does talking about an attempt to instigate major change through music equate to the same thing as actually doing it. Does the fact that my five year old nephew has chosen Slipknot as his favourite band suggest that perhaps their muddy message is reaching the wrong people?

And does anyone really give a flying fuck for the theory and meaning behind the mixed messages of Slipknot's music?

A week later and I'm in Glasgow's infamous Barrowlands venue where, in a few hours time, Slipknot will be playing their second ever UK show – their first outside of England's famously too-critical capital. Glasgow is a tough place, but one full of fire. A working class city that likes to have fun. The Barrowlands is no different. It's the only venue in Britain I've been too that has metal detectors on the front doors. I hear knives are pretty popular around these parts. Knives and drinking. Where better a place to get to know Slipknot?

The interview takes place with percussionist, co-founder and ideas man, Shawn 'The Clown' Crahan, an expert welder and father of three whose main interests are nihilism, welding and art (the Impressionists and Cubists being particular favourites). We're also joined by drummer Joey 'Superball' Jordison,

Crahan's sidekick. Jordison is five foot five in his stocking feet and hits the drums harder than anyone else you'll ever see. Both men alternate between speaking succinctly and matter-of-factly, and barking out random obscenities like Tourettes' kids on a bad amphetamine binge, despite the curious fact that neither are drug-takers and only one of them indulges in alcohol.

Bear in mind that Joey and Shawn are the band's elected spokesmen – those best at articulating what this whole mad circus is about – and you can only imagine what the other seven are like. But I can't help coming back to the one same question: are they true heretics out to question the society that spawned them, or are they just wrapping the American Dream in dumb clothing and selling it as pre-packaged angst to *Buffy* generation kids who know no better?

And if that's the case, why do I like them so much?

These interviews are extracts from conversations that took place in February 2000 in Glasgow, December 2000 in Manchester, May 2001 in Lisbon, Portugal, and October and December 2001 on the phone.

Hello chaps. Are we ready to begin?

Joey Jordison: "Listen, first of all, number one: no! Number two: fuck space. Number three: fuck Egypt – Egypt and space are the same thing. Number four: eat pussy. Number five: lose my mask and die. When you die you're just fucking done, you're toast. Number six: fuck hurricanes. Number seven: basements – don't ask. Number seven: fuck Ron, our old bus driver. Number eight: don't ever fucking put your hands near my mouth."

Nice to meet you too. What in the devil's name are you on about?

Shawn 'The Clown' Crahan: "It's the rules of Slipknot, dude. If you see a backstage pass tonight, look at the back of it and you'll see what we mean. It's nice to meet you by the way."

Thank you.

Shawn: "Are you coming to see us in London? We're going to kill people. You better be there."

Joey: "We'll do it standing on our heads and then we'll get naked."

Great. So how did the in-store signing go earlier on?

Shawn: "It's always fun. I can't speak for everyone but I don't like to get into my 'special place' more than twice a day because by the third time things would seriously start getting... killed."

Your 'special place'?

Shawn: "Yeah. That's when The Clown takes over me."

I think you are what psychologists would term, 'fucking mental'.

Joey: "Oh yeah, I wake up and I am mental. I go to bed and I am mental. I am mental within my dreams, I am mental within my normal state. I get fucking wasted out of my mind – piss drunk – and I'm worrying about the frequencies of my kick-drum. I am out of my mind."

Hmmm.

Shawn: "It's true. I, on the other hand, order things for the band then go mental wondering if they're going to be there and, if when they show up, they are going to be what I want. I'm the organiser and it makes me mental."

Joey: "Yeah, like if our passes had turned up today and the pentagram had been the wrong way round, I would have been mental."

Shawn: "Everything is a non-stop battle with us because we're so anal, but then that's what this art-form requires. That's who we are and that's why we'll last forever and kill everybody else."

Joey: "…unless we kill ourselves our first, which could very easily happen."

Shawn: "Yep. Someone in the band is definitely going to die."

You think so?

Joey: "Oh yeah, and we think we know who it is, too."

Someone is going to die by their own hand, you mean?

Shawn: "Come on, dude. Your job is to get a percentage of rock stars who die for any reason – whether it's drugs, car accidents or whatever, right? OK, now remember that there are nine people in this band who are off their fucking rockers and you just have to do the math…"

Joey: "When I get out of bed I am mental. When I open that first eye I'm, like, 'What can I do for this band today?' It's the first thing I ask myself every fucking day."

Shawn: "It never stops. On and on. It's so sick. You get towards the end of a tour and you feel like you want to go home and lay in your bed, but then when you get there you're like 'why am I not on the road?' This band just never stops. The Anti-Christ is alive by the way. He's right here and he's at least 30 years old."

Really? The Anti-Christ is here in Glasgow?

Joey: "Yeah, and he loves our band. Anyway, listen, I remember reading an interview one time with Bruce Dickinson from Iron Maiden and he said 'I don't wake up and say I'm the singer in Iron Maiden'. Well I do wake up and say I'm the fucking drummer in Slipknot and I'm not going to fucking cheese it! Do you know what I'm saying, here? I've got to do everything to my fullest potential otherwise, Christ, then I would be mental. I had corn flakes at six in the morning by the way."

Hardcore. Back to the in-store signing. Those are some pretty deranged fans that you've got there.

Joey: "Yeah they are, but I'll still personally chase them down the street to sign autographs for them, that's how much they mean to me because I'm a fan myself."

Shawn: "Yeah. But we all deal with them differently. If they know who I am and they want to talk to me I'll spend as much time as possible with them. I'll give them a chance. Because of the masks people never recognise me anyway. They are always, like, 'Hey! Do you drive the bus?' "

Are your fans in Britain more fanatical than in America?

Joey: "I think the reaction is much the same: mental."

Shawn: "Shall I show him my foot?"

Joey: "Yeah. Show him your foot."

Shawn: "Do you want to see my foot?"

Yes, show me your foot.

[Shawn pulls down his sock to reveal a swollen, black ankle.]

Shawn: "This is what I'm dealing with today. See how fat that is?"

Joey: "He's not going to be taking it easy tonight, either."

Shawn: "It's broke. It's fucked up, dude."

How did that happen?

Shawn: "Being a madman".

Joey: "He's mental. We wake up and we're mental. The dude has broken himself! That's how it is with this band."

But tonight is the first night of the tour, so how did it happen?

Joey: "You seen his head scar? Twenty-three stitches, bud. Knocked himself clean out."

So how did that happen?

Shawn: "It was the last show in New York."

Joey: "What about the Ozzfest when you fucked yourself up?"

Shawn: "No, the Ozzfest show was a different injury."

How many injuries have you acquired amongst you?

Joey: "Dude, you don't have enough fucking tape to record it all."

Shawn: "We want to start an injury list on our web page."

Joey: "...and The Clown will definitely be king."

Shawn: [Quietly] "My Mom doesn't like it, though."

Your mother? Why, does she worry about her Clown son?

Shawn: "No matter when I call my Mom, the first thing out of her mouth is always 'Are you alright?' If I arrive home from tour without telling her I'm back, she'll assume something has happened or something has gone wrong and I really don't have the heart to tell her I'm slowly going insane. I guess she'll find out all about it when she has to bring me flowers."

Tell me about your fans then.

Joey: "Oh yeah, the maggots. We've toured America a lot and when we get the chance to come over here and play for fans, thousands of miles from where we live and where we wrote these songs purely to have fun in our basement, it is a genuinely humbling experience. Just seeing the way they have embraced us is very flattering for all of us. It's so... so, grand."

Shawn: "Plus they're fucking crazy over here, man. Kids in the UK are not spoilt as much as they are in the States. You've got to understand, our kids back home go beyond the call of duty for us, but if they came over here they'd see that the reaction is different and they'd step it up. I'm not slagging them, but there's so much bullshit going on in the States right now that I think it wears kids out, the way things are sold to them and so forth. They're up to speed because they catch onto stuff early but they need to get back in love with what it's all really about. They need to get away from the materialism of it all. Over here, I don't think things have got quite as perverted yet. They wait for the successful bands from the States – and it is generally successful bands because it's expensive to do and you really have to want to do the mission – and when you do make it over they appreciate it. Dude, if you would have told me two years ago that I was going to come to Scotland I would have told you to go fuck yourself. Fuck. I'm in Scotland and I can't believe it. It's weird, but, you know, the story is really not that different wherever. What we've got here today is a club with a sound system, a band who are going to be up there living their dream and there's going to be a whole load of kids who need music to escape for an hour, to live."

Joey: "The best thing about it is that we get to do it tomorrow. And do it again. And again. And make a new record. We just got back from Japan and Australia and I swear to God they were the best crowds we've seen. We couldn't walk the streets of Japan."

Shawn: "Wait, I got to do this to you. [Pulls out a toy monkey and wiggles it in my face.] *Wap!* It's a funny monkey."

Yes, it's funny isn't it? So anyway, would you say that your first album was such a success because those issues that you talk about – alienation, self-loathing, destruction... funny monkeys – are an international language for teenagers?

Joey: "I think we speak directly to the kids, whereas a lot of bands talk right over their heads. We're all kids ourselves. Even with this current success of the band we still go through the exact same things those kids go through every single day."

Shawn: "I finally came up with a good way to explain the importance and the impact of our album. It's the first time I've thought of this since putting the band together all those years ago.

"If you took this table right here and put a wall around the rim, then took a top and spun it as hard as you fucking could with all the love in you, it would just bounce off the walls and that would be it. It would be normal. It would be expected. With Slipknot you take the fucking wall off, throw that top on the table and at any given second it could go overboard. It's so uncontrolled and you don't know what's going to happen. All the fans are the same – they're fucking mental, they hurt, they love, they hate. Everything that this spinning uncontrolled thing that is Slipknot is, they feel. We try not to talk about religion or politics because we'd rather talk about growing up, living, being a human and just trying to deal with life – whether you love it or hate it – by trying to wake the fuck up in order to do something about it. The only thing that we preach is that, hey, you exist and if you believe in yourself you can have anything you want. If I'm in a bad mood or my foot hurts there's all these people who [psychotically punches his own head twice]... know me, you know? I haven't met them, but they know me. When I start hitting myself to get it all out on stage – my DJ Sid and I do it quite a lot – I've got all these kids in front of me in the crowd who are doing the same thing, but they don't stop until their knuckles are bloody and their eyes are becoming blackened. I talk to these kids after the show and they're smart kids, you know? They understand us and the reaction within them is insane."

Joey: "We've been through so much shit within the confines of where we come from and we've got so much fucking shit to work out that we're good for another five albums. We have barely touched on what we can do. You'll see."

Shawn: "We'll take everything to a new realm and change things up for ourselves. It's a good feeling. We're just getting started."

Joey: "The way I see it, this current world tour that we just did was the one where we gathered up our people – our army – and now it's time to fucking literally change the world. Destroy everything. You wait, you're going to shit yourself. You'll love it. Recently, I've learnt to step outside of the perspective of our band and look at it and I see that we have got a lot of fans. I'm a rabid music fan and have been all my life and because I have loved so many bands and seen the way they have certain types of fans, I've never seen a legion so sick as ours. It's fucking crazy."

Have there been any dangerous encounters with fans? Any junior John Wayne Gacy's[2] maybe?

Joey: "Honestly, no, because they understand what we're really about. They see beyond the masks, beyond the exterior. Well… maybe there have been one or two incidents."

Shawn: "Once in a while you let down your guard and you forget how sick everything is, but you can be sure someone will step up to remind you otherwise. That's the Slipknot experience. I had a girl come up to me at an in-store signing in New York and fucking head-butted me, grabbed me and said [whispers] 'I'm going to fucking kill you tonight!'"

Joey: "She told every member of the band she was going to seek them out and kill them. Even just today in the Virgin Megastore I had a girl begging, pleading…"

Shawn: "…To piss on you? Was that what I heard?"

Joey: "Yep, she wants me to piss on her."

Shawn: "Are you going to do it?"

Joey: "Absolutely. Absolutely I'm going to do it. Like dogs."

Shawn: "Well I'm going to film that shit when it happens."

Joey: "I can't wait. And I'm going to be jerking it when I do it."

I think I'd like to join Slipknot. It sounds interesting.

Shawn: "Oh, you could get in the band real easy but if you suck we kick you out and beat the fuck out of you."

Joey: "Yeah. You can get in real easy, but we'll fucking nail you."

Shawn: "You won't walk out."

Joey: "It's like a gang thing. First you're fired then you get your ass kicked by nine crazy motherfuckers. That's one bad day to come home from!"

Shawn: "It's not like a job or something – you'd be glad to be merely fired from Slipknot. That would be getting off lightly."

What's the harshest criticism you've received so far?

Shawn: "None, because we've got the Mafia on our side and everybody knows we'd just have them murdered. Yeah, there's criticism man, but the way we look at is, failure is where criticism comes from. I mean, I don't feel anything for you and I don't give a fuck what you write, I don't care – but we're still kind of part of the same team. We all like music. This isn't some watered-down salesman shit I'm talking here, I just mean we're working hard and we're giving you our real lives. We're not trying to buy you or anything. We do what we do because we love it and I think people know that because it shows. It's hard to criticise that, but everyone's got their opinions."

Joey: "Take the good with the bad. We won some magazine awards from both *Kerrang!* and *Metal Hammer* but we also came in on the worst band categories too and that fucking rules!"

Shawn: [Shouting into the tape recorder] "I'D LIKE TO STATE THAT HALF THE PEOPLE WHO HATE US ARE PUNK MOTHER-FUCKERS! AND GUESS WHAT? I FUCKING LOVE THE SEX PISTOLS TOO, SO SUCK MY DICK!"

Joey: "Yeah… um… and so when I'm playing drums and I see someone that has written a bad thing about us, I play just as much to school that motherfucker as much as I do my fans. It's the same love."

What do you mean? You're talking in riddles, man!

Shawn: "We like to convert people. Back home we had a whole ska-punk crowd come down to our shows and they hated metal but they loved to watch us go off. It wasn't the show, but the way that we play our instruments. They thought, 'Jesus, not only are you a great drummer but you're going fucking psycho while doing it!'"

Joey: "Right. It's like Shawn always says to his son, if you're going to play drums fine, but play them like… this!" [Starts throwing punches.]

Shawn: "Yeah! I tell him, I don't give a fuck what you do, be a ballerina, drink Coca-Cola, write for a paper, but just do it like… this!" [Mimes a dramatic fit.]

Joey: "Feel it. If you don't feel it, FUCK OFF! You have nothing for me. Nothing! Do it right. If you don't, well… never mind."

So do you think that makes you more punk rock than most punk rock bands?

Joey: "Yeah, we are for sure. I think Slipknot has the highest punk rock ethic you're able to find. We started from nothing, our record has curses and obscenities coming out of its ass and the next one will have even more. The next album will be harder. We're not polished and radio-friendly. We were in the studio throwing stuff and not caring if the fucking tape machine got scratched up or if anything got smashed. It's just equipment. There's so many fuck-up's on the first album… but it rules because we've never been about making it note-perfect. You can't when you play as hard as we do. I fuck up all the time because I am a human."

Shawn: "We just got to play the Conan O'Brien show in the States and I think pretty much everyone in the industry and probably our fans too really thought that we were going to use the opportunity to be fucking assholes and pull some sort of stunt. OK, here's the deal, man: if I want to take a shit on stage, I'll do it regardless."

Joey: "And he did, by the way. And he threw it at me. They wrote in *Kerrang!* that I took a shit in Shaun's room and he didn't speak to me for a while, but you know what? He stepped it up and took a shit onstage and then threw it at me."

Where was this?

Joey: "This was in Virginia Beach. The thing is, yeah, he got the shit on me but I made a spectacle out of it. I played with his own shit and when I took a shower that night there was a shit stain on my sock that I'd been walking around with for fucking ten hours! So I go, 'What's sicker? You took a shit on stage, but I played a show with it!'"

Shawn: [Mumbling] "Yeah, but I ate it."

Joey: "Huh? Yeah, that's true, you did eat it. And you didn't do it G.G. Allin-style, all fucking whacked out on drugs. You did it completely sober. Anway, we've got off the subject again."

Shawn: "What you've got to understand is, if the feeling was right on Conan O' Brien to do something, we would have done. Instead though we went on and played our song. We felt that Slipknot playing on that particular mainstream, prime-time TV show was probably the biggest ever victory for heavy music ever. We like to think that we're there at the beginning and that in the future you'll be able to see Neurosis or Hatebreed or Napalm Death on TV. We go with the moment and we play to the best of our ability. I never tell people to be careful before we go onstage, because that's when we start getting hurt. We just go out there as if it's a fucking war."

Joey: "There's no faking it because it's all emotion, it's all heart. When Sid [Taylor, DJ] goes up on the top balcony at the fucking London Astoria and flips off, do you think he's worrying about whether he's going to get hurt? Hell no."

What's your nickname?

Joey: "It's Superball. One time I came offstage after a horrible show and I was literally bouncing off the walls and bouncing ten feet in the air. I was fucking airborne. I was so mental I could have given Michael Jordan a run for his money."

What were you like at school?

Joey: "There was a teacher I had a huge crush on and I'd always try and look up at her skirt. I guess that made me a teacher's pet, right? I got decent grades but mostly I hung out by my locker with my headphones on. I was extremely introverted."

When did you lose your virginity?

Joey: "Oh, this one is good. The girl was 14, I was 17. She was mental and I was just trying to get laid. Cathy, she was called. So I go over to her house and make it into her room. She's throwing Twizzlers at me, tries to throw a clock at me, and she's cranking Madonna on the stereo. Then she turns off the light, throws a rubber at me and it hits me in the forehead. I didn't realise until she was getting herself ready that she had a broken leg and I was like 'How the fuck am I going to do this?' I'm trying to get her fucking pants off like a moron and finally I get in there, get in three or four strokes and then blow a load and say, 'You know, maybe we shouldn't be doing this?' I pull out and leave her lying there with her fucking old gimp leg hanging out, pull on my pants and wear the rubber all the way home. When I get home I fill it up with water to see that there aren't any holes – that's how mental I was – then let out the biggest scream you've ever fucking heard.

"It was the best sex I've ever had. Nothing has topped it yet. I fucked a charity case."

What's the best pet you've ever had?

Joey: "I had this cat that used to go out and fight dogs then come back a bloody fucking mess – tail half ripped off, trails of blood. He was called Not My Cat. He ruled. I used to dress him up all stupid, hang cigarettes out of his mouth. He dug it, but then [wistfully] he disappeared one day…"

Who are you attracted to right now?

Joey: "Fiona Apple. I'm completely obsessed by her. I'll tell you a story. I was meant to be in the same studio that she was in, but I got there a day late and she'd already gone. Apparently she'd just been hanging out with a bottle of wine – when I heard that I was completely and utterly depressed for a month. I met her once though and she flirted with me. She didn't even look at Shawn, but she flirted with me."

And who deserves a smack?

Joey: "Fiona Apple, on her ass when I'm doing her doggy–style."

What's been the most embarrassing ever moment in your life?

Joey: "One time in school we watching TV and I puked up my lunch all over my desk. I was so embarrassed that I tried to cover it up by scooping it up with my arms but it was running out on the floor and stuff. I was embarrassed but ultimately it ruled because I caused a vomitory and a few other people started puking too."

What's your drug of choice?

Joey: "Should I be honest here? OK, I don't do drugs. I suppose I'd have to say caffeine."

What interests me most about Slipknot, is the split-personality disorder that appears to run through the collective ranks and which is best personified in the band's most vocal member, Shawn Crahan. Exuding the general sense of an aggrieved roadie who, like all roadies, views the world beyond the parameters of heavy metal with contempt, Crahan is talkative and intelligent although also prone to resorting to chimerical Charles Manson-esque phrases. He is the first to admit that his skills as a musician are limited. Indeed, he's far more likely to be heard proudly showing off his work as the welder and designer of Slipknot's stage set than any neat paradiddle that he's pulled off during the actual show itself.

In short, he's the idea's man, the reformed alcoholic whip cracker, the one who originally drew together a disparate and desperate group of musicians – from former teenage drug addict and sometime porn shop worker Corey Taylor to their LSD-fried English hip-hop/drum 'n' bass DJ Sid Wilson – in Des Moines in the first place in order to make his vision real. He's also a typical hard-working mid-West husband and father of three who has built his own house by hand and likes nothing more than discussing the brush-strokes of Monet – all of which makes for a contradictory profile of a modern metal warrior.

When the Clown mask comes on though, it's a different matter. To borrow from a standard horror movie plot-line, it's The Clown who unlocks the door to

Photograph: Martyn Goodacre

the basement of his mind, deep down where the demons lurk. Fittingly, it was Crahan's childhood Clown mask that inspired the direction of Slipknot; the sympathetic, pleading eyes seeming to give way to a darker, deeper character with a gonzo smile that looks more like a lascivious leer. When the portly percussionist puts on his mask and becomes The Clown, he's unleashing the beast inside.

A few months after encountering a relatively green Clown, I caught up with a world-weary Shawn in a reflective, though no less agitated, homely mode for an end of year type interview. The Clown made an appearance too.

As the year comes to a close, how would you describe the general state of mind within the Slipknot ranks?

Shawn: "Well, I can only speak for myself, and personally I feel like I'm no longer going to co-operate with people. I am not going to try and beat you over the head to get your attention – either you're with Slipknot or you're not, and if you not I'm not going to be around you. All I've got to say to everybody is that Slipknot is the greatest band that there has ever been in the entire world; our philosophy, our well-being, the way we present our life, the way we live our life, the way we project our life to the kids. Everybody else can fuck off. Simple really."

Have any other bands influenced the recording of the new record?

Shawn: "The only shit I'm listening to is noise: Today Is the Day, Neurosis, Merzbow – the more distorted and fucked up it is, the better my head is going into the album."

Are you looking forward to hitting Europe again?

Shawn: "Absolutely. But if someone doesn't take me to a fucking gallery next time I come, man… if I don't get over there and see some real fucking culture I'm going to flip out. Let's do it. All someone has to do is grab me early in the morning, wake me up in my bunk and say, 'Clown, I'm going to take you to see some art, your mind will be blown but we'll be back for soundcheck.' Believe me, those three hours will make my whole week. That's the thing I love about touring. We recently went to a gallery in Spain and I got a chance to see a bunch of original Dalis and Picassos. OK, so it might not be heavy metal, but Picasso was a serious artist who created art that was as intense as any musical form, plus he had technicians and managers so that he could take his show on the road… and years later it's still on the road impressing the fuck out of people."

So what has been the highlight of the last 12 months for you?

Shawn: "A couple of things. It was a highlight to play Reading Festival. It was a lot of fun because it was a big show and if it never happens again I was still a part of it. It was also pretty special because we played with Rage Against the Machine there, shortly before Zack left. I feel pretty honoured to have done that. Coming full circle was the real highlight though. Originally, I left my wife and kids in order to make an album and to be in the best band in the world, and two years later I came back from Europe with an award stating that the maggots thought we were the best band in the world, so I decided to mark the occasion by driving all the way home in order to complete the cycle, to close the chapter. And let me tell you, I had a lot of revelations driving home and reflecting on all of the things that we've done in a short space of time – four European tours, success without depending on radio or TV, forcing people to pay attention to who we are and what we think about life. The last two years turned out slightly different to how I planned, but they've been pretty exciting none the less."

So what has upset you this year?

Shawn: "People not paying attention to the right things, people not using their brains. It upsets me because on the one hand there are people who love you as a musician and pump you up, but then they'll go away and do their job – specifically I'm talking about 'critics' who will use things against you because they see it as their job. My stance in life is I do exactly what I want and if I get in trouble doing it, then so be it. The low point of the past year is the sudden realisation – or confirmation – that most people within music willingly conform to the ways of the industry and by extension of that, society as a whole. It's the same fucking bullshit day in and day out. We all have to live by certain laws but this stupid fucking industry is full of people who are not giving 100% of themselves to change it. I have no respect for people like that and hopefully I can destroy every one of them."

Who do you admire as a person?

Shawn: "Again, it's got to be my wife because she allows me to do all this whilst still having a family. She's been sick for the past couple of days and I've had to take the kids to school two days in a row. Let me tell you, it's not an easy thing to do. You have to get up at six, dress two kids, take them all the way across to town to one school, then wait an hour and wake up the youngest and get her ready for a whole different school. Four hours later I'm back to pick them up. So while I'm out being a fucking stupid rock star my wife is normally taking care of the real important things."

Have you made any new enemies recently?

Shawn: "Only myself – it's my biggest battle. I always lose too. I'm in a constant battle with myself every day – I like to live, I don't like to live, I like to be in the band, I don't like to be in the band. It's a lot of pressure."

Does The Clown still attract the strangest Slipknot fans?

Shawn: "I can't speak for everybody, but Clown fans usually want to punch me in the face or they want me to hit them. They bring me dog balls and cow heads and hearts. It's not really weird to me."

What's the one thing you take with you wherever you go?

Shawn: "Interesting. I guess it has always been my wedding ring. I have to take it off when we play because it cuts me. I have a giant callous and my finger got all cut when I played drums on the last tour. My ring was made for me by my wife and I once lost it for three years. We were recording an early version of 'Spit it Out' in a studio before we got signed and I got in a big fight with the engineer and was spinning around because I was so pissed off that I left without it. One day out of the blue three years later, they found it. It's the one thing that reminds me of who I really am in life, no matter how bad it gets or how cut up my face gets or how many dead cow heads are all over the place. When it gets like that I look at my ring and realise that I have something that most people don't have: happiness with a family who love me."

Tell me a joke.

Shawn: "A joke? There are a couple of jokes that have just gone on and on, one of which is 'The Dudes'. It's not a typical joke, it's a drawing that was done by an affiliated worker of the band. It's a homosexual comic book drawing and it's funny as fuck, but done in good taste. It's not making fun of anyone or anything but it's the most wrong, most sickest, most hardcore drawings ever. It has made it all around the world and the band live to see The Dudes every day. When we get up and The Dudes aren't in the dressing room we're fucking mental. Each one of us has made it into an episode and it's brutal. Little things like that keep us going."

What should Slipknot do next year?

Shawn: "Well, in response to all those other bands who've answered this question, I think Slipknot should fucking kill every one of you people. Jesus Christ. I personally am taking a stand against everyone and everything. It's not about rock 'n' roll any more – none of this is. I don't care about interviews, awards or any of that. I care about the world we live in and if we all hate the things we're hearing and seeing why aren't we changing them? If that means me beating everyone in a face with a baseball bat from now on, that's what I'm going to do. It seems like everybody has got an opinion about us, but no one likes to talk to my face. I might bite and punch… but I listen too."

What would you do with Britney Spears if you met her?
Shawn: "Stick a plunger up her butt-hole, maybe. I think she's good for a head shaving and a demoralising three months in a closet, bound and gagged and reconditioned. Fuck her."

What do you want for Christmas?
Shawn: "To be in my new house that we're still fixing up. My wife and I like to construct but it takes time and I'm leaving in less than 30 days to start the album. We have a dining room now where we can sit as a family and eat dinner together, and I can't remember the last time we did that religiously. I can sit down and look at my kids and ask them what they've learnt at school – no TV or anything, just a family sitting down and talking together. The American Dream."

Slipknot's second album, the much talked-up and heavily marketed *Iowa*, was recorded on the back of two years touring. The band had gone through the madness years of roughing it on the world circuit, developing their image, building a fan base and trying to (unsuccessfully) control all their press, and were now at the stage where the Slipknot entity had become a major commercial opportunity for all involved. A sizeable chunk of money had been invested in keeping nine band members plus crew on the road for months at a time. Those backstage tube socks and M&Ms don't come cheap.

Recorded relatively quickly with nu metal zeitgeist-meister Ross Robinson at the controls, *Iowa* was to be the album that would see Slipknot go mainstream – on their own terms. They'd vowed not to 'cheese it' by softening things for radio, MTV and general mass consumption and would instead take their soupy sound in the other direction – towards white noise and black metal dynamics, if their utterings were to be believed. This was to be an album by a band of hicks whose eyes had been yanked opened and clamped wide like Malcolm McDowell's in their beloved *Clockwork Orange* (itself an obvious influence on Slipknot's, ahem, 'anti-image') due to the sudden exposure to the belching, farting music biz beast. This was to be the album that told the world who these shadowy[3] calculating psychos were and where they'd come from: Des Moines, deep in the musical hinterlands of Iowa.

Upon the album's completion, it went straight to the top of the charts in the

UK and Top 5 in most of the major countries. Soon afterwards in 2001, I talked to singer Corey Taylor, an ever-grimacing Crahan and exuberant pint-sized drummer Joey Jordison.

Your second album *Iowa* is done, dusted and out there – how has it been received?

Corey Taylor: "Well, I think the kids love it and parents hate it – which is just the way all good music should be. Parents can't fucking stand us. It's the usual case of the older generation not getting it and the younger generation grasping something they can really relate to. I totally appreciate that because – as much as we love playing – if you can't relate to your audience you'll disappear. Good popular music should always have a bit of danger to it and apart from Britney's Spears's fucking clit piercing I doubt there's any real danger out there."

As the band member responsible for the lyrical output how do you approach your writing?

Corey: "A lot of the stuff that I write starts as small ideas, which might come to me on the road. We usually get the music together before I start writing because we change things so much – something I write which might be relevant one day might be totally pointless the next. Making the album I jotted down pages and pages of stuff, then in practice I'd adapt lyrics and rework them into songs. I came up with concepts – 'Wait and Bleed' from the first album started as a kind of story, but the problem is there's so many fucking clichés out there in music, the aim is to come up with something which avoids that but is both entertaining and provoking. Sometimes it's a fit of passion that comes out in eight lines, other times I'll write 12 pages – it all depends on the inspiration.

"Lyrically I'm proud of the whole album because as a writer you're always striving to say something the best way and put it in the best words you can. To be able to express something the way you want to is something to be proud of. I feel like I'm getting closer to my goal, which is to write the ultimate song. I doubt I'll ever do it, but…"

Tell me about the song 'Iowa'.

Corey: "'Iowa' is really the first Slipknot love song. As sick as it sounds, it is still definitely a love song. Why? Well, love is relative, man. Love is in the eyes of the beholder. A serial killer and his toy? Why not? There's love there. John Wayne Gacy loved his children, for fuck's sake. Sure, the serial killer thing has been done before, but to look at it from the point of view of the love that he is full of is a different approach. Love can be ten times more angry than hate any time, so I thought it was a good idea for a song.

"The only song Ross [Robinson, Slipknot producer] wasn't beside me screaming his head off on was *Iowa* because I told him on purpose that I didn't want him in there. We did two takes and the vibe of the song was extremely sick. We turned all the lights off in the studio, lit all these candles and I stripped down and sang the song naked. I started cutting myself with all these broken candles just to put me in that destructive mind-set and the thing was, I felt no pain. It was all adrenalin, it was all release. I could actually see these imaginary people sitting there man, – one of them was a malicious bastard of a killer and beside him was his victim who he had meticulously taken care of. And this guy wasn't treating his victim as a person, but as an object, a sexual toy. It was a really sick, sick vibe."

Ross Robinson has quite a reputation. He has pretty much single-handedly managed to define the latest metal sounds by working with the best and most extreme new bands around.

Corey: "Ross Robinson is definitely the best person I've ever worked with to record vocals because he wants you to go so hard and so real that he'll have you sing the song over and over and you never know which take he's going to use. He gets in your head beforehand by sitting down with you and asking what the song is about and how it makes you feel. It's a beautiful thing because it's pure creativity. Ross pushes you to express yourself as hard as you can, you know? A lot of people tend to go for the numbers, the easy win – they're looking at it with dollar signs in their eyes. Ross looks at you with his heart. He'll get in your face and he'll scream in the background while you're singing and it's so much fucking fun. He's in there with you the whole time. Like, on the song 'Disasterpiece' I had six people in the room with me and we were all slamming and going for it, whereas on *Iowa* I had to get in that spot where you can almost rise above yourself and become so detached that ultimately you empathise with this person who you're singing about."

Shawn: "What do you want me to say about Ross? Ross is Ross, dude. I have a blast when I record with him because we both have the same philosophy: we like the shit that the rest of the world doesn't think makes sense. We go for the purest of art, the noisiest noise. When we work together it usually means we're working on something weird. I get hell for my back-up vocals sometimes, but Ross brings the real side of me out and he accepts it. I also like watching him and Corey. That world is so surreal to me. When Corey and Ross are together it's best to stay away, give them their privacy and just pay homage to two nut-jobs at work."

Joey: "Me and Ross came up with something called The Run to the Border, which is taken from a slogan from the Taco Bell food chain. It involved me running a mile from the studio down to Taco Bell with Ross – who had damaged his knee – riding his bike alongside me. Then we'd run back and start recording the drums right away. I don't like to slick shit up and make it over-produced because our band is very raw, very brutal and very abrasive. I see us kind of like the Andy Kaufman of metal bands. Fuck man, I had to exercise to make *Iowa!*"

Shawn: "I'd watch that kid [Joey] play so fucking hard every single day. Sometimes he'd only to do three takes because he was physically gone. Do you know how much concentration it takes to create something that's going to last forever? When you're sitting there and you're hooked up and plugged in, it's forever man! And when is doing something that you've waited your whole life to do it's serious, man, it's not a fucking joke to us. We're reflecting society today, we're the ugly mirror of truth. I don't know what else to say to convince people of our intentions."

How long did the album take to do?

Corey: "The way we work is we pretty much write and record everything to put on a record – no extra songs – just like Metallica used to back when they were good, ha ha! They'd write what they needed and that would be the album. But then they changed. The record company fucking hates that because they want more so they can sponge off you as much as possible. The song 'I Am Hated' was originally just for the *Rollerball* soundtrack but at the last minutes we thought, fuck it, let's not keep a good song off the album, so we put it on."

Shawn: "For myself, I can't really say that the recording of *Iowa* was that enjoyable, but it was how it needed to be. Personally, I was really consumed with the artwork and the research involved to take Slipknot up a step."

Being in a recording studio is generally a boring time for bands with everyone having to do their parts at different times, so it must doubly bad for a group the size of Slipknot. What did you do to kill time?

Corey: "One of the main sources of entertainment was this lounge that we set up called the Tiki Bar that was done up all Hawaiian and shit. When we were done we'd start pounding booze, hanging out and having a good time. When we weren't doing takes we were in the lounge watching bullfights and really bad porn. It was a good time. We were hanging out with other people who were recording there, like Ben Harper and Unida, who we're big fans of. We just met a lot of really cool people. The whole feeling was pretty subdued though and not as crazy as people would probably think. We were pretty removed from the whole Hollywood bullshit scene because the studio was in the Valley. But at the same time we were still right in the pit of sin, so there was a still a sick vibe going on. One night Ben Stiller showed up to hang out."

Ben Stiller? Is he a Slipknot fan?

Corey: "I don't know, because I think we kind of freaked him out before I really got a chance to find out. He was, like, 'What are you guys doing? You're puking on each and other and bleeding everywhere, Jesus Christ…' and I was just like 'Yeah, sit down, have a drink, godammit…'"

Joey: "Casey from Amen came in for a little bit and a couple of the Queens of the Stone Age were there once in a while but mainly we watched the Playboy channel pretty much all day every day when we weren't working."

Shawn: "We'd stay up until eight in the morning, walking the streets and taking pictures of bugs, of signs… anything. We were researching light by walking in darkness. It sounds weird, but it was what I had to do. It was what was keeping me sane. I didn't even bring my wife and kids along with me because I had to work to do.

"I was getting up and doing Tai Chi, getting my blood going. We had this guy Rory who came in with loads of herbs and stuff to get in shape and clear ourselves up. I was working out a little bit, but mainly concentrating on stretching and breathing. I also got into a lot of strange worlds, like photography. Like, I would just pee somewhere and… um, make a whole photo shoot out of it."

Iowa is surely the heaviest album to ever get to number one in the UK?

Corey: "Yeah, I think us getting to number one with a record like that is a statement in itself. We'd done two tours of duty but I still wasn't sure whether anyone would like the album, so when we heard we were number one in the UK and Canada, number three in America, number four in Japan and number two in Australia it fucked my head up. It's a testimony to the fact that music doesn't have to be soul-less and awful. It can be heavy. It was a victory for extreme music and it showed that there's a much wider market for extreme music than a lot of the record companies and critics of supposed anti-social would care to admit. And I'm not talking about mall-rock[4] – the music that's supposed to be heavy, but really is a load of crap – I'm talking about true heavy music. All those mall-rock bands need to fuck off because they're giving so-called heavy music a bad name. They're at the other end of the spectrum as far as I'm concerned."

Given Slipknot's appearance, you're a band more open to impersonators and impostors than most – does this ever happen and do you get recognised much?

Corey: "People recognise me for my tattoos, but I'm generally pretty chameleonic. I change my appearance a lot – I change my hair, grow a beard, shave my head, whatever. But still I sometimes get recognised, just not as much as you would think. Recently there was a guy out in the audience in a ski mask signing autographs as me so one of my buddies from the band No One beat his ass. Things like that happen and it hurts because people are taking advantage of these kids. I don't want that to reflect on our band. I'm out there every night for a couple of hours signing things and hanging out with kids. I'll beat anyone's ass who jeopardises our relationship with our fans or attempts to rip them off in any way."

How did the concept and title of *Iowa* the album come about?

Corey: "The title of the album was a mutual decision. On our second European tour we came up with the idea of using a really crude, crayon drawing that The Clown had done of this dog with its leg cocked, pissing everywhere. We were just going to scrawl *Iowa* across it in big, poofy letters. When we were doing instores, we left these drawings everywhere and that's how the idea germinated. We realised we could turn it into a statement about where we come from – a statement for kids who come from small towns anywhere. There's a lot more darkness going on in these small towns than a lot of people out there realise. When you think of Iowa you think of corn fields, farmers, cows and all that bullshit, but any true music aficionados will know that's where Buddy Holly died or where Ozzy bit the head off a bat. What else is there to know? Not much. Kids are born with no future and they have to fight for anything. There's no opportunities, it's like being dead on arrival. So, we decided to call the album *Iowa* as a tribute to where we come from and a tribute to no-hopers and misfits like us everywhere."

Joey: "That song does something to me, man. We did that song in one take. A two inch reel of tape is 16 minutes long and we were so in 'the zone' that we didn't know when the song was going to end because most of it was improvised. Our engineer started freaking out because it sounded so awesome, and when we got to the end of the song and the final note faded out there was about a two second gap before the tape snapped. It was fucking scary, man. We did that song with the masks on and the whole vibe was really, really eerie. I can't say we weren't on any substances at the time, too…"

So what has the reaction been back in Des Moines? Are people offended of flattered by your portrayal of the place?

Corey: "There's one gentleman who keeps bringing us up at the city council meeting who wants us banned from the area, from our own home town. He wants us rounded up, arrested and driven out of Iowa. It's funny though, because at the other end of the spectrum the mayor was talking about having a Slipknot day, a state-wide holiday once a year. It would be funny, but ultimately I think it would detract from what we stand for. It might be nice to get the key to the city someday, but in the end is that going to save me any money or parking tickets? I don't think so…"

Joey: "We might have recorded in California but our sound was pure Iowa. It rained in California the whole time we were out there, anyway."

Have you all established your own non-musical roles within the band?

Corey: "There are very different personalities in Slipknot. You've got the class clowns, the chiefs who take care of a lot of the business and you've got the guys who are just enjoying the life. But when it comes to crunch-time, we'd all die for each other because we're all after the same thing. We don't fuck around."

Does being Slipknot ever feel like 'work'?

Shawn: "Not in the conventional sense, no. We took our time making a record and felt no pressure. The label stayed away and left us to it – they could tell us what to do if they wanted but I'd tell them to suck my dick and go fuck themselves. I don't care. Our record label is a bank – that's all."

Onstage you're The Clown, giving the crowd the finger and playing with yourself. Who are you in the studio?

Shawn: "I have never understood the studio situation until this last album. The reason I was able to get my vibe on was because I was able to research what I wanted to do. I was able to implement a lot of ideas that I have about percussion, which is something I've never had the chance to do before. I've started to play the guitar. I'm going on a lot of interesting different journeys with photography, with learning guitar, learning stuff from Joey… so Clown is always there live and Shawn is there when we're recording, but Clown turned up in the studio too. They're both in there somewhere and the tough part is trying to find myself – the true me within it all. To me every song is a little epiphany about our own existences."

To get the other side of the *Iowa* story, I spoke to producer Ross Robinson a few weeks after the album went to number one. Through his work on the first two albums by nu metal pioneers Korn, Robinson is the man most responsible for the sound that is currently booming across the States and beyond.

He quickly distanced himself from the burgeoning genre as it swan-dived into the mainstream with baseball cap askew, via the malignant rap-metal of Limp Bizkit, whose *Three Dollar Bill Y'All* he also produced. From his Californian Indigo Ranch studio, Robinson has earned a reputation as a man who draws on the energy, insecurities, anger and ambition of his performers and turns it into something tangible, something marketable. His contribution to albums by Soulfly, Machine Head, Sepultura, At the Drive-In, Glassjaw, Amen and, yes, the Vanilla Ice comeback album, have made him one of the world's most in-demand producers. Refreshingly, he remains as approachable and passionate about his work as ever.

Ross Robinson: "For me, the making of *Iowa* was the biggest challenge of my life. Shortly before we started, I broke my back riding motor cross but still decided that I was going to produce this record no matter what – it almost became something bigger than my body or my physical life. This feeling permeated into the band and I think, in a strange kind of way, they were almost happy about the injury because it made everything more real, more painful. Nobody was allowed to show up late because I would be there on time every day, ready to work despite what had happened. It brought more a feeling of humility to things, rather than being consumed by fame, success and the usual rock 'n' roll distractions.

"I saw a huge difference within the members of Slipknot from making the first album [Slipknot, 1999] and starting work on *Iowa*. They'd been out and seen the world and they were finally beginning to sound like who they really were. It's hard to transfer yourself into the rock stardom thing where everybody is kissing your ass and I think that stuff affected them in this next chapter of their lives. It's sad to see the wide-eyed, brand new baby grow up, but despite the added pressure on them their intentions were still honest and pure and they have kept their integrity as a working entity. I think they'd definitely lost the innocence that was there on their first record – that's the big difference between the two albums. The first was intense, but also strangely innocent. Plus, they write better riffs now.

"There was times when I'd be in the room with Corey when he was doing his vocals and when he hit the high notes it'd just be like 'Fuck!' and the pain in my back would go. I think that when you're giving it that hard it can be healing. Those vocals had healing powers! They really brought me into the moment and it was incredible. I was basically just there to support him and throw shit around. It's the craziest thing, but I don't remember the names of songs on any

Photograph: Martyn Goodacre

of the records that I've done. So, for me, it's not about favourite songs on albums, but favourite parts or moments during particular songs. Like, the night before they came into the studio, Sid's grandfather died. When he came in I put him behind the mic, just to vent, to let it all out doing background vocals on 'People = Shit'. There were other voices with him, but it's his that you can hear the best screaming throughout the chorus. Him doing that was special to me.

"Shawn devoted his whole life to the artwork and aesthetic of the album, so he wasn't around too much during the guitar over-dubs or whatever. Laying down the drums they all did it together, but everybody was cool with him pursuing another role because he's so important to the progression of Slipknot. He breathes life into them.

"There really weren't many people visiting the studio during the entire making of the record and if somebody did come by Mick [Thompson, guitarist] would be fucking pissed off. I don't want to mention any particular band names but, you know, Slipknot are their own little island. They're not the kind of band to take on somebody's else's vibe because they have such an overpowering one of their own. Long may they reign."

Back on the road again. Lisbon, Portugal. Some wood-panelled enormo-dome down by the harbour. Day One of the band's second touring cycle. The *Iowa* album was hitting Europe and Slipknot wanted to hammer the point home with a show to talk about. Outside in the baking sunshine kids in customised boiler suits mill around smoking cigarettes and looking mean. Armed cops in stiff wool clothes – the Policia do Exercito – mill around smoking cigarettes and looking mean. An over-dressed British journalist lies in the shade of a lorry looking fucked[5].

Inside, I endure rock 'n' roll's own form of the Mandarin water torture – the soundcheck. Hairy men in ill-advised shorts running around with jangling wads of keys hanging from belt-loops. The crew erect a Satanic stage set which is heavy on goat imagery, pentagrams and Old Nick's personal phone number, 666. The lighting is deep red and their seems to be metal everywhere – runways, galvanised percussion sets, potentially fatal sharpened spikes randomly jutting out from Sid Wilson's DJ stack (or whatever you call it – decks?). Clearly the *Iowa* stage show is The Clown's welding wet dream made real.

With the soundcheck winding down, I retire to the highest back bleechers of the venue to shoot the shit one more time with Shawn Crahan, full of doomsday enthusiasm for his role as American heretic.

Have things changed much for you since we spoke a year ago in Glasgow?
Shawn: "We've made a few changes just to make things a little more comfortable for our bodies. My whole life dude, I would go to giant venues like this one here to see Kiss and right when the lights go out and

the band walk on, was always my favourite part. It's that moment of uncertainty when the band walk up onto to the stage with flashlights, the idea that anything can happen up there. That's exciting, inspiring. Of course, none of this is the way that I envisioned it, mainly because there's more of you guys then there are of us."

What do you mean by 'you guys'? It seems unfair to assume that everyone involved in music who doesn't perform is out for their own gain or something.

Shawn: "Currently, the industry is still winning and that's something I have to deal with every day. It seems people will only let you succeed if you play their game. I have to question everything that we're doing because all of this to me is an absurd dream and I'm more certain than ever that this is going kill me.

"Early on I tried to use my personality, my intelligence, my charm, anger and hate to reach out to people who I thought I could trust but I've been burnt time and time again."

By the press?

Shawn: "By the press, the media, the label, by friends and other bands. It's a weird trade-off man, because essentially we're saving kids' lives by providing an outlet for their worries, but I also have to sit back and watch the media turn around and say things like, 'How can The Clown be so nuts but still have a family?' I understand you have to ask questions – that's cool – but they shouldn't be turned into hypotheses.

"So now I've decided that I'm going to start hurting back. Everyone's obtainable."

What do you mean 'everyone's obtainable'.

Shawn: "Well, you're obtainable. I know that I can find where you live and I can turn up at your house on a Sunday afternoon and say, 'Hey dude, it's time to be responsible because you've got to deal with me now.' How can you win a Best Band in the World award, yet people will still write lies? I don't understand how a magazine like *Kerrang!* can worship us one minute, then talk shit about us the next."

But I think you're...

Shawn: Look, I don't care. From now on I'm here to destroy. Anybody who comes after me and my brothers and tries to be all artistic for their editors, but won't take responsibility for the things that they've written, I'm going to call them out, dude. Don't try and get anything past us. We don't have to give all the time – this could quite easily be the greatest band that never was. We don't have to do this, but we choose to and we're a band that gives a lot.

"We suffer, dude. At the end of the day I'm fucking bloody and bruised. My legs are ripped from my knees to my ankles and I've got a calcium build-up on my third vertebrae. In ten years time they've going to have to drill through my neck to get rid of it. I'm done, I'm fucking dying here and it's all self-inflicted because it's what our art demands. This is killing us. Once, there used to be some young boys in a band called Slipknot who liked to jump around pulling their hair out. We were out of our minds then, but now it's all about focus and violence... and everyone knows that violence kills."

So how does the attitude within the band differ now you've tasted success?

Shawn: "When you're a new band you have no money, no power and no say, so you go out there and you murder with your music, as we did. Now we have the opportunity to say what we want. I got all the lights, drums, masks and outfits that I want because we worked for this, but you know what? Dude, now it's so much harder. Oh, this is so much harder..."

You definitely seem to be the man who gets things done in the band...

Shawn: "I'm hurting so much every day, man. Take that stage for example. When you're designing things you have to worry about how much it costs to send to Europe, will it fit in the venues, does it look right? My drums took eight months to put together and it took six weeks just to design the three-pivot hydraulics on Chris's drums and now I've got a patent on the motherfucker so that no other band steals our ideas. See that drum set on the left of the stage? In pre-production it threw someone ten foot in the air across the barricades onto his back. This is all serious shit and it takes up your life to organise. I was on the phone every day for the seven months when we supposedly had some time off the road and I was mental as fuck. This band is still taking me from my wife and kids. I locked myself in the basement of our new house and I literally spent five months sitting from midnight until five in the morning just sitting there, thinking, buzzing, writing and figuring it all out so that 40 people can go out on the road again. I thought the break was going to be good for us but it just made us more insane. We're just a bunch of jack-asses who are out of our minds – every last one of us. And because of this one of us is going to die. We're beginning to understand that these are not normal lives that we're leading, this is something for ever. I just hope that kids can come and see us then go home and draw a picture or whatever and without realising it will have been influenced by what we do in some way, even if it's just a little energy boost. Dude, when I'm 50 and can't move, I'm going to have generations of people that were inspired by the philosophy of the 'Knot'."

Will you personally ever be happy with Slipknot?

Shawn: "You know what I really want out of life? What I really want, is for this to stop before it ever has a chance to suck. We'll really have won when the others in the band go on further and do things that won't suck. Right now, I see us as several impressionist painters, all with different brush strokes and different colour choices. Some do still lifes, some do nudes. Some do social, some do surrealism – whatever. I'd like to see the Slipknot family branch out and do better things beyond the band. The thing is, I'm worried about all of them. I stopped caring about myself a long time ago and I know that when I check out of this world it'll be because I don't take care of myself and because I don't give a fuck. That's OK, that's who I am, but I worry because there's a lot of guys in this band who are the same way and I know we have so much left to do. It'll be interesting if a voice like mine can be heard in other directions because, dude, I'll turn the world upside down. This right now is just… peanuts."

Perhaps you should move into politics.

Shawn: "A lot of people have been telling me that, but I'm not sure that I could because of all the shit that I've done in the past."

All the more reason to get involved in politics – you might actually be believable. Or entertaining at the very least…

Shawn: "Well, I'd tell things straight up. I'd say 'fuck all this bullshit, here's the truth as I see it'. This is who I am and what I've done. I'm afraid they're coming for me now already though. People are starting to point the finger and people are starting to die. We had a girl back in Iowa who committed suicide and when her parents found her she was wearing Slipknot gear and blasting the album. The coolest thing about it – although there's really nothing cool about a young girl losing her life amongst the disarray of the world right now – was that her Mom went up to Corey and said that we were the only thing that the girl believed in, the only thing that made sense to her. She said that while we may have helped her make that choice, at the same time in a world full of pain, some pleasure is better than no pleasure at all."

What are you hoping to achieve by doing this? Is seems like you have greater goals than the average rock band. It seems like an obsession with which you will never be satisfied.

Shawn: "I don't like being blatant and I don't like to go purely for the shock factor. With Slipknot, I want to draw lines of confusion. I want to make you work for the art, I want you to have to think. People are tired of the shock factor. I'm trying to teach kids that music is art and it's the only vibration that brings us all together regardless of colour of skin or any difference in language. I do know though, that when they misinterpret us they're going to come for me. It's my face they'll be waving their guns in, it'll be me that the parents will point the finger at. Somebody has got to do it though, and I'm finally fine with being that guy."

When I spoke to Marilyn Manson he said he knew for certain that the F.B.I. had been tracking him and had an open file on him.

Shawn: "We have an F.B.I. file on us too. Anybody who has any power over mass quantities of people has a file. That's alright, I don't believe in this world anyway. I wish I'd never been born. I know that's a terrible thing to say, but I'm tired of all the hurt that's going on, I really am. I think life has always been hard and man has always questioned it, but I suspect that life could have been a lot easier a long time ago. People have been asking the big questions about life and God for thousands of years, but they didn't have to deal with what we have to deal with in the world today – things like human cloning, machines that talk, cockroaches that carry cameras in hypodermic needles. Everything is so much quicker, faster, cheaper – we're killing ourselves slowly and we're destroying this place too. Mother Earth has got all the time she needs – she'll wipe us out and take ten billion years to recreate herself – but it's us who will be fucked."

I've had this conversation with other people and no one seems to be able to face the reality that one day humans will be gone, even if it's way beyond our restricted concept of time. We're not going to stay as we're are – we'll be tomorrow's dinosaurs.

Shawn: "Yeah, I think the film *The Matrix* said it best: we're nothing but a bunch of filthy fucking viruses that consume beauty and shit it out. This world is going to be full of empty carcasses, shit piles, bone buildings, piles of junk, filth and fucking crap.

"I'm not going to sit here on the pity-pot and say that no one understands me, because I don't understand what's it's like to be the kid whose parents are divorced and maybe he thinks he's gay… that pain I don't know, but I know that he's a human being. My wife is the only person that I have right now. I don't even have my brothers in the band because they're fucking mental too. All I can do is tell you what I think and hope that we see eye to eye. That's what communication is."

Knowing your interest in art, I brought you this book about the Italian Futurist art movement. They believed in chaos and a multi-media bombardment of the senses – pretty much what Slipknot do, only 80 years ago. They had people rioting at their exhibitions.

Shawn: "Excellent. These are the people who have walked through our past. There's so much truth in art and that's why I'm such a fanatic. I like people who un-think what has already been thought. I like people who reinvent themselves and refuse to bow down to the usual bullshit. I've been doing a lot of photography recently and have got into a real weird place because of it. I've been doing a lot of self-portrait nudes because I hate myself so much, yet through photography and art I'm able to feel a bit better about myself, I'm able to heal myself a little and make some changes, you know? It might be a future career for me. I have a lot of pain, but at least now I'm trying to document it and analyse it as a means to overcome it."

Is it tough being away from your family for long stretches of time?

Shawn: "Very tough. Sometimes I hate it. I always speak of my wife of the highest regard in interviews, yet still I go home and punish her because I'm going nuts. I don't get to go home and be in control these days – I'm out here. Whatever. All my wife and kids do is show love. Some rapper – I can't remember who it was – recently said that when he comes home there's nothing but love waiting for him and… [his eyes start watering.] …Shit, it's fucking me up just thinking about it now because it's my wife's birthday today. This life is so fucked up, but if you can learn to give love back then you'll be OK. I haven't learnt how to do that, but that's my goal. I'll always be angry because I was born into this fucking filth. I was born with a penis so I have to live in the man's world. Jesus Christ, this world tries to kill you from the moment you come out of your Mom's vagina. It's not your parents fault because they're just doing what they think they should do. It comes from century upon century of conditioning. Bullshit. You have this thing called a skull which is the armour for the mass, the mass is the mind and the mind is the soul, if it exists. The shell is just a tool for the mind to get places. Dude, you don't even need a dick to have sex anymore! The brain creates the chemical that controls your libido. The mind is everything, the shell is nothing. This is something that I'm learning. I've realised that none of us have had a chance since birth because we're thrown down into our own worlds and by the time we've worked out what it all means it's too late. By then you're probably working in a job you hate and your life is set in stone. That's probably why I used to be an alcoholic. I used to drink a lot and I had all these ideas that I wanted to share but everybody thought I was a dreamer who couldn't focus or hold down a job – 'Oh, it's Shawn being drunk again.' Then finally… *boom!* I pursued my dream and now that I've got it, I'm not even sure that I want it anyway. I don't know whether anyone is even listening to us as a band and what we say."

I'd say they probably are.
Shawn: "I'm this close to not doing any more interviews because I don't need anyone sucking my dick.

"This isn't like fucking Kiss or Alice Cooper, this is Slipknot. What pisses me off is that people think they can comment on our lives and our ideals, but unless you've eaten my shit, fucked my wife, changed my kids fucking diapers, sat in my bunk, had pneumonia, spinal meningitis and felt such pressure from the world around you, then you've got no fucking right to say a goddamn thing about us unless you've tasted it, felt it. I'm coming after people because people have got big mouths. Don't get me wrong, we're being rewarded and we're thankful, but there's still a lot of hurt being cultivated here."

How long are you going to keep this up?
Shawn: "I really don't know. I've got a lot of issues to deal with, like the fact that my parents are getting older and aren't going to be around forever. Giving to the world takes it out of you. I honestly don't know how long I can do this for."

What would you do if you left the band?
Shawn: "I'm not afraid to work. I'm not afraid to go back to Des Moines, Iowa, away from all of this. I've done it before and I can do it all again. Still, I'm real excited about my new lights. They move up and down."

At least you're inspiring a lot of people to ask some questions about themselves and their lives. Surely if you can effect people on that level, you're getting somewhere and should be proud.
Shawn: "We are proud, man. We have excellent wives, girlfriends and families and we've even got a lot of friends in the press, so you'll get to

see good Clown, but you'll also have to deal with bad Clown. I just want people to be responsible for their actions. You can go away from this interview and say that you listened to what I have to say and, ultimately, you think The Clown is full of shit. That's OK, I'll respect you. That's your opinion. I'm just tired of people turning our vision upside down and trying to destroy things for us. If it continues... I'll have to get out."

Notes

1 The full Slipknot squadron is: 0 – Sid Wilson, DJ (gas mask); 1 – Joey Jordison, drums (kabuki mask); 2 – Paul Gray, bass (pig mask); 3 – Chris Fehn, percussion ('dick nose' mask); 4 – James Root, guitar (demonic court jester); 5 – Craig Jones, samples (spiked diver's helmet); 6 – Shawn Crahan, percussion (clown mask); 7 – Mick Thompson, guitar (Hannibal Lector-style iron mask); 8 – Corey Taylor, vocals (zombie).

2 Serial killer. Fond of painting pictures of a clown/alter ego called 'Pogo'.

3 And they're definitely that. The few times I've been around the band, most have only ever been half there, drifting in and out like strange sceptres. Interviews suck. Waiting around sucks. Catering sucks. Rocking fucking rules.

4 Like the strip-lit Utopias that pepper the American landscape with everything-under-one-roof retail outlets that possess all the charm of a Third Reich sterilisation clinic, mall-rock is the heavily marketed, cliché-addled, designer-branded music favoured by many of America's young, white and, generally, middle class mall-rats, and whose success in the early zeroes show no signs of waning. Perpetrators include the likes of Creed, Godsmack, Staind, Puddle of Mudd and Nickelback. Awful shit. Kurt Cobain's suicide vision of commodified 'grunge' is now very much a living reality.

5 Self-induced – I'd had a late night and an early start.

Fat Mike (NOFX)
punk in drublic

*"It's true punk rock, it's elitist
and I love it…"*

*"MTV – quit bugging us
Major labels – quit bugging us
Commercial radio stations – quit
 playing us
We've been doing just fine all
 these years
Leave us the fuck alone! Assholes."*

Sleeve notes from *Heavy Petting Zoo*

(Epitaph, 1996)

NOFX ARE AN INTELLIGENT BAND – way more so than most people probably realise. Dumb punk drunkards rarely become influential musicians, never mind empire builders, yet the leading lights in the second (or are we on to the third or fourth or who-gives-a-fuck-anyway so as long as their noises are glorious?) generation of West Coast punk bands have done just that. With little in the way of a career plan, but in the capable hands of erudite frontman 'Fat' Mike Burkett – who isn't really fat – NOFX have gone from unknowns in the mid to late eighties (a musically arid period right across the board), scratching out a living at such a basic grass roots

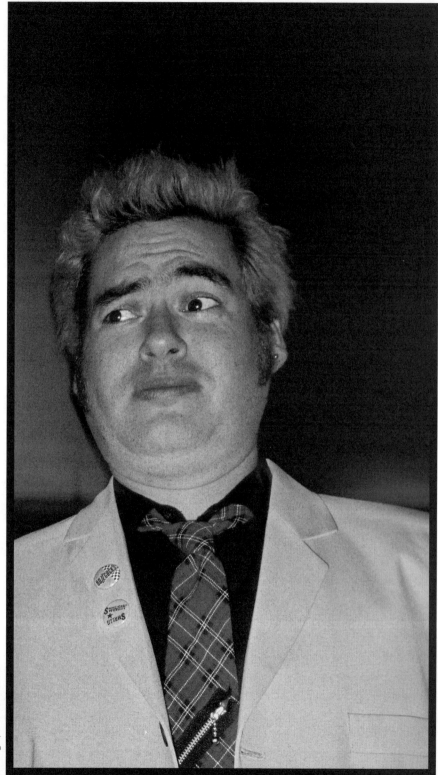

level that they were on first name terms with worms in most US states, to being one of the most respected independent bands currently in existence.

Inspired by Black Flag's heavy duty road work and the socially conscious, harmony-laden sounds of leading SoCal heroes Bad Religion, NOFX hit the road with a basic set of songs and a thirst for beer. Management, record contracts and all the various other cluttered trappings that ensnare more mainstream acts were not an option. That wasn't punk and besides, NOFX weren't that good, as early releases clearly illustrate. But there was something there – a sense of fuck-it-all fun mainly. Blasting through pun-addled caustic sideswipes at everything in sight – the government, gender politics, capitalism, beer, the various slackers, yuppies, West Coast deadheads, and punk rock snobbery – Fat Mike has made sure that NOFX shows and releases are always memorable affairs, with plenty of food for thought on offer to soak up the booze; where dogma and preaching is out, but belligerence, crowd baiting and a general refusal to go through the usual rock 'n' rolls motions is most definitely in.

And somewhere along the way NOFX got good. They learnt to play, they made a lot of friends across America, Europe, Australia and beyond and signed up with the burgeoning Epitaph records, the label started by Bad Religion guitarist Bret Gurewitz and which went on to become the most successful wholly independent label of all time (apparently bigger than Motown, even). When Green Day and NOFX's some-time support band and label mates The Offspring hit pay-dirt in 1994 with their respective *Dookie* and *Smash* albums and punk looked like becoming the mainstream music's replacement for grunge (after its main punk-reared-but-corporate-suckled exponent, disillusioned with the appropriation of his music into mainstream American entertainment, had chewed on a shot-gun) NOFX were already the true punkers' band of choice anyway, the Godfathers you wouldn't necessarily want at the wedding. And nor would they want to be there. Or if they were, they'd be pissing in your ice tray. Crazy Americans.

With the success of those bands less bothered about the ethics of it all, the big labels inevitably came sniffing. NOFX laughed it off and carried on doing what they were doing. Touring, recording, drinking.

In the early nineties, Fat Mike started his Fat Wreck Chords label to release the occasional NOFX single and a few acts who, it must be said, sound a lot like his own band – ranging from the great (Propagandhi), to the seminal (Snuff) and the one dimensional (Lagwagon). A fresh alternative to turgid unit-shifting rock, the new punk sound appealed to everyone from pre-teens to skaters to students to the old skool fans who like it raw, the past decade seeing it grow to such an extent that every large label now has its own pool of young punk bands ready to endorse the latest free threads, appear on the Saturday morning kids' show with the puppets and the Britney karaoke, and do whatever it takes to 'shift product'.

But thanks to both a genuine passion for the music and keen marketing, Mike has turned Fat Wreck Chords into a formidable and highly profitable business which continues to document the ever-changing sounds and ethics of modern punk rock.

And as certain factions of this new punk music becomes wimpier, danger-free and quite content to spread its goofy videos across eMpTV and stretch its music across endless multi-formatted single versions for guaranteed chart placings, in true punk rock style NOFX have released everything from early censorship-baiting single 'The PMRC Can Suck On This' to the 13-song seven inch single 'Fuck the Kids' (1996) to the 18 minute one-track EP, *The Decline* (1999) as well as pun(ch)-drunk albums such as *Liberal Animation, Ribbed, Punk in Drublic, Pump Up the Valuum* and *White Trash, Two Heebs and a Bean,* the latter a reference to the band's White-Hebrew-Hispanic heritage. Musically, they've delved into ska, calypso, jazz, lounge and swing, but have found a stock sound in fast melodic, incisive and impressively produced punk rock with a message[1]. All without the help of the usual shady paymasters, pluggers and pimps.

Most importantly NOFX don't do interviews. So when Fat Mike offered to have a chat, it seemed rude to decline...

This interview took place March 2002 on the phone.

Well, first off – let's get the obvious out of the way. You're known for not doing interviews with any mainstream publications.

"I don't do NOFX interviews, but I will do ones about my record label. Plus, this is for a book, so that's cool. Basically, I got really sick of being in these stupid magazines that misquote me to sell issues. I don't need to be more popular. I like to get my own opinions across, but I don't feel any great need to be more popular. That's not what this is about."

Was there a certain point where you decided that you didn't want to go down that route?

"Yeah, it was probably in 1996 after we started seeing a lot of punk bands get real big. We just thought they looked so stupid. I won't mention any names, but we'd see them in these magazines like *Rolling Stone* and *Spin* and they'd be coming out with all this bullshit that they thought the kids wanted to hear and I just thought, 'I don't want to ever be that person up there.'"

Do you still get approached to do a lot of things like that, or have people finally got the message?

"They pretty much get the message now, but I know that *Spin* have just approached me to do something. Obviously, I won't be doing it."

To go back a few years, I wanted to ask you about the first band you were ever in – False Alarm.

[Laughing incredulously] "Yeah, False Alarm! That was back in 1983, I guess. We just played stupid, mindless hardcore and only ever did one show at a party. I didn't really write anything, I just played bass for a while. But it was a start."

What was it that turned you onto punk rock in the first place?

"I'd heard punk rock here and there, but very little of it really. Then one night when I was 14 – so I guess it must have been 1981 – a friend of mine said, 'Let's go to the Whisky to see this band Killing Joke,' so we did and it was completely crazy. Everyone was dancing and I just thought… this is rad. So I started going to see X and the Go-Go's and everything followed from there."

Do you think punk rock is generally discovered by teenagers because that age is one full of turmoil and confusion as to what the future may bring?

"Sure. I wasn't even in high school when I first went to see punk rock bands and that was it for me, you know? I started buying records like crazy. Probably the first record I went and bought was *Urgh! A Music War,* which was a compilation featuring Devo, The Cramps, Pere Ubu, X, 999, Gang of Four, that type of thing, then it was the Sex Pistols *Nevermind the Bollocks*. That was it for me. I was sold."

What are your memories of NOFX's first show?

"That was in Hollywood. We were all drinking outside and I'd just beer-bonged a 40-ouncer of Old English before we played, but it didn't matter because we only had four songs at the time. This band, I think it was Justice League or maybe it was Unity – some straight edge band or another – let us use their equipment after they'd played their set. I think there were about 50 people there at most. It was awesome."

I know that a lot of the band's early shows involved playing keg parties – a social phenomena that we don't really have in the UK. How did they work?

"Playing clubs was never a good idea for NOFX because we weren't very good and never pulled many people so when we did a tour in 1986 or '87 we said 'fuck it' and just called up lots of kids who we'd met here and there and asked them to let us play in their garage or their back yard. We'd buy a keg of beer and charge people two bucks to get in, and we actually made more money doing that we ever did playing clubs. We'd make, like, $75 or $100 – way more than that in the clubs. But, you know, we're all drunks anyway, so it was perfect."

NOFX almost seemed proud of their incompetence, particularly in the early days – how long did it take you to reach a level of professionalism in what you were doing?

"I think by 1989 we were pretty good – and this is after we started in '83. So, six years."

So six years of drunkenness, then.

"Well, we're more drunk than ever at the moment, but it did take us six years before we began to understand what a melody and shit like that meant."

And how long was it before you were all able to actually make a full-time living out of NOFX?

"About 1991. I think that year we each made $8000. That was just about enough to live off."

You also went to college during those early years – was that to do a business degree?

"No, I never took any business classes. It was mostly human sexuality classes. I could well have become a sex therapist if punk rock didn't work out."

Is that where a song like 'Vanilla Sex'² came from?

"Yeah, we have a lot of sexually explicit songs, or songs looking at sexuality."

Although some people probably think it's a big joke, I've noticed that you often write from a female perspective, which for a testosterone and beer-fuelled punk band is quite subversive.

"That's because I'm obsessed with lesbians."

Aren't all men?

"No, no. Most men like to see two girls together, whereas I like to see lesbians. Butch chicks in leather. Girls who want nothing to do with men. It's not the normal male fantasy."

Do you think it's because seeing two diesel dykes at it is something totally unobtainable to you as a heterosexual man?

"You know what? That's exactly it. And it's the same thing with punk rock. When I started going to shows I thought, 'God, these people are so fucking weird and different', but it was immediately a scene I wanted to be accepted into. In San Francisco the lesbian punk rock scene is crazy. It's a scene that I can't be a part of because there's no way I would ever get in. You've got all these cool lesbian punk rock chicks with mohawks and their own bands doing their own things. It's true punk rock, it's elitist and I love it."

Again, that's because even though you're Fat Mike, one of the leading lights of punk, you're still ultimately a man with a dick and therefore immediately exempt.

"Right! The hottest chick – girl, woman, whatever I mean – ever is Joan Jett, you know? And now she's bald, man. Anyway, me and my wife saw her play a really small show in front of, like, 300 people not so long ago and afterwards my wife got backstage to meet her and hang out, but I couldn't. All because I'm a man! As a man it's a strangely attractive club to want to be a part of."

Excerpt from author's diary: 27 May 1991: Hungover. Played with a band from California called NOFX last night. We were even worse than usual. My bass broke in the first song. I hate guitars. I hate them because I can't play them. But NOFX... that was a different story. They pulled up in a van that they had been living in around Europe for the past month. They laughed at our dry-ice machine – "Fuck! We haven't seen one of those things since LA in the mid-eighties! So gay!" – and at the fact that they had flown halfway around the world to play to 30 drunk Geordie punkers. I think NOFX will do well. One day they might even play a place that has a stage. My band will amount to nothing.

Fuck it. I can always become a journalist.

School tomorrow.

I've no doubt that you get asked this a lot, but I was wondering what you think about the recent boom in commercial punks bands? The last year has seen bands like Sum 41 and Blink 182 – who were directly influenced by NOFX – sell huge amounts of records for any genre.

"Well, I will say that Sum 41 are super-cool kids and we did a lot of drugs together on the last Warped tour, which was great. A good time had by all. But all those commercial bands really kinda make me sick. Not so much musically, but the fact they're all singing songs that are safe, singing things which won't offend people – which was the very reason I got into punk rock in the first place. To me, it was always about saying stuff that pissed people off, but made them think too. All these commercial bands are just singing about girls and things we really don't need to hear about. It's commercial, it makes me sick and I personally think they're ruining punk rock."

These are the bands in the pockets of the record companies – those who have to play the marketing game of constant promotion, sponsorship and so forth.

"Suddenly there's all this punk rock and nobody is offending anybody. It's the exact opposite of what it's supposed to be."

So who is doing the offending these days?

"Well, sure, I like to think my band sings about things that offend. I piss people off all the time without even intending to. I'm just trying to express ideas and if that pisses people off, then so be it. Bands like Propagandhi[3] are doing it. Man, I don't know, I don't have a list of bands in front of me. Randy from Sweden are one of my favourite bands at the moment and they have the habit of kicking people's asses."

One of the greatest strengths of NOFX has always been your refusal to have your videos broadcast on MTV, the only real reason other bands make videos in the first place. This is an extreme rarity these days. What do you think of MTV at the moment, given that it has such a huge influence on the teens of America?

"Well, MTV is not even worth discussing, it's such a joke. We have never wanted to have anything to do with something that commercialises punk music. It's what we as a band are against whole-heartedly. We're a popular band – we can't help that – but we don't go through commercial sources. I mean, I can't discuss MTV because it always sucked and now it sucks worse than it ever sucked."

It sucks alright. And yet it seems to be growing like a cancer, spreading images of beautiful G-string clad people whoopin' it up at Florida beach parties or whatever across the TV screens of the world. MTV seems to be projecting a lifestyle that is make believe and it's extremely depressing.

"It's horrible. Commercial radio is the same. There was only ever one station that was good and that was Radio Free Hawaii. It was a station that had ballot boxes across the island so that people could call up or put in requests for songs that they wanted to hear played. So one day you'd hear Operation Ivy, Frank Sinatra and the Go-Go's, whatever you wanted to hear they would play. It was the obvious way to run a cool station,"

And is it still going?

"No, it got bought out by a big corporate radio station, surprise, surprise. The first good radio station in the world and it's gone."

You've been running Fat Wreck Chords for ten years now – did you set out to turn it into the highly successful independent label that it has become?

"No, it's totally weird. A lot of labels have bigger plans, but ours is just to survive. Things are going OK, but between the internet and more and more people burning off their own CDs at home, I believe the music business as we know it will collapse over the next few years."

Because people can get their music direct form the source?

"Yeah, and I think that all the major labels are going to go bankrupt as a result. We'll try and stay afloat, but you just never know. It's hard to say what an average Fat Wreck release will sell as some bands sell 300,000 albums, some sell 3,000. It just depends. Right now, the biggest band on Fat Wreck is Me First and the Gimme Gimmes[4], funnily enough. That's not including any NOFX releases that we put though. NOFX releases always do more than any others."

Maybe the music industry needs to be destroyed so that it can have a clean start and be completely restructured?

"Yep – and I can't wait for it because people will have to go out and discover music that they actually like instead of being force-fed it."

How involved are you in the day-to-day running of Fat Wreck Chords? If, as you say, the music industry is about to collapse, do you see labels like yours staying the distance?

"I come in for a few hours a day. I've got 16 people working here so I don't have to be in all the time. As for the collapse of small labels as well as the majors… sure. A lot of labels have one big distributor that is inevitably owned by a major label and if they go under, then the label's going down with them. With Fat Wreck we have about 50 distributors worldwide, so if we lose some of them we'll still do OK. Try not to keep all your eggs in one basket."

I know that the past few times that NOFX played in London you had a lot of problems with people spitting on you, so much so that you didn't play

here for a number of years? Do you find that some misguided people still think that this is a 'punk rock' thing to do?

"It happens occasionally but London is always by far the worst place for it, for sure. I get more pissed in London than anywhere else because people speak English, so when I'm pleading for them to stop doing it they should really know better."

I saw a video of a NOFX show on the Warped tour where you personally refunded the crowd for the show being so sloppy – do you think this is something that should be made compulsory for, say, all these terrible major label saps we have to endure?

"Well, the only reason we did that was because it was supposed to be at an outdoor show in Texas where the sound would have been pretty good but it was actually in this huge warehouse. It sounded so terrible that you couldn't hear anything that the band was doing and I felt bad about it so I got 5,000 singles – dollar bills – and said, 'Here's our share of your money back 'cos you got ripped off,' and threw it into the crowd."

Given that I first saw you play in a tiny community hall in the north-east of England, I bet you must have played some shitty places over the years?

"God, there's been quite a few. We had a show in Moscow once and they wouldn't let us out of the airport. That sucked. They said it was something about our paperwork not being right and we even tried giving them $8,000 in bribes and they still wouldn't let us out of the place. Another time, we had a show in Sarajevo that we never made it to because we got stuck behind a bunch of tanks. Just weird stuff like that."

Even though you're relatively young, it's coming up to 20 years since NOFX started. Doesn't that automatically make you, like, The Grateful Dead of punk?

"However long we've been around, I always look at Bad Religion because they've been around way longer. They've still got a few years on us!"

Financially, I'm assuming that NOFX no longer need to tour. If it's not the money, what drives you to keep playing endless tours to gobbing punk kids?

"After this many years, I really don't want to play shows if I'm not loaded any more. If I'm not drunk or on something I don't want to play, 'cos for me punk rock should never feel like a job. It has always been my intention to avoid that, but when you've played somewhere between 1500 and

2000 shows over the years, it does begin to feel kind of redundant. Especially when you have to play 40 shows in a row."

But can you drink 40 nights in a row?

"No, it's very hard because you start to get pretty run down. But if I'm not drunk, I feel like I'm cheating the crowd because I'm not having that much fun doing it. I've been playing some of these songs for 15 years and I'm not going to pretend I'm having a good time when I'm clearly not. So when I'm drunk, I actually am having a good time, you know what I mean? I don't want to be up going 'Hey! Alright! Y'all having fun!' if I'm not. Fuck that."

But whether you're drunk or sober, I'm sure the crowd would be into it because either way you're still playing NOFX songs and they can still jump around and do the drunken macho mosh-pit thing.

"Well yeah, but I'm not doing it for them. I never got in a punk band to please the crowd. I did it because it was fun for me."

If you could go back, Is there anything that you would change about the way you have done things?

"I think our name is terrible. Just… terrible. I don't know what I'd call us now given the chance, but names like Dead Kennedys, Circle Jerks, Suicidal Tendencies – they're good punk rock names. NOFX is terrible."

You tend to be viewed as one of the few true independent figureheads in this new generation of punk bands – what do you think is the biggest misconception that people have about NOFX?

"I think everyone thinks that we're just a joke band when lyrically and socially I'm political. I mean, I think our lyrics are very socio-political, but people don't think of us that way because of some of the other subjects we sing about and the way we sing them. When we play we're drunk and we have fun so people automatically think 'Oh, they're just a bunch of idiots.' I spend a lot of time trying to educate people on how the world should be and how we as individuals can change things."

I'd say that you've got progressively more political too. I mean, there's not that many drunkards in bad shirts singing about, say, the American economy or sexual mores?

"Well, you get older and you learn stuff. Also, now that we're a popular band we have a social responsibility. Beforehand we didn't, but now I can't help thinking that we do. That's the very reason why I've been a vegetarian for five years. Although I do eat fish so maybe my convictions aren't that strong."

What do you do for non-musical, frivolous fun at the moment?
"Well, it sounds kinda weird but I really like fucking my wife a lot."

There's nothing weird about that.
"Well, after ten years, you know…"

Hey, be grateful – at least you're getting it.
"Yeah! I spend a lot of time on the golf course these days too."

Golf? Jesus.
"Yeah, well, you know. I've got my handicap down to about a 12."

To finish up with, what would you say has been the band's greatest achievement?
"I'll tell you a couple of things that I'm really proud of. The first is having never been on MTV. I mean, we got a gold record in the US for *Punk in Drublic* and that was completely without MTV. I just think that bands like Fugazi and NOFX show that you don't have to go through commercial means to make a living doing music. You can do it by your own rules and still be successful. You know, we don't have to kiss ass for anyone. We don't have to answer to one person in this world. We're self-managed – and always have been – and we've still sold around five million records. I'd say that's pretty good going."

Finally, what do you weigh these days?
"Oh, not too much. I'm down to about 170."

Notes:

1 The crux of which appears to be social change through the medium of satire – see the world for what it is, laugh at it, then go set about trying to fix things. That's what NOFX's music says to me, anyway.

2 Anti-censorship/pro-pornography song from *S & M Airlines* (1989).

3 Canadian melodic punk band who owe more than a little musical debt to NOFX. Unlike many other pretenders however, Propagandhi are a well-informed anti-capitalist activist band who also run their own G7 Welcoming Committee Records. The label's website (www.g7welcomingcommittee.com) is crammed with vital, incisive information on numerous worthy causes (their essays on US foreign policy, the F.B.I.'s war on the Black Panther party and veganism are particularly informative, as are their recommended reading lists) and whose multi media approach is everything that punk rock should be in the new millennium. Say the band: "We have to re-examine our societies' institutions and be willing to work to radically reform or even remove them if they don't measure up to the values of freedom and democracy that most of us claim to live for and be willing to die for."

4 'Comedy' side-project band formed by Fat Mike with members of Lagwagon and No Use for a Name, where easy listening/MOR favourites (John Denver, Barry Manilow etc) are butchered in a punk style.

Henry Rollins
one man army

"I cast off ballast as I go…"

"6.15.85 Tampa FL: Drove all night. Woke up sweating — clothes and blankets wet, a bowl of something dumped in my shoes. I got out of the van and pissed in the road. I walked around, trying to figure out where I was. I walked down an alley — rats darting for cover, garbage and old cars. Another slum…"

Rollins diary excerpt, *Get in the Van,* 1994

IN 1981 AT THE AGE OF 20, Henry Garfield gave up his managerial position at a Washington branch of Häagen-Dazs ice-cream store, changed his name, became the singer for his favourite band, Black Flag, and embarked on a cultural carpet-bombing mission that is still going strong two decades later. Black Flag set a new standard for hardcore punk's DIY ethic and musically expanded the genre along the way. Through relentless touring and releasing their own records, they helped form a nationwide network for a new generation of alternative bands, many of whose efforts reached high levels of commercial fruition. Nirvana, for one, would undoubtedly not have existed were it not for Black Flag. Police harassment, lengthy legal battles and a frugal existence meant that the

band's survival was a day-to-day battle with America itself.

By the time the band split in 1986, Rollins already had a reputation. He was the intense looking guy who liked to lift weights and write poetry. Weird. Poets in rock generally either belong to the preening purple velvet pantaloons brigade or the gritty sub-Bukowski/Waits mob. Rollins was neither. The shifting landscape of life on tour and the constant harassment from punks and police alike having provided ideal writing material, he began to self-publish his own journals and poetry through his own 2.13.61 company. He also went on to form the Rollins Band, a more metallic influenced, riff-based band who (ironically) in the wake of Nirvana and MTV's sudden appetite for all things heavy, enjoyed a taste of mainstream success and have sustained a hardcore following ever since.

Rollins is someone who has divided opinion all along. The critics often hate him for the very same reasons that so many feel compelled to devour his prolific Renaissance Man output – his blunt demeanour, his obsession with physical strength, his unerring ability to bypass trends, his (relatively) Neanderthal-sounding music, his subversion of the sex-drugs-rock-'n'-roll clichés (rock stars just do not talk about how much they've bench-pressed that morning when they should rightfully be presenting heavily exaggerated accounts of the previous night's hedonistic escapades) his chiselled prose, his relentless self obsession and his general refusal to lay down and eat shit. That and the fact he once wrote: "If we were in the jungle they [critics] would be in the pot and I'd be stirring – that's for fucking sure."[1]

The past decade has seen Rollins refine his spoken word routine from the furrow-browed performance poetry diatribes of yore, through the intensely personal outpourings that followed him witnessing the fatal shooting of his friend and Black Flag roadie Joe Cole in 1991, to a cosier, though no less spittle-flecked series of post-Bill Hicks anecdotes and observations accrued at the same rate as his 'frequent flier' air miles. Endorsements of products such as Apple Mac and acting roles in numerous Hollywood films saw Rollins lose favour with some of the old punk guard in the nineties, but seeing as it was those very same people who pulled his hair, grabbed his balls and put their cigarettes out on him on a nightly basis throughout the previous decade, he was not unduly bothered. He was reaping what he had sown. He knows he got his wings the hard way.

Some simply dislike Rollins for not following the standard rock 'n' roll career path (a route perhaps best captured in comedian/actor Denis Leary's summary of Jim Morrison's creative parabola: "I'm-drunk-I'm-nobody-I'm-drunk-I'm-famous-I'm-drunk-I'm dead. 'Big Fat Dead Guy in the Bath-tub' – there's your movie title."[2]), an act of defiance which is rule-breaking rock 'n' roll by definition.

In reality, he's an American original, an archetypal frontiersman transported to the urban jungle, pushing the mental and physical beyond the imagined boundaries and moving on into the dark unknown hinterland of the American dream-cum-nightmare, each scribbled page of prose a slice of journalism of the soul. Rollins's experiences – from police harassment to soured relationships to his many archetypal 'American abroad' tales – are shared ones and form the bulk of his creative output. It's a selfish approach and one in which Rollins is always the central character, the put-upon anti-hero, but all art is vain and indulgent, so surely it's better for the artist to immerse him/herself in it whole-heartedly, rather than try and fake it. "This is not my hobby until I go to college," he writes in the 'Afterword' to arguably his best-written work, *Get in the Van: On the Road with Black Flag.* "This is what I do. This is who I am." In which case, Rollins is the latest in a long line of American creatively-minded men (who include Walt Whitman, Henry Miller, Jack Kerouac, Lou Reed and Clint Eastwood's Man With No Name) whose ongoing analysis of themselves and their surroundings is seemingly the one thing that keeps them sane. Only this time, he's squeezed into one rapidly perishing pair of sports shorts and is wandering the high plains of the twenty-first century. He's one of the rare few who made a conscious decision to live the dream a little and see what the world and its many flavours had to offer.

This caffeine-fuelled interview took place in a London hotel room in June 2001.

I've just finished your latest *Black Coffee Blues* book, *Smile, You're Traveling* and it's clear that hotel rooms like this one play a big part in your constantly moving life.

"Oh yeah. I've spent more time living in vehicles and hotel rooms over the past 20 years than anywhere else, I can tell you. I'm not like Duke Ellington though who loved hotels and did 50 years straight in them. What are you asking: do I get a bunch of women in there and break shit?"

No, I'm asking whether you enjoy spending your life moving from room to room across the world?

"It's nice to have a place where you don't have much stuff to worry about – you know, you just unpack your little suitcase, build your own environment and then pack it away again the next day. Often in hotels the air-conditioning is really righteous and in the summer-time, on a night off, you can get a good night's sleep, which is always my basic plan in order to recover my voice. But then you always have the maid trying to come in and look at your stuff. That's life."

You seem to thrive off your own self-imposed regimentation – do you have a routine to your day?

"Sure, right now I have a really simple daily routine: walk in, grab a few clothes, throw 'em in the sink, wash 'em, roll 'em up in a towel, dry them off and see if you can get some clean laundry. That's what I did last night when I arrived in London. I ate some food around the corner and came back and did three days of laundry. I've got to be here today and tomorrow and then fly back on Saturday, so I want some relatively clean clothes to fly home in so I don't blow away my flying neighbours. That's my ritual."

There seems to be an obsession with cramming activities into every second of the day – is that true?

"Yeah. Wake up in the morning, go to the airport, fly to the next city, get in and unpack and see if there's time to go to the gym or hit some record stores, or get a nap. Whatever I need to do. I go to the venue at 6pm and do a very quick soundcheck. After that I hang out and get my head together, hit the stage at eight, finish the show and go back to the hotel to unwind and eat whatever food I manage to take from catering. At night I watch some news, go to bed and hit the airport the next morning. It's boring; I'm a machine. At midnight, all I can think about is the next show and what time I have to get to the airport."

It's that old tour saying of 'hurry up and wait'. Bands have to frantically rush to be somewhere, only to find they have hours to kill. Is this generally the case in your decades of touring?

"See, that's the thing with the spoken word shows that I've been doing. There's never that much time – I'm just looking for time to get a work-out in, or hit the record store. If I go to a store I'll have, like, 20 minutes so you have to hit them real quick. Sometimes there'll be people going 'Henry, can you sign this?' and I'm, like, [pretends to manically flick through a record rack] 'No, not now! I've got to get to The Ramones section! I've been waiting to come to this store for four months and I'm on a mission. I'm not going to sign your record, OK? I'm on a mission.' If I'm doing a work-out, I think 'what can I do in 40 minutes?' and I go in there and hit it. That's how it is: 'I have 20 minutes to enjoy this cup of coffee. Ready? Enjoy!'

"I'm not trying to make this sound like I'm Mr Tough Guy, but my schedule gets super-compressed. I'll get up early and be fucking tired, just so I can get to the airport early and not have to jam, just so I don't have to run. I'll drag these tour managers to the airport for an 8am flight and they'll be there at 6.30 going, 'Why are we here, Henry?' and I'm, like, 'You know what? You can sleep late tomorrow.' I like to sit and not have to move and sweat for an hour because this is the only time that I have off, because the rest of the day is taken up with getting to the venue, the hotel or whatever.

"Also, there's just a lot of everyday stuff that you have to deal with that gets really frustrating."

What type of things do you mean?

"Me and the world – me integrating into the world. I've been in a different country every day for the last ten days. Do interviews all day, fly at night, get to the new country at midnight, eat, go to bed at two, up at eight, interviews all day, back to the airport, new country. That's what I've been doing since the speaking tour ended – this promotional tour began the very next day. I'm jamming constantly. Like last night, I ate at a place around the corner and when I went to the convenience store there was these two people there. They get their stuff and they see me and they just stand there. They're waiting for me to pass so they can get an autograph or something. They're watching me and all of a sudden I feel like I'm on display. The store is really small, they're between me and the cashier and they're making me feel like some dog with his ass in the air, so I just stand there feeling stupid with a bottle of mineral water. I'm waiting for them to leave. I'm looking at them like, 'can't you tell I'm just waiting for you to leave so I don't have to be observed as I shop?'"

I suppose shopping is possibly the most inane thing you could be watched doing.

"Yeah, it's like, 'can I just have a normal moment today?' So they finally leave and I buy my stuff and of course they're waiting outside. I just went off on them. They had the autograph book out, so I just said, 'Is that what that fucking Broadway production was about in there, where you don't even let me out of the fucking place? You make me feel like such an asshole, like I'm on display.' These two punters, a girl and a boy, they had no idea what they were in for. I let loose on them. I told them that they make motherfuckers like me feel really self-conscious when they do things like that and then I kicked a pile of garbage into the street I was so pissed off."

But they weren't actually bothering you, so what does it matter?

"Yeah, well, you know. You've got to let off steam. So anyway, there's that kind of frustration which is a factor of my day right now."

Does that happen in every city that you go to?

"It's just part of being recognised. As Dave Lee Roth once said: you buy the land, the Indians come with it. Some days the Indians piss me off. So that's my normal thing on tour: I'm very focused. For me, the only reason I'm there is to do a great show. You're right though, I owe that audience… not much – only everything I've got. No big deal, it's just that the only reason I'm in town is to be on that stage so everything else revolves around it to the extent where every bite of food is considered, at 3pm I stop talking and then later it's time to go out there and break them into pieces, because that's what the job is. I'm not saying you should hate the crowd and hurt them, I mean that you should go out there and be so devastating that they leave going 'that kicked my ass' – which is exactly why I go see bands."

The last time I saw you doing spoken word was at The Barbican in London and what impressed me most was that I sat down at 7.30pm and stood up three hours later without my mind wandering once – almost as if I'd lost all concept of time.

"That is about the highest compliment that I get paid. The best thing I can hear is that you think it's 45 minutes and you're going 'what a fucking rip-off!' until you look at your watch and you realise that you have sat on your ass for three hours without even realising it. Once a week someone will say that to me and I'm, like, 'Yessss!' That's what I want – the time to fly by. That's always the goal."

You have the image of being something of a modern-day warrior, hitting all territories for six then leaving on the first plane. Are there any essential items you always carry with you on your travels to make the mission smoother?

"Well yeah, sure. Travel clock, toothbrush, razor, socks, shoes, pants, shirts, dental floss, microphone. I'm trying to think of everything that is in my suitcase… some books, some work projects, CDs, a CD player – you know, The Walk Discman scene. Past that, just the normal male toiletry items. Nothing weird. I'm really boring, man. When I'm doing all this work I go super-minimal. As few things as possible. I take three pairs of socks which I burn through real fast, so I'm always doing laundry, but I've been in Australia, Thailand and Europe for 11 weeks now and if you're carrying everything every day then it better be well-considered.

"I carry a lot of nutrition, a lot of Met-Rx bars[3], just because I'm not going to eat that airplane food. When I'm in the hotel at night I get real hungry, so I eat a protein bar. I basically cast off ballast as I go. I started off this tour in Australia and my duffel bag was heavy with food. I had 50 Met-Rx bars and now I'm down to one."

I don't suppose you can buy them in London, can you?

"You can, but they're expensive and, besides, they sponsor me so I get them for free. I'd rather load up at home when they send them out to me.

Aside from that, I have my lap-top, notebooks, pens and the bare essentials: lifting belt, gym shorts, chalk for my hands when I dead-lift… and that's it."

Do you get much time to work on 2.13.61, your publishing empire, when you're away for such long periods of time?

"I have an employee, an… [laughs] I have Carol, basically. I'm the boss, it's my machine but she runs it. She's been there since 1995, she rocks and she's one of the more amazing people I've met in my short life. She checks in every once in a while and says 'things are great. Making money, doing great, nothing's burning down, everything's cool, this book is going back into reprint, you just sold another 5,000 copies of that book, this one is going into Chinese and German, all is well, call me if you need me.' No news is great news. Every couple of weeks I'll call her up for a one paragraph report. I'll see her on Monday when I get back to LA and go into the studio."

What albums do you carry around with you?

"Let's see, there are a few albums that always go on the road with me. There's The Damned's *The Damned* and *The Black Album* – a great post-gig album. I've been listening to that record at night on and off for 21 years. Thin Lizzy's *Jailbreak* is always with me, *The Crack* by The Ruts is a perfect album, and The Buzzcocks's *Singles: Going Steady* is another amazing collection of songs."

You can never tire of the Buzzcocks. They'll never be out of date.

"Oh God, how can you? They're just too good! There's all these vintage live albums coming out and they're ridiculously good. They keep coming out because I guess they need the money but, hey, I keep buying 'em. I play them over and over. The other album is by King Crimson, and it's the one that the critics hated: *Three of a Perfect Pair*. It came out in the summer of 1984 and it's a pop album. Black Flag bought a cassette of it at a gas stop in England and Greg [Ginn, guitarist] just came in, like 'Oh, hey, I just bought the new King Crimson record.' After a few weeks, I kinda hijacked the tape and it went into my back-pack, where it's been ever since. For me, it's a great night-off tour record. But is it a great record? I don't know. I just know that I've been playing it for so many years that I love it."

Maybe you've lost all sense of judgement – and if you've been carrying a King Crimson tape with you for 17 years I'd say you have – but then if you

like something, fuck it.

"Well, exactly. In my line of work you've got to be careful about what's good and what's not. Like when we brought in the backing women on some of the band's new songs [2001's *Nice* album] it was my manager's idea and he said, 'why don't you just try it out?' He'd worked with them on another record and he thought they were amazing. I was, like, 'OK, I don't hear backing vocals on our record but, shit, I'll try it' – because if I don't like it I can always just press 'mute'. So they came in and they sang their asses off and that night I went home and played some rough mixes and loved it. But is it any good? Or is it just that I'm so jazzed by hearing chicks going 'Yeahhhh!' on one of our songs that I'm just tickled by the gimmick of it, like 'Ooh, there's a snow whistle on there, oh boy!' But is it any good? That's the question. So anyway, I played the songs all night and loved them. The next day I went into the book company and told them to sit down and give me seven minutes of their undivided attention. I played the staff these two songs and they went 'Oh my God Henry, that's so cool.' I went to the studio, the engineer liked it so we kept it and made the mix. But I'm real careful about all these things – just because I like something doesn't mean it's good. I look for other people's opinions and try to be objective. There's a lot of that in my line of work because I'm releasing stuff into the public. Is it any good? Is it any good? You better check it out and listen with clean ears, give it a week of not listening to it and then go back to it because it's like the girl you go to bed with: she's cool for the moment, but then you wake up in the morning and realise that you are in fact insane…"

> *"This is not a book. This is libel, slander, defamation of character. This is a prolonged insult, a gob of spit in the face of Art, a kick in the pants to God, Man, Destiny, Time, Love, Beauty… what you will. I am going to sing for you, a little off key perhaps, but I will sing. I will sing while you croak, I will dance over your dirty corpse…"*

Henry Miller, *Tropic of Cancer,* 1934

I'm interested in your writing career. When did writing first become a compulsion. Did you receive much encouragement at school?

"No, I didn't. Well, yeah, there was the one teacher Mr Clinger, who I'd write really fucked up stuff for before school and give to him after class. He'd tend to say, 'Well... I think that you can use better language than 'fuck' but I like that you're writing creatively.' He told me not to show it to my English teacher – at that time he wasn't teaching me – because he would rat me out about the language. Mr Clinger told me to keep that kind of writing up and to keep showing it to him, but not to hand it in to anyone else. I wrote that stuff because I knew that I could give it to him without being reported, because my school was a military one and you could get in trouble for anything. He encouraged me to write freely and to just write whatever. You want to kill somebody? You hate somebody? You love somebody? Whatever, write it out. With Mr Clinger, it was all OK and that was just the encouragement that I needed."

Who were your early literary influences?

"It tended to be a lot of stuff like *One Flew Over the Cuckoo's Nest, The Red Pony, The Pearl, The Grapes of Wrath, The Old Man and the Sea*[4] – cool stuff, but straight down the line. The type of stuff you read in high school, but doesn't exactly make you want to burn your house down."

So what inspired you to broaden your tastes and begin to start documenting your own thoughts?

"It's the early eighties, I'm in Black Flag and all of a sudden I'm seeing so much stuff that I've never seen before. I mean, you're young and you're on the road and your eyes get opened very wide so I started keeping a little journal. Maybe I overheard a conversation between these two men who had sex with a hooker and snorted a load of cocaine and bragged about all the booze they drank, so straight away I'd be, like, 'Reporting from a shitty bar in New Orleans where I'm going to be playing in four hours...' I'd just sit there writing these things down because you have so much time to kill. That's why a lot of bands get bad habits because you spend so many hours just hanging out. So I started writing.

"Then when I read Henry Miller's[5] *Black Spring* in 1983, that book just blew my mind. I'd never read anyone who used language like that, who was that free, that honest, that flagrantly unrestrained and so I said, 'OK, that's it. I'm writing.' I was so inspired and very young – I was 22. It was, like, 'Oh man! Wow! This is the shit!'"

Miller seems to have to have that effect on everyone who reads him, I know he certainly did with me around about that same age.

"Oh yeah. He's the one that makes you think that you can do it because, you know, he was just writing about his life. It's not as polished as an F. Scott Fitzgerald or as momentous as a Dostoevsky but, man, he's right in the strike-zone. Damn! He's right in the pocket. Then of course, when you start to write yourself you realise that what he's doing isn't easy at all and it makes you love him even more because, shit, it's hard work. I thought, I'm not gifted like he was and this is going to be a rough climb but I might as well enjoy it because it'll be worth it in the long run. Achieving that level of ultimate honesty in your writing, you find out that it's a matter of being brave. You can be honest or dishonest and the reader will never know either way. Maybe Miller was just a lying bastard – we'll certainly probably never know now – but, hey, it was good lie if it was one…

"I got so much from that single book and that single guy. I've read all the other Miller books… well, not all of them. *Sunday After the War,* I don't think I've read and *Big Sur and the Oranges of Hieronymus Bosch,* I don't remember reading, which means it either wasn't very good or I just didn't read it. Some of the older stuff didn't rock my world as much as books like *Quiet Days in Clichy,* the *Tropics*… books and *The Rosy Crucifixion* series *Sexus, Nexus* and *Plexus,* which I finally got to in '85. I read them all. There's one that his buddy Lawrence Durrell begged him not to release – it was *Nexus* or *Plexus* – and it's pretty rough. I remember reading *Sexus* first and going 'Yay, cool!' then reading *Nexus* and going 'cool' and then reading the third one and going 'Thirty pages on how much you like Dostoevsky?!? Fuck this!' Either way though, Miller told it how it was.

"For me, the next high-point was his book *The Air-Conditioned Nightmare,* which was him encountering America after being away from it for so long, and a lot of the observations still stand true today. That book had the urgency of his Paris writings but then he kind of settled into his career, almost like late-period Hemingway where he's Henry Miller the Writer writing about Henry Miller the Writer. With his early stuff, he's writing and he's covered in lice, he's broke, he's fucking everything in sight, he's writing a million words a minute, he's writing love letters to Anaïs Nin on napkins, you know? Crazy stuff. He's living that life that you can only maintain for 18 months before you either get rich, die, or go corporate. Everyone has had that summer where they've lived like a dog and it was great, but then, six months later, it's like 'Fuck this place!' By the time he got back to America he got all cleaned up and finally had some money."

There are obvious comparisons to certain band's careers there too, whether it's the glory of the struggling artist or the opulent creatively-bankrupt one. Was it this spare existence that you could relate to, given your hand-to-mouth experiences with Black Flag in the early eighties?

"Yeah, I just think you can maintain that kind of fury, that lean, flesh-bone-muscle, no fat thing for a while, and then you change. I've definitely seen a different style of writing come out of me. When I was eating one-and-a-half meals a day in Black Flag everything was intense. I was 22, 23 and I had no money. Everything was intense and pushed to the limit because the music meant so much to us. Each gig was like the last gig on earth every single night. It was insane how much we were into it. I'm still into it now, but I can put it into perspective too. You do a show and it's a 8.5 out of 10, the crowd thought it was great, but you knew it was a little croaky and the band was a little rough 'cos they're all jet-lagged. In Black Flag though we'd be [grunts furiously in disgust] whereas now you tend to just accept that tomorrow's another night. I see my writing reflects that change and I see a lot of my early writing like Miller's Paris writing – not in talent, but in that super-urgency. I was in the same position for a while because I was starving. I was screwing, I was broke and everything was vibrant because I had no resources. I could walk up to the most beautiful women in the whole club and just hit on her with all my courage because it was either that or sleeping in the van with my head in the drummer's arm-pit. There was nothing to lose, so I'd march straight up and say, 'Hi, my name is Henry. Er, you're beautiful,' and… shit, seven times out of ten I'd be going home with her. She's blown away because I had the balls to walk up and introduce myself when everyone else was too scared to talk to her. Things changed for me though. As the world encroached upon me, I became a bit more withdrawn. I used to walk down the street unrecognised and no one wanted my autograph, whereas now it's a different deal. I can walk to the convenience store to buy water and suddenly I'm too self-conscious to buy some crackers because these people are staring at me. So… your world changes."

Do you think that maintaining the level of solitude that you clearly thrive upon has become harder – purely because your face is more recognisable these days?

"Yeah, there is that. Your world becomes smaller and your windows become bigger so that more people can look in. But also there's the thing where I'm walking out of this store and I'm very angry because these people were looking into my world and I'm going to huff and puff and complain as I walk into… a five-star hotel. I said on my last spoken word record that for me, it's always been a mission, but when you're flying business class it's not a mission, it's a 'mish'. 'I'm going out on a mish, I'll be back in a while! Take my baggage, thank you James!' you know? So now I fly business class, I stay in nice hotels, I can afford any restaurant that I want and I can look at any car and I can buy it. I'm not saying I'm a big rich guy, but I can afford to eat and I have a house that I paid the mortgage on, no problem. So that lean, up-against-it thing for me is over and to pretend it's still there would be living a lie. I mean, I have a BMW 540-i. Yes, I bought it used, but it is still a BMW and it cost me a shit-load. I no longer need to take the bus any more so that urgency is over. I no longer roll out of whatever I slept in and go, 'Fuck, bring it on!' I still have it in me, but it's different now. That kind of stuff makes for great writing because you go home and go, 'Fuck it, I'm going to show you some honesty, I'm going to beat you to death with it!' Nowadays, my honesty consists of something like, 'Today I got in the back of a Jaguar from Heathrow' – which I did – '…and was driven to this nice hotel that I can somehow afford.'"

So that element of catharsis is no longer necessary for you now?
"Well, also I'm older. That cathartic need you have as a 22 year old when a girl leaves you has gone. Nowadays, it's more like, [wistfully] 'She left me. Oh. Huh. Yeah, they always leave. Time to go put on a Tom Waits record…' I mean, it doesn't make me go, 'Arrrggghh, how will I survive?' It makes me go, 'Ah shit man, let's go eat,' because I've been there, done that 50 times. It's sheer repetition. And I don't sweat gigs any more either. Don't get me wrong, I still take them as seriously as a heart attack, but only insomuch as I don't want to let the crowd down, whether we're in Chicago or Bumfuck, Idaho. It's just a case of going to work and beating the shit out of people with the music, only now I smile more when I do it because it's a happy ritual for me. It's an age thing and to not admit that is wrong. Have I got fat and complacent? No. Do I have the energy and capacity to make music that's vibrant and ass-whoopin'? Well, the proof is in the pudding. There's the new record. I think it takes care of the ass-kicking quotient for the year. Is the band ready to go out and rock that shit? Absolutely. Will we devastate? Oh yes. Has that part of it left me? Hell no! I'm going to be training hard, eating hard and thinking iron thoughts to get ready for the next Rollins Band tour. Am I going to write a 30 page indictment when the girl dumps me next time? No, it'll be a footnote because it'll be, like, the eight hundredth girl. As I live my life, that part of me has changed. To not admit that change would be selling out. To try and recapture all that would be an artificial version of me –

just like when we saw Bryan Adams dressing like Kurt Cobain a few years ago. What was that album? *Sixteen Forever?*[6] Like, Bryan... Bryan? Hello? Have you ever hung out with a 16 year old? They're idiots, Bryan! They're dumb fuck-heads who you don't want to talk to. I'm not trying to offend any 16 year olds, but I remember myself as a 16 year old dumb fuck-head and I had the time of my life being ignorant to most things in the world. I don't want to be 16 again, nor would I be want to be 16 forever. Christ..."

How did recently turning 40 affect you?

"That's the mid-life crisis right there – when you question your role. It's been an amazing revelatory 18 months for me."

In what way?

"Finally becoming an adult. Going to a show and realising that every single person in that club is not in my age group, realising that none of the girls want anything to do with me, although I've never really been pursued by women anyway. I've met a lot, but I'm not Brad Pitt or Mr Blink 182 guy. I would love to say it really happened for me like that, but it never did. Not really. So now I'm walking in there with my grey hair and 40-year-old ass to watch Mother Superior – the guys who are my backing band – do a show. I realised that they were all kids in there and I was the only adult. Then I started to look around me at things like the advertising world and it was, like, shit, 'Am I the only old person around here?' Look at all these ads with their young skinny girls [reaches for a nearby glossy magazine]. Shit man, this magazine makes me feel old. If I stepped up to this girl on the cover of this magazine do you know what she would do? She would laugh in my face and say, 'Get away from me you fucking dinosaur, you father, you fucking... uncle!'"

You think so?

"Yes, absolutely! Look at me with my grey hair! I've got more grey hair than your Prime Minister, my friend! You realise, shit man, you're at a different stage in life, things are different now. None of this magazine is about me – it doesn't concern me. Some of these chicks in here are professional porn stars, but even if I look at a Calvin Klein advert I know that world doesn't concern me. You walk down the street and all the people in the adverts are half your age. So that makes me wonder, where's my food group? Where are the real adults? I saw this thing with Nick Cave in the newspaper the other day and when they asked him if he liked being an adult he said, 'Yes, thank God. I don't have to hang out with young people any more.' Me and my road manager are both the same age and urgently heterosexual men who like women… but where are they all? We go on the road and I'm, like, [whispering] 'Mike, Mike, where's all the women our age?' We joke about it all the time because all the women who come to my shows are college students. Girls want to meet me, sure, so I can sign their book and they can ask me about this thing I wrote. But they don't want me and I don't want to get into bed with a 22 year old either. They're pretty, they're cute, but I want a woman. We go for weeks at a time without meeting any women. I don't know, perhaps they're all on Mars on something."

Are all the women your age married or busy having kids then?
"Every once in a while I'll ask a woman, 'Where can I meet cool ladies like you?' and they usually tell me that they're all getting married or they're professional people and they don't go to gigs. They have to get up at six or eight in the morning. I meet women all the time – interviewers, air-flight attendants, whatever – and it's always very jovial, so I ask them where I can meet their friends. They admit that they're hard to find because either they've found Mr Right and they're off the scene so they're not going to go to a rock gig at ten at night to watch me at eight hundred million decibels while they get run over by some aggro punk kids. So they say, go to a club, go to a bar, a party, otherwise in your day-to-day life you won't encounter them. So then you start to think, 'Fuck man, there ain't nobody around here for me.' Also, what music is being marketed to me? Limp Bizkit certainly aren't. In no way am I putting them down, but it's not for me. Don't tell me a Slipknot record is marketed towards me. Maybe I'd like it, but look at the people buying the T-shirts. I'm twice their age. My Australian agent said, 'Think about what music is being marketed to us,' and I couldn't answer."

Bryan Adams.
"Damn! There's Bryan, Sting, Tracy Chapman… phew. That's it."

U2?
"Yeah, the 'mid-life crisis' album[7] they're calling their latest one. I thought it was a washed-out piece of shit. A well-produced boring record. But who else is there? What gig do I really want to go see? Wow man, popular culture is not for people my age. I guess that has been the biggest revelation of being this age. I'm not bothered about the grey hair –I've been getting grey hair since I was 27 or whatever. I'm not going to dye it. I have lines on my face that make me look like I've seen some rough

road. I don't look like I've been a drug abuser – I just look like I don't sleep enough. I know it. I'm at the end of a tour. But when a photographer shows me a Polaroid I usually say, 'Christ, I look like death, people will think I'm on drugs if you print this.' Shit…"

Fortunately though, your career doesn't rely on some Calvin Klein aesthetic – your work is not about your image – it's about the words you write and the things you say.

"Sure. And I'd rather stand on my words than stand on my cheek-bones, 'cos all that goes. Your hair's going to go, it happens to everyone. It's been interesting becoming an adult and watching some of my friends kind of shrink back and sort of retire and walk away from The Thing. I don't know exactly what I'm trying to say… I guess they get mediocre. They put on, like, 18 pounds. What the fuck man?"

Are you talking about contemporaries of yours?

"Yeah, my friends, people of my age group. You see them and they're all round and soft. I tend to think, 'Don't you work out? Don't you move your ass at all?' Most of them have a wife, three mouths to feed and they're really busy all of a sudden. They get up at, like, five and have a work-load that is really terrifying and unenviable. That seems to be the 40-year-old male experience and it's weird. I don't have a lot of friends and I don't have a lot of enemies – at least hope I don't – so I don't hang out much. There's not a lot of people I can call up for a chat, but there's a lot of people I know from playing in their venues for 20 years and what-not and I've watched them blow up and cool out. They're all like, [softly, resigned] "Well Henry, my wife…' Your wife?!? Huh? You're talking Swahili to me, pal. It just makes me see that I'm not going that way."

Do you think perhaps, that people in their teens and twenties think that they can take over the world – or at least change it – but later they slow down, get fat and give up the battle?

"What it is, is they get a little success and they get comfortable. I could live a lot more comfortable than they do, I can afford it. I'm not a millionaire but I could take a lot more time off, I could do a third of the gigs I'm doing right now and get by fine. I'm not trying to brag, but I could make my income just from the talking shows or the band or the book company alone. I could get by, eek it out and get a little bohemian on that motherfucker."

What would you do with all that spare time though?

"Read, write, think. I could plausibly do it for six months, but that's not me. To keep it going you've got to be vigorous, you got to keep it jamming, you got to keep the wire taut – that's part of the job. I could take it a little easier but I consciously choose not to. My manager is always encouraging me to take a month off. I say, 'Richard, you don't understand. Just humour me and book me.' Then he'll be like, 'Henry, you got all these frequent flier miles. Why not find a nice girl, fly first class to Bangkok…' and I just tell him that it sounds like a living hell hanging out with some chick on a beach. Yeah, the sex would be great, the sun, the fun, the room service, but I'd want to be getting back to the war. I really like the war, the struggle, the thing. I'm obsessed with it. I'm one of those guys who prefers the work over love, over sex, over glory, fame, money… work knocks everything into second place and has screwed up every relationship I've ever had. The work has come between all of it. As soon as the women blasphemes the work – 'If you really liked me…' – I'm, like, 'Oh my God, you got to get the fuck outta here. You just told me I shouldn't go to band practice? I'm sorry. In the rulebook you gotta go. In the name of Al Green and all that is holy, you must leave.' I can't hang with that."

Do you intend to keep up this pace as long as people are still interested?
"Yes, as long as I think I'm vital. As long as it occurs to me to do so. I can't tell you how long I'll go but right now I'm really digging it, I'm maxing out. I think I'm firing well on all cylinders – the last book was good, the new record is great, the band is primed and I think I'm in good shape. I think we're doing good stuff out here and so I want to keep the ball in the air because I'm having such a good time. I'm in love – it's a love affair. I'm deeply in love with what I do; it's not a woman, it's the work. I love that audience, I really do. In my mind I owe them everything, it's true. I live on other people's approval – you're kind of in the same boat too because if you write shitty stuff, you're fired. You're doing your work. I live on people going, 'Yay!' every night. I've been getting, 'Yay!' and paying for my dinner for 21 years so you gotta remember who puts you where you are. Them, not me. I created something that they like, but if they didn't like it there would be no music. It's turned into an interesting love affair that I have with these people. I don't know them and sometimes they piss me off – like last night – but I'd walk a mile to please them, you know? As long as I can keep that up, I want to. You've seen those people – Don Rickles, Frank Sinatra, John Lee Hooker. They did it until they dropped off. BB King. That guy did 100-plus shows at the age of 67!"

I heard BB King actually averages 300 shows a year.

"James Brown was doing it like that too. I met the country and western singer Tanya Tucker once and she said, 'Honey, we only come home for Christmas...' Damn man!

"Another time, I was in a Starbucks at an airport in Canada and I heard someone go, 'Hey, Henry.' I just glanced over and saw some Caucasian shape, then I realised it was Rick Nielsen[8]. Him and his band tour relentlessly and he was, like, 'How many shows you do this year?' When I said '96 shows,' he said, 'Well, you still have a few weeks left...' He knew he had me 'cos he'd done 100-plus shows. He got me. That said, I've averaged 104 shows a year for the last 21 years. Most years I do more, but then there's the year where you write the album and do fuck-all. One year we did seven shows, the next we did 140. This year there'll be 150 – it'll be big. And you've only heard 12 of the 30 songs we recorded. In my mind I'm already on the next record. I emailed the band the other day to see if they were ready and they said, 'Man, we're exploding with new ideas.' We'll have a tour break in November and then I imagine we'll be straight back into the studio. While touring our last album, [*Get Some Go Again,* 2000] we had five days off and we recorded half of the new album. Five days later we were in Sydney, Australia, still on it."

You see all these bands who spend five years making one record. There's really no excuse for is, is there?

"I think your audience will leave you if you don't stay on it. A lot of bands have very normal lifestyles. A guy like Sting – he's got kids, you know? Bono is onto kid number four. I guess they have to go home and be dads at some point. Bono can't tour like me, nor would he want to. Me? I've got fuck-all else to do. I live a weird lifestyle and in a way I'm a loser – I don't have a life. Well, I got one, but this is it. I come home to a house full of dust, little piles of receipts and different coins from different countries from the last tour, stacks of CDs I haven't had a chance to play, books that I'll someday read... I unpack, I do my laundry and eight to forty days later me and that suitcase are gone again. Then I come back to the house again – dark and dusty, the toilet water is brown from the rust, gotta buy the groceries and make sure there's nothing living in the refrigerator. I hope there's no science experiments in there right now. If there was milk in there when I left in February, I'm in trouble now! No one misses me, no one says, 'Henry please come home,' so what else do I have to do? A week and a half after I'm back at home, I find myself saying, 'Well, that was nice, now book me some more shows.'"

Well, I hope you can keep it up. Knowing that Rollins is out there means a lot to people. It's comforting to know that you're not going to do an acoustic album and that you're still waging a war against mediocrity.

"Here's my thing. When The Ramones stopped playing I remember being so thoroughly bummed because somewhere in the world that night Joey Ramone was not going to be going, 'Good evening, we are The Ramones!' It was the end of an era because The Ramones are a part of me. It was good to know that they were out there guarding the coast. Then when Joey died the other day, I was like, 'Jeez man…' Part of me died too. I saw those guys when I was 18, so I had to sit it out and think about it. I've got stock in that company. I just hope that somewhere out there I'm that for someone else."

I'd say you probably are.

"I meet people who are so proud of having seen me. They say, 'Dude, 35 shows!' I worship these people. What better way to say you like me than enduring 35 nights of my bullshit? That's a lot of cash, time, desire and sheer tenacity. People say that as long as I keep showing up they will too. That's all I need to hear to keep me going for the next ten shows."

Well, having flown to England to see Black Sabbath on your time off, you can obviously appreciate why music fans can be so fanatical about their favourite artists.

"It's knowing those people are out there and they're just not going to stop. Every Led Zeppelin, Van Halen or Ted Nugent record that came out I bought. I saw the tours, everything. Same with punk rock. [Fugazi's] Ian MacKaye does a show and I'm there, four feet away from him right in front of the stage. I'm loading the gear in, I'm carrying it out. If someone looks at him wrong I throw them across the room. I'm that guy's biggest fan. Whenever Bad Brains played we would go through hell and water to be at that show every time. We were loyal motherfuckers because that was us up there. These days though man… look at the career of Hootie & the Blowfish: fourteen million sold, two million sold, half a million sold, back to the clubs. Maybe it's the way they are marketed, people just don't stick with bands any more. You've got to wonder what they think about it all. Frank Black? Lou Reed? J Mascis? I'm there. Good record, bad record, I don't care. I buy it just to show support. I just wish there was more bands who had that going for them now. You see bands go huge one moment and then suddenly side-lined the next."

It's wrong.

"It's not wrong — it's marketing. It's the way the music industry is. So many bands are nowhere near done with what they want to say, but their cheekbones are sagging. I've been lucky because I've never been huge. There was one moment in 1991 when that 'Liar' single got lots of airplay, but that was it."

But at that point you had already spent ten years establishing yourself on the underground. You were already a 'made man'.

"Yeah, I just never had very far to fall. These bands have big ups and bigger downs, but I'm always curb-high. When I fall I only cut my knee, then I get up and keep jamming, just like Neil Young does. It's not up and down, it's ebb and flow. He knows there's 25 more records to go — that's how I see it too. I see it all as a long road ahead and for me this next record is just one of three that I already have in my mind still to do. No one's done with Mick Jagger or Sting yet — the trick is to keep people around. I've been lucky — the worst I've had is a crowd of 500. But then it goes up to eight or nine hundred. I've been right in there at club level and learnt that is the way to survive. I don't get really rich, but at least I've got shows on Thursday, Friday and Saturday. I'd take that any day over hanging out with seven million in the bank, aged 28 with my career behind me and all I have is a bunch of money to hang out with for the next 50 years going, 'I was something once…' I wouldn't want lawyers and marketing people telling me that my shit's over with — I don't want some guy in a suit or MTV telling me when I'm done. That's why I'm so glad I never depended on those people for my attendance. It's a rough road without those guys. When MTV were smiling upon us it was pretty fascinating for us. We were all very cynical cats in the band so we knew that the clock had started on our 15 minutes. Within a week we had 800 more people coming to see us. Then when the next single came out we put our key in the elevator to get up to the penthouse and were told that the code was invalid. Our crowds immediately went back down to normal and that was it for us. We didn't even go gold, yet people called our follow-ups commercial flops, like we were even interested in that. We had a foot in the door, but I couldn't tell you what the furniture was like inside. Shit, I'd rather be broke and still doing it than be rich and have it all behind me."

Notes

1 From Rollins's *Get In the Van: On the Road with Black Flag.*

2 From Denis Leary's interview entitled 'Nicotine Age Riot', *Melody Maker,* 1993.

3 Met-Rx: "The high protein aspect of the Original Drink Mix… in the convenience of a food bar! Can complement a total nutrition program when combined with the Drink Mix. Engineered for serious athletes who want to augment their program." Information taken from www.metrx.com.

4 By Ken Kesey *(One Flew Over the Cuckoo's Nest),* John Steinbeck *(The Red Pony, The Pearl* and *The Grapes of Wrath)* and Ernest Hemingway *(The Old Man and the Sea).*

5 Born in Brooklyn in 1891 to German parents, Henry Miller's early years were spent working first at his drunken father's tailoring business then sweating it out at the Western Union Telegraph Company. This early experience of work and his burgeoning family life were enough to make Miller realise the security of the nine-to-five was not for him and provided him with a philosophy that was central to his body of work, and which has attracted young and/or free-thinking fans every since.

It was only when Miller put some distance between America – or the 'Air-Conditioned Nightmare' as he later labelled it in his 1945 study of the same name – that he found the liberation he was looking for. Diving headlong into the Parisian underbelly of the 1930s, soon establishing himself amongst artists, prostitutes, hustlers, dreamers and ex-patriot writers such as Dos Passos, Cummings and Hemingway. It was here that Miller and second wife June embarked on their infamous ménage a trois with diarist Anaïs Nin.

Realising the power – and shock value – of literary truth, Miller developed his unique prose style, riddled with endless digressions, proclamations and a life-affirming belief that the only true God is the individual. The result was a body of work that's still being uncovered today. France reciprocated Miller's love for its capital by being the only country to openly publish Miller's work for close to three decades. *Tropic of Cancer* (referred to as his 'fuck everything' book) was published in 1934, having been written as free-flowing, feverish prose. Working in great bursts, much of Miller's work is based upon his experience and explodes with orgasmic digressions of delights as he suddenly remembers an incident in the New York streets of his childhood, a particularly glorious meal after days without food, or the fine odour of the female genitalia. Chain smoking Gauloises, a fedora perched on his head and music playing, Miller was prepared to open his mind and lay it out for all to see 30 years before the Beat generation embraced the concept.

Described by William Carlos Williams as "a whore with her pants off for purity and candour," in *Henry Miller: A Life* by Robert Ferguson, smuggled copies of *Tropic of Cancer* remained unpublished in America until 1961 when the public got to see what the fuss was about. Finally, at 69, Miller was a world renowned writer, adored and vilified equally. Since the sixties, the likes of *Black Spring* and his sprawling trilogy *Sexus, Nexus* and *Plexus* have all been reissued and have been in print ever since, allowing him to retire to Big Sur, California to fend off the thousands who flocked there to visit the man who opened their eyes. He died in 1980. While the Beat generation picked up on Miller's wanderlust spirit, low-life Charles Bukowski recognised Miller's importance as a true voice, and latter-day writers/performers such as Rollins and Lydia Lunch have embraced Miller's mind-expanding ideas, adrenalised prose and sexual progressiveness. Rollins even published *Dear Dear Brenda,* a collection of letters written by a wrinkled Miller to friend and Playboy model Brenda Venus, through his 2.13.61 imprint. In short, Miller was rock 'n' roll before rock 'n' roll was invented, and a true American Heretic.

6 He means *18 'til I Die,* 1996.

7 Both critics and singer Bono (specifically on the song 'New York') have referred to *All That You Can't Leave Behind,* 2000 as the band's "mid-life crisis album."

8 Guitarist with over-rated Illinois power-pop rockers Cheap Trick.

American autopsy/the heretic remixed

(compressed dub-plate version)

american threat / fucked up situation / burnt-out contemporaries / industry machinery / painstakingly / organically / revolutionary / kicked up a stink / kicked people's asses / rage / blue lights flashing / night sticks connecting / asphalt dialogues / alternative sources/back-stabbing bullshit / frustration and anger / empowering groove element / culturally resistant / assimilate information / terrify / commodify / sweatshops all over / death row fusion / commercial fruition / contention /anti-police sentiments / first amendments / political engagements / civil disobedience / rocking the white house / where naked black men are a regular occurrence / amen / sick vibe / hand jive / drive-by / freak show / lunatic shit / physical hit / hostility / humility / endorphin high / see me cry / like jacking off / you know / like the manson murders / sweaty palms / high school shootings / ironic iconic / LSD / don't blame me / fight fight fight / fucked in the teeth / political monkeys / absinthe obituary / public enemy / start the loco / funk soul punk / the new worldwide religion / a different cadence / don't pretend to be stupid / dinosaur system / fuck that shit / internet situation / a perfect fit / vocal power / final hour / drunken or high / he got game / when the shit hits the fans / bust that ass into jello / twin towers / watergate starfucker / glitterati fanatic / crackpot dictator / kill the poor / down the river / with nails through his eyes / and a bible / it's a dirty job / an obscenity trial / a black cloud / but someone's gotta do it / drive-in hardcore / know the score / dusty institutions / supercharged / electrified / hard-line / classic style / road miles / earthquakes shakes /napoleon solo / texas sex / a definition of jesus / tightness of trousers / the macho brutality / narcissistic / like his body hung on his bones / 100 per cent real / clowning around / fuck space / eat pussy / be mental / don't cheese it / broken bones / broken homes / dog balls / cow heads / maggots / britney / butt plug / gimp leg / killer / thriller / with no effects / male fantasy / punk chicks with mohawks / expressing ideas / thousand dollar bills / stuck behind tanks / way longer than us / social responsibility / eggs in one basket / suck worse than they ever suck / iron the black flag / eight hundred million decibels / ass whoopin' schedules / ballast / muscle / hit it / bullshit / american heretics / remix / scramble / i can see cheri's ear stem / her rican tie meat / her tic can arise me / ace martini cheer / over / save / exit / abort / END

Bibliography

For researching or name-dropping purposes, I read the following books and recommend them to any aspiring Heretic, American or otherwise:

Gina Arnold, *Kiss This: Punk in the Present Tense* (Pan, 1997)
Jason Arnopp, *Slipknot: Inside the Sickness, Behind the Masks* (Ebury Press, 2001)
Michael Azerrad, *Our Band Could Be Your Life: Scenes from the American Indie Underground 1981-1991* (Little, Brown & Company, 2001)
Gavid Baddeley, *Dissecting Marilyn Manson* (Plexus, 2000)
Roland Barthes, *Mythologies* (Vintage, 1993)
Angelo Bozzolla and **Caroline Tisdall,** *Futurism* (Thames & Hudson, 1977)
Vincent Bugliosi and **Curt Gentry,** *Helter Skelter* (Arrow, 1992)
William S. Burroughs, *Naked Lunch* (Flamingo, 1993)
Andrew Calcutt and **Richard Shephard,** *Cult Fiction* (Prion Books, 1998)
Chuck D and **Yusuf Jah,** *Fight the Power: Rap, Race and Reality* (Payback Press, 1997)
Bret Easton Ellis, *American Psycho* (Picador, 1991)
Robert Ferguson, *Henry Miller: A Life* (Hutchinson, 1992)
Harmony Korine, *A Crack Up at the Race Riots* (Faber & Faber, 1999)
Stewart Home, *Confusion Incorporated: A Collection of Lies, Hoaxes & Hidden Truths* (Codex Books, 1999)
Hanif Kureishi and **John Savage** (eds), *The Faber Book of Pop* (Faber & Faber, 1995)
Beth Lahickey, *All Ages: Reflections on Straight Edge* (Revelation, 1998)
Legs McNeil and **Gillian McCain,** *Please Kill Me: The Uncensored Oral History of Punk* (Abacus, 1997)
Marilyn Manson and **Neil Strauss,** *The Long Hard Road Out of Hell* (Plexus, 1998)
Henry Miller, *Tropic of Cancer* (Flamingo, 1993)
Henry Miller, *Black Spring* (Flamingo, 1993)
Henry Miller, *The Air-Conditioned Nightmare* (New Directions, 1970)
Michael Moore, *Stupid White Men... and Other Sorry Excuses for the State of the Nation!* (Harper Collins, 2002)
Friedrich Nietzsche, *Thus Spoke Zarathustra* (Penguin, 1961)
James Parker, *Turned On: A Biography of Henry Rollins* (Phoenix House, 1998)
Henry Rollins, *Black Coffee Blues* (2.13.61, 1992)
Henry Rollins, *Get In the Van: On the Road with Black Flag* (2.13.61, 1994)
Henry Rollins, *Do I Come Here Often? (Black Coffee Blues Pt. 2)* (2.13.61, 1996)
Henry Rollins, *Smile, You're Traveling (Black Coffee Blues Pt. 3)* (2.13.61, 2000)
Jon Savage, *England's Dreaming* (Faber & Faber, 1991)
Daniel Sinker (ed), *We Owe You Nothing – Punk Planet: The Collected Interviews* (Akashic, 2001)
Martin C. Strong, *The Great Metal Discography* (Canongate, 2002)
Everett True, *Live Through This: American Rock Music in the Nineties* (Virgin, 2001)

www.allmusic.com has proved to be an invaluable source for checking song titles and release details.

In writing this book, I am also indebted to the following publications, not least for inadvertently providing an education (and in some cases, an occupation): *Kerrang!, Melody Maker* (RIP), *Bizarre, Careless Talk Costs Lives, Maximum Rock 'n' Roll, NME, The Guardian, Flipside, Mojo, Uncut, Spin, Punk Planet* and the many under-acknowledged shoestring-budget fanzines who continually pump new blood into the worlds of music and writing.

Index

"Have a nice day!"

Popular American saying